# MEXICAN AMERICAN BASEBALL IN EAST LOS ANGELES

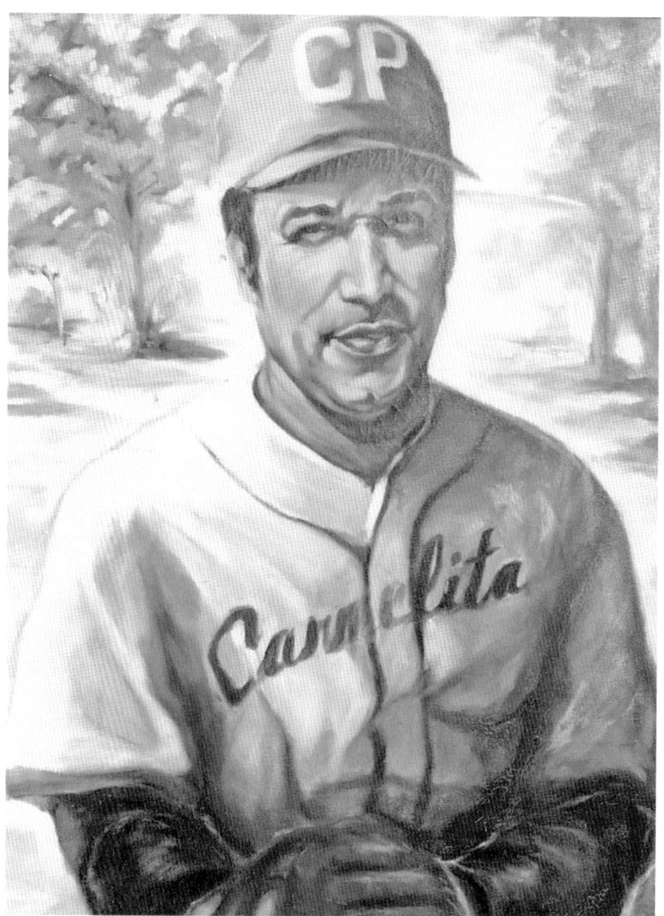


On April 4, 2016, Richard Peña, one of the coauthors of this book, passed away. Richard was one of the original players who helped establish the Latino Baseball History Project in 2006. He, Al Padilla, and Bob Lagunas have been the heart and soul of the project since its inception. We are all indebted to Richard's passion and tireless work promoting the long and rich history of Mexican American baseball and softball. Heaven now has an outstanding left-handed pitcher. His coauthors dedicate this book to his wonderful memory. Rest in peace—*descansa en paz*, compadre. (Courtesy of Richard Peña.)

**FRONT COVER:** Al Padilla was an outstanding pitcher and hitter in the late 1940s at Roosevelt High School. He is seen here in his famous swing. He coached at Roosevelt and Garfield High Schools and at East Los Angeles College. He has been inducted into the Occidental College Hall of Fame for both football and baseball. (Courtesy of Al Padilla.)

**COVER BACKGROUND:** Mexican American youth teams were sponsored by neighborhood playgrounds, churches, merchants, American Legion posts, social agencies, law enforcement, recreational centers, mutual aid societies, charitable organizations, and generous individuals. Baseball and softball taught boys and girls the everlasting skills and life lessons of playing a team sport. These values and a code of conduct gave them a head start to successful careers in American society. This photograph was taken in 1940 at Wrigley Field in Los Angeles. (Courtesy of Ray Alderete.)

**BACK COVER:** Baseball and softball taught boys and girls the everlasting skills and life lessons to be successful, including responsibility, cooperation, good judgment, common sense, cleverness, self-assurance, perseverance, teamwork, will power, self-control, listening skills, the value of hard work and practice, and sacrificing oneself for the collective good. One such youth team was this 1940s Órnelas Market squad. (Courtesy of Richard Peña.)

# MEXICAN AMERICAN BASEBALL IN EAST LOS ANGELES

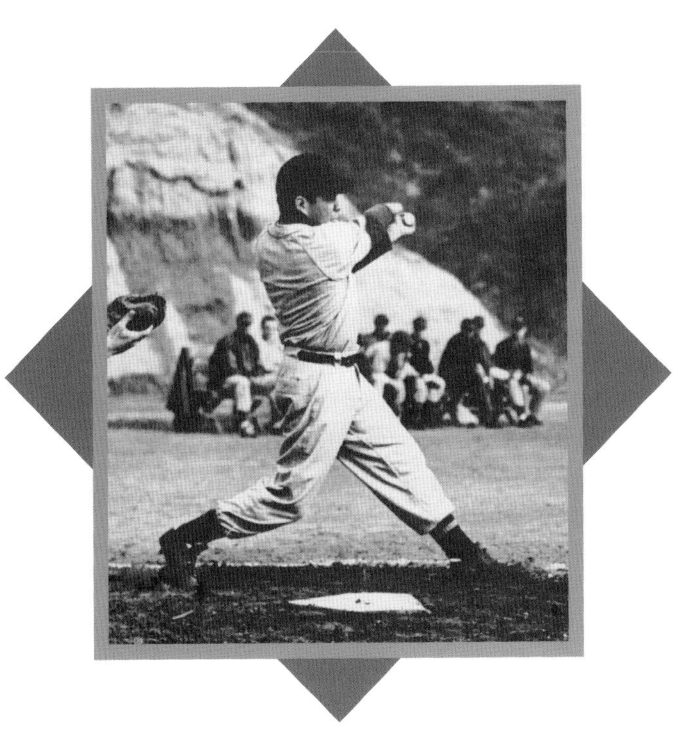

*Richard A. Santillán, Richard Peña,*
*Teresa M. Santillán, Al Padilla, and Bob Lagunas*
*Foreword by Edward J. Ávila*

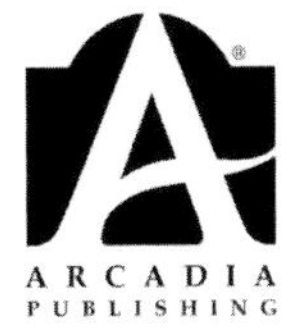

ISBN 978-1-4671-2471-3

Published by Arcadia Publishing
Charleston, South Carolina

Printed in the United States of America

Library of Congress Control Number: 2016954890

For all general information, please contact Arcadia Publishing:
Telephone 843-853-2070
Fax 843-853-0044
E-mail sales@arcadiapublishing.com
For customer service and orders:
Toll-Free 1-888-313-2665

Visit us on the Internet at www.arcadiapublishing.com

*To my father, Carlos, who graduated from Roosevelt High School in 1942; my mother, Rachel, who grew up in the "Flats;" my brothers, Charles and Joe, born at the Lincoln Hospital on Soto Street; and the East Los Angeles institutions from my early life, including the White Memorial Hospital, Dolores Mission, Our Lady of Lourdes, Belvedere Elementary School, St. Mary's, the Floral Drive-In, Belvedere and Hollenbeck Parks, and the First Street Store; and lastly to my precious and unforgettable wife, Teresa.*

—Richard

*This book is for everyone who has ever loved and played the game of baseball.*

—Coach Al Padilla

*To my husband, Richard, for his love of baseball and for his tireless work and passion for each of the books in this series, and to our three children, Anthony, Dianne, and John, and our three grandchildren, Alec, Román, and Rhiannon. They have played ball in Alhambra, El Sereno, and East Los Angeles. Finally, to my siblings, Lilia, Salvador, Martha, Julia, and José, and our loving parents, Cresencio and Guadalupe Ávila Holguín.*

—Teresa

*To my dad, Robert "Lakes" Lagunas; brother Art; son Robert K.; grandson Jay; and cousin Rudy Viera; to all of the coaches who had an impact in my life from youth to college: Art Bartless (Pico Rivera Pirates), Jim Reeder (Los Angeles State College), Windell Pickens (Orange Coast College), Manuel Moreno (Maywood), and Jack Danridge and Tom Keough (El Rancho High School); and to my old baseball buddy Conrad Muñatones.*

—Bob

# CONTENTS

# FOREWORD

I was born at the Beverly Hospital and grew up in Boyle Heights on Soto Street. I attended St. Mary's Elementary School, Cathedral High School, East Los Angeles College, and Cal State Los Angeles, where I graduated with a degree in political science. I was an avid baseball fan, although I personally played only on the school playground with friends. I still fondly remember my father, José, taking us in the 1950s to the Pacific Coast League Angels games at Wrigley Field and to the Los Angeles Memorial Coliseum when the Dodgers first moved out to the West Coast. Through friends, my brother Joe became the batboy for the Angels.

I grew up at a time when a political revolution was taking place in East Los Angeles. After World War II, Mexican American servicemen and defense workers, many of them women, escalated their pre-war struggle for civil, economic, and political rights. That struggle led to a watershed moment when World War II veteran Edward R. Roybal was elected to the Los Angeles City Council in 1949. Roybal was a great baseball fan and knew many of the players, coaches, umpires, and teams from the eastside. The Ávila and Roybal families, both from Boyle Heights, came to know each other in those days. My sister Esther had gone to Ramona Convent with the Roybal daughters Lillian and Lucille, and our families became close.

After military service, about the time I completed my master's degree in 1968, I received a call from US congressman Roybal about interning in his office. Working for this amazing man who I had idolized since childhood was an incredible opportunity for me. I soon became his field deputy, and later I became involved with his other trailblazing efforts, including the establishment of the National Association of Latino Elected and Appointed Officials (NALEO). Roybal asked me to be its first executive director, which took me to Washington, DC, in 1979. NALEO celebrated its 40th anniversary in 2016.

Congressman Roybal is remembered today as the father of Mexican American politics in the Southwest. He heroically stood on the side of the people of Chavez Ravine when their properties were confiscated to build Dodger Stadium, he bravely led the fight against the Los Angeles Police Department for its discriminatory practices against people of color, and he was on the side of the students during the 1968 educational blowouts in East Los Angeles. Among his friends were Pres. John F. Kennedy, Cesar Chavez, Martin Luther King, and actor Anthony Quinn.

In fact, Congressman Roybal was an institution in East Los Angeles from the 1930s, when he graduated from Roosevelt High School, until his death in 2005. His daughter Lucille now serves in Congress. The congressman loved sports, especially baseball, and represented East Los Angeles during its golden age. He was often seen on the field talking to players at Evergreen, Belvedere, and Fresno Parks and at Wrigley Field and Gilmore Stadium, the home of the Hollywood Stars.

This extraordinary book on the long love affair of East Los Angeles Mexican Americans for baseball and softball pays tribute to the men, women, boys, and girls who played the game, and to Congressman Roybal, who combined his passion for politics and sports with his fight for a better world.

—Edward J. Ávila
President, Project Restore

# ACKNOWLEDGMENTS

The foundation of this project to publicize the rich history of Mexican American baseball and softball in East Los Angeles is due to the remarkable work of the Latino Baseball History Project at California State University, San Bernardino (CSUSB). Others who support this effort include the following individuals and staff at the CSUSB's John M. Pfau Library: Dean Cesar Caballero and Sue Caballero, Jill Vassilakos-Long (head of archives and special collections), Iwona Contreras, Ericka Saucedo, Amina Romero, Carrie Lowe, Manny Veron, Brandy Montoya, Hayley Parke, John Baumann, and Stacy Magtedanz.

The authors are indebted to the players and families who provided their cherished photographs and amazing oral histories. These dedicated individuals and groups include Ron Regalado, Al Padilla, Richard Peña, Fred Scott, Gilbert and Alma Gamez, Ray Alderete Sr. and Jr., Victor Pimental, Bobby Recendez, Joe Gaitan, David Olmos, Art and Bob Lagunas, David Escarciga, Monte Pérez, Joe Ronquillo, Rosemary Olmos Esquivel, Henry R. Mendoza, Sally Hernández, Al De La Rosa, Kelvin Paz, Anthony Luna, Gene Aguilera, Ray Ruiz, Jaime Longoria, Frank De La Rosa, Richard Télles, Christine Gonzáles Gillett, Damon Farfán, Raymond and Julia López, Carlos and Rachel Santillán, Richard Lugo, Mary Robles, Marcelino Saucedo, Ernie Rodríguez, Art Velarde, Rodolfo Martínez, Jackie Arenas, Victor Gamboa, Ray Lara, Ray Loya, Nicky Escamilla, Rudy Castoreña, Ron Baca, Raúl Cardoza, Lauro Montes, George Caro, Carmen R. Reyes, Pete Barrios Jr., Jaime Castel De Oro, Jo Galindo O'Dell, Conrad Muñatones, the López family, the Ralph Núñez family, Chris Kolotzis, Gil and Lucille Pérez, Saúl Toledo, the Regalado family, Charlie Sierra, Ernie Blanco, Armando Pérez, Gil Gamez Jr., Fred Martínez, Elías De La Rosa, Gabe Peña, Jim Gonzáles, Rod Martínez, Christopher Docter, Mimi Poon, and Tom Pérez Jr.

The authors also thank the following high schools for giving their time and valuable resources to make this book possible: Garfield, Roosevelt, Lincoln, Wilson, Cantwell–Sacred Heart of Mary, Cathedral, Salesian, and Sacred Heart of Jesus. We also thank East Los Angeles Community College and California State University at Los Angeles.

The authors thank Tomas J. Benítez for his outstanding poem on pages 8 and 9. Tomas has been an arts and cultural advocate for over 40 years, including 20 years as an arts commissioner for the County of Los Angeles. He currently serves on the board of California for the Arts, is a member and chairperson of the Latino Arts Network of California, a founding member of the Latino Baseball History Project, and a member of the Baseball Reliquary.

We recognize once more our in-house editor, Elisa Grajeda-Urmston, for her spirited and untiring professional work, and our heartfelt appreciation and gratitude again goes out to our technical consultant Monse Segura. Finally, the Latino Baseball History Project extends thanks to Arcadia Publishing, and especially to our longtime editor and friend, Jeff Ruetsche, and editor Jim Kempert for their extraordinary commitment to our series, now at 10 books, on the long and rich history of Mexican American baseball and softball.

# Baseball in East Los Angeles

Echoes of a past time, long ago. Sounds in the air, trapped in a memory:
WHACK, the crack of a bat, WHOMP, the sound of leather hitting leather. In that moment and time, we were young forever, in our memories, and for the rest of our lives.

*La pelota*, baseball. *Los peloteros*, the players, the games played in the sleepy town streets in little *pueblitas* all throughout Mexico. When they came to East L.A., they brought the game with them.

*Cruzando la linea*, the border. *El Norte*, they came here in waves, *la onda*,
Across the water, first the Rio Grande, then the L.A. River, to the Eastside.

They played in English Spanish and Spanglish, and they also spoke *beisbol*.
*¡Dame la pelota! ¡Hechalo! ¡Honrun!* Throw me the ball, eh!

Los Aztecas, Las Aztecas, Los Chorizeros, Los Chicanos. They were far from the homeland but they wore their pride on their chests. Baseball, the American game, played by Mexicanos.

They settled into their new homes and neighborhoods, creating barrios like Boyle Heights, City Terrace, Lincoln Heights, built in the shadows of the downtown buildings and centers, across the river, on the other side. East.

Undaunted by segregation, eminent domain, or urban renewal, they played on. And they played their game. On Sundays, all day, at night, all year long.
They became more American day by day, inning by inning, living the dream in a parallel universe.

Parks and playgrounds; real uniforms with raised letters. Organized teams.
Now decorated with the names of their barrios and hoods, like flags in a parade, a place to be from, a home to defend with bat and ball and glove.

But also pickup games on those hot summer nights, playing in churchyards, community centers, schoolyards. There was always time to play ball out in the streets in front of our homes.

Just a bunch of neighborhood guys; Mexicans from here, from there, Jews, Japanese, living together, playing for the love of the game. We called ourselves the Evergreen Comets, champions of the world and everything else, eh.

Heroes emerged, legends were born; a cadre of good ballplayers that played into the hearts of their neighborhoods and our memories. They created their own history of the game. They played the game as good as anyone else, they were ballplayers.

They played for love, they played for pride, and sometimes, they played for money. Los Chorizeros, the New York Yankees of East L.A. After high school, maybe some college ball or the army, maybe in Mexico, anywhere there was a chance to keep playing ball. But there was one more option:

Factory teams, teams sponsored by *los patrones*, patrons of the art of baseball. Play baseball good enough, and you could get a good job, what could be better? El Paso (the shoe store), Ornelas Market (the market), the chance to keep playing ball.

Brothers playing together, fathers and sons played together, *tios* and *primos*, men among men, the best players no matter. But what about the women?

There would be no Mexican American baseball legacy in this country—much less East L.A.—without the women.

Like the Adelitas following the battle camps, they were there in the parks every Sunday, tending the children too young to play yet, and feeding the men, smelling like the delicious food they were cooking all day.

*Como las soldaderas de la revolución*, some of the women played the game too. Baseball *y* softball, they played the game, and they played it very well.

Oye, look, that girl over there, look at her, she throws like a man! *¿Sabes...?* Yeah, well she's purdy damn good! She can hit too. *¡Déjala!*

But they still had to play in knee-highs and shorts or often in pleated skirts; add a little lipstick, honey. They did what they had to do to play the game.

Yes, they played baseball in Chávez Ravine, four little barrios nestled into the hillside just outside of downtown L.A. They played baseball all day long, until they had no place to play. Eminent domain. "Just move the Mexicans from their homes why don't you?" So they did, *cabrones*. "Make room for the Dodgers coming to town." So they did, *pinche cabrones*.

But Mexicanos love baseball, and soon they loved the new team in town.

1960s in East Los Angeles, the new decade, a reborn city, new freeways, Kennedy and Sputnik, a new world. And a new team to go along with it.
Los Aztecas, Los Chicanos, and then, *al final*, the Los Angeles Dodgers.

Then in 1981, Mexicanos and Chicanos sitting together, talking to each other in English and Spanish, about one thing, one person, El Niño, El Toro, The One, at last: Fernando Valenzuela! *Fernandomanía* changed baseball forever.

"...And a child shall lead them!" voiced Vin Scully in his most honeyed dulcet tones, exalting after another incredible win for The Rookie in that magical season of '81. "*¡El Niño héroe de Echahuaquilla, Navajoa, Sonora, Mexico!*" echoed the great Jaime Jarrin. The *voz* of *los Doyers*. He bridged the Spanish-language audience with the English language talking about the national pastime, another line crossed.

100 years of béisbol in East Los Angeles. From old forgotten dirt roads to sprawling neighborhoods, baseball has been a part of the emergence of the Mexican American community in East L.A. Local heroes keep playing the game. From the sandlots to the 1970 Wilson Mules, city champions. From the playgrounds to the 2014 Lincoln High School Tigers, city champs.

That first wave of young boys became old men, and now, many have gone on to the greener field of dreams. Generations have followed, playing ball, staying young in our hearts and minds forever. Baseball is a timeless game.

As Mexicans came to Los Angeles, the game allowed them to become more American. In turn, as Mexicans have stayed and continued to flourish in Southern California and the United States, they have made the game more Mexican. Baseball in East L.A. is the American game, and it plays on and on.

—Tomas J. Benítez

# INTRODUCTION

The history of Mexican American baseball dates back to the massive immigration of Mexicans into East Los Angeles during the first two decades of the 20th century, mainly due to the Mexican Revolution. East Los Angeles was then a vibrant melting pot of ethnic groups. It gradually evolved into the largest Mexican American community in the United States. Its residents often refer to this area as East LA, the Eastside, and, with affection (*con cariño*), as East Los. East Los Angeles is located east of the Los Angeles River and is linked to downtown Los Angeles by several concrete bridges built by the Works Progress Administration during the Great Depression. The community is both flat and hilly and is divided into several distinct subcommunities, including City Terrace, Boyle Heights, Belvedere, Lincoln Heights, El Sereno, Hazard, Estrada Courts, Maravilla, Ramona Gardens, Pico-Aliso, Russian Flats, Tortilla Flats, and Hillside Village. More important than geography, Mexicans and Mexican Americans are linked politically, economically, culturally, linguistically, and spiritually.

Mexican Americans found employment in and around East Los Angeles in packinghouses, railroads, tire companies, hardware stores, hospitals, produce markets, foundries, garment shops, steel and auto plants, hospitals, and trucking companies. There were countless Mexican-owned businesses, including restaurants, barbershops, beauty salons, printers, hardware stores, meat markets, fruit stands, furniture and clothing stores, jewelry shops, auto repair, television and radio repair, cleaners, record stores, bars and liquor stores, construction, waste management, auto lots, art galleries, and landscaping. A few lucky ones found employment with the City of Los Angeles.

East Los Angeles has witnessed major political events since the 1930s, including the Great Depression and Repatriation Program, the Zoot-Suit Rebellion and the Sleepy Lagoon case, World War II, Korea, and Vietnam, the postwar civil rights movement, the election of Edward Roybal to the Los Angeles City Council and US Congress, Bloody Christmas, the Viva Kennedy Clubs, the attempts to incorporate East Los Angeles into a city, the emergence of La Raza Unida Party, the rise of the Chicano movement, the walk-outs and Chicano Moratorium, the death of Rubén Salazar at the Silver Dollar Bar, the establishment of Chicano studies, the renaming of Brooklyn Avenue to Cesar E. Chávez, the election of Gloria Molina to the Los Angeles Board of Supervisors, the election of Antonio Villaraigosa as mayor of Los Angeles, the rise of the immigrant rights movement, the ongoing battle against physical displacement by freeways, urban renewal, and gentrification, and so much more.

This book explores 100 years of Mexican American baseball and softball from 1917 to 2016 in East Los Angeles. Obviously, it is impossible to highlight all the preeminent players and renowned teams that graced the fields in East Los Angeles. That prodigious task would require volumes of books. Instead, this is a mere glimpse at the long and rich legacy of baseball and softball. More than a game, baseball was a political instrument designed to promote and empower civil, political, gender, and cultural rights of Mexican Americans confronting head-on the reactionary forces of prejudice, discrimination, intolerance, sexism, and xenophobia. Today, family members still play on the same fields where their hard-working ancestors brought joy and honor to their neighborhoods a century ago.

# Youth

For decades, baseball youth associations had no official sponsorship in East Los Angeles, including Little, Pony, or Colt Leagues or Babe Ruth teams. Instead, Mexican American youth teams were sponsored by neighborhood playgrounds, churches, merchants, American Legion posts, social agencies, law enforcement agencies, recreational centers, mutual aid societies, charitable organizations, and generous individuals. Credit also goes to the talented managers and knowledgeable coaches who selflessly mentored young players into accomplished athletes with baseball knowledge and technique.

Seasoned managers and no-nonsense coaches found time after a long, hard day of work to practice with the kids. These thrifty coaches dipped into their own pockets to subsidize equipment and uniforms. They taped together old bats and balls that could be used over and over again. They bankrolled the construction and maintenance of the fields where young people perfected their skills. This was an era before state-of-the-art pitching machines, batting cages, batting helmets, aluminum bats, mini-tractors to smooth the infield, electronic scoreboards, speed guns, pitch counts, stop watches, and immaculate fields.

These baseball architects instilled all-embracing values and a code of acceptable behavior in their young protégés, preparing them to be successful in life. Managers and coaches had sons, nephews, and godsons on their teams, discouraging them from straying into a life of crime. These revered coaches spoke the language of baseball and stressed fundamental mechanics, and they did not tolerate showboats and big heads. For some boys, these coaches were surrogate fathers. Eventually, girls and young women became part of this rich and vital network.

Baseball and softball taught boys and girls the everlasting skills and life lessons of playing a team sport—responsibility, cooperation, judgment, common sense, empathy, intuition, gumption, cleverness, accountability, self-assurance, perseverance, teamwork, sportsmanship, competition, will power, self-control, protocol, fair play, listening skills, the value of hard work and practice, and sacrificing oneself for the collective good. These survival tactics were rarely taught to Mexican youth in schools. These skills and values gave the players a head start to successful careers in American society.

Former players have given back to East Los Angeles as teachers, carpenters, counselors, coaches, principals, truck drivers, construction workers, business and political leaders, priests, doctors, plumbers, dentists, nurses, auto and steel workers, professors, reporters and broadcasters, gang workers, law enforcement officers, the military, labor leaders, artists, poets, writers, and many more blue- and white-collar occupations.

This chapter explores the long-ago youth teams and players who blessed the diamonds in the largest Spanish-speaking community in the United States. Players continue to bring dignity and reputation to these sacred fields of East Los Angeles. Youngsters today still practice until dog tired, still play on Saturdays, and still keep their army of fans on the edge of their seats. And like a century ago, a gutsy core of dedicated managers and qualified coaches are still producing gifted players and future community leaders en masse.

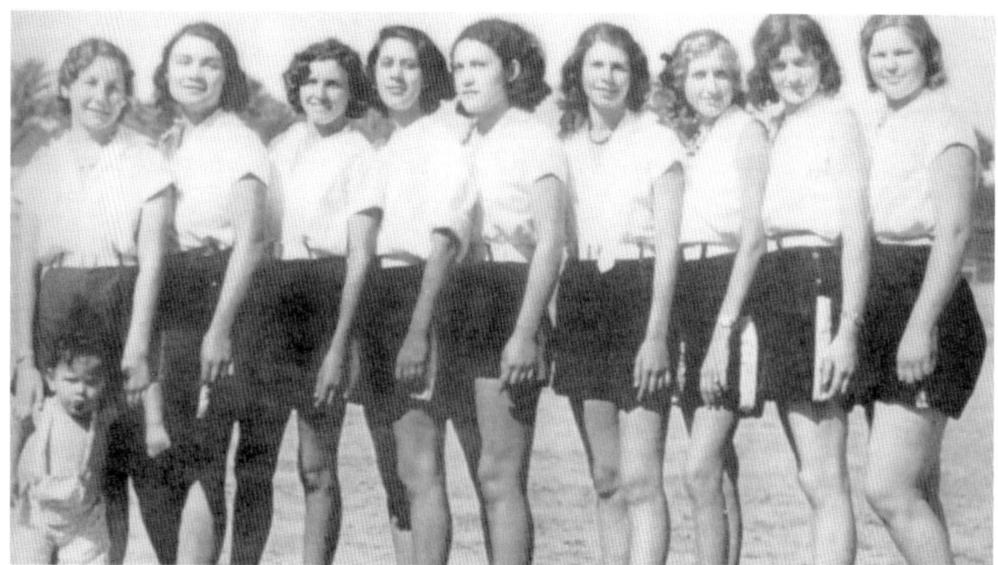

This 1931 team played in the Pecan-Utah section of East Los Angeles. The team manager was legendary Manuel Regalado, who coached several teams throughout Los Angeles. Only two players are identified: Mary Talvera (third from left) and Annie Faldman (fourth from left). Regalado asked famed photographer Dick Whittington to take this picture. It appears that the team was sponsored either by a local church or the parks and recreation department. Today, Dolores Mission and nearby Pecan Park sponsor sports for neighborhood youth. (Courtesy of Ron Regalado.)

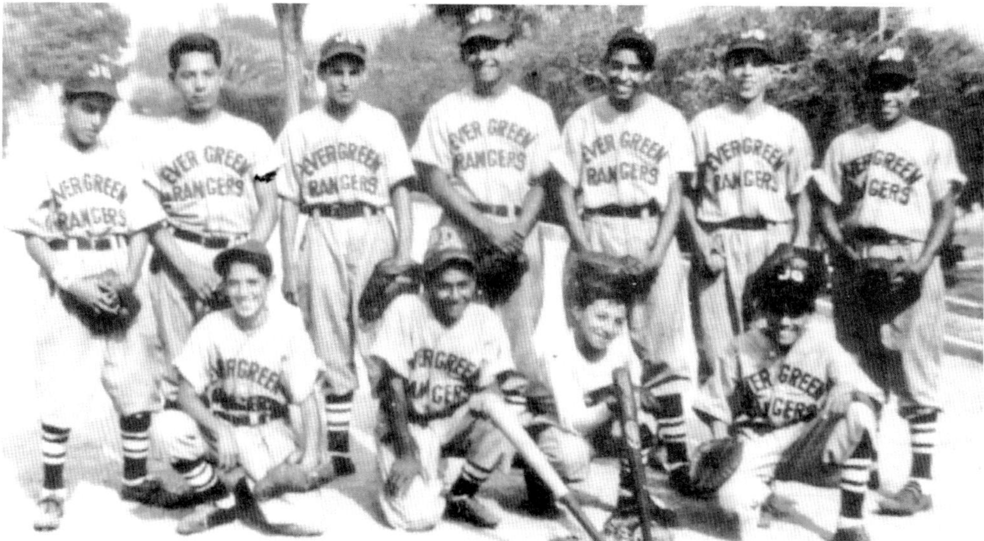


Most Mexican American high school and college players began on youth teams and leagues in East Los Angeles. Among these teams was the 1944–1945 Evergreen Rangers. Youth teams had dedicated coaches mentoring players with both baseball skills and how to be better citizens in their communities. From left to right are (first row) Andy Saís, Robert Ontiveros, Albert Ortiz, and Gilbert Mendoza; (second row) Johnny Mendoza, Sócrates Selicio, Dick Duran, Manuel Flores, Robert Duran, Robert Ortiz, and Al Padilla. (Courtesy of Al Padilla.)

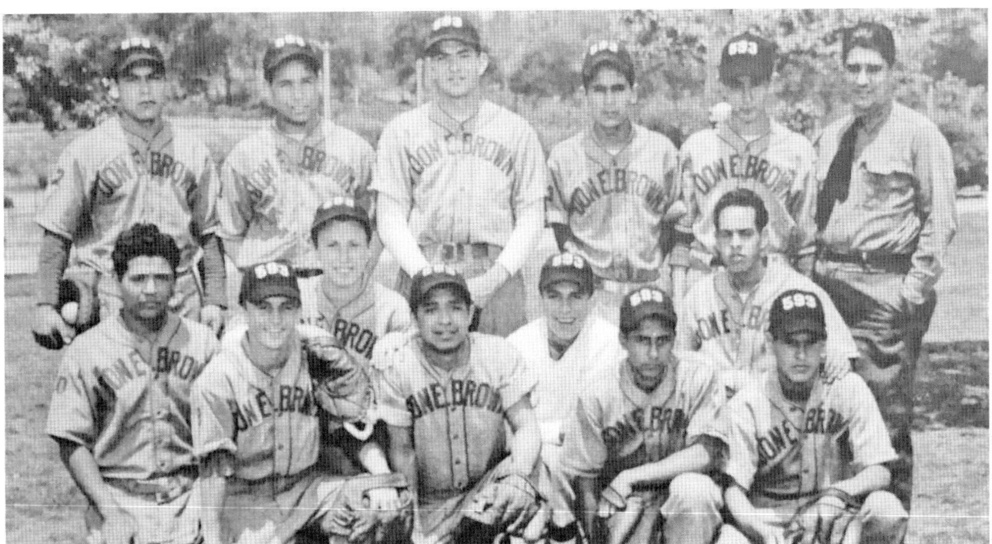

American Legion Don E. Brown Post No. 593 was a prominent youth club in 1949. Famous actor and comedian Joe E. Brown was a sponsor, fan, and advocate for youth baseball. Brown sponsored teams in low-income areas in the name of his late son, Don, who had been killed in World War II. From left to right are (first row) Manuel Flores, Andy Saís, Jimmy Miller, Johnny Robles, Robert Ortiz, Victor Ontiveros, Robert Duran, and Dick Duran; (second row) Johnny Peña, Al Padilla, Charlie Chávez, Pat Molina, Vernon Brady, and manager Andrew Saís in his Boy Scout uniform. (Courtesy of Richard Peña.)

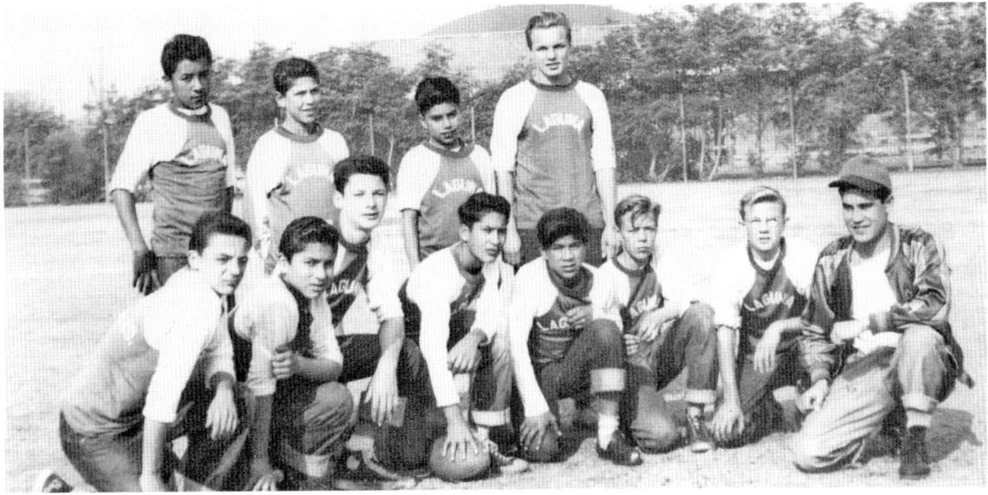

This 1940s Laguna Park youth football team included several players who later became outstanding baseball players at Garfield High School. From left to right are (first row) Dave Beadles, Bill Miranda, Jimmy Pérez, Ángel Figueroa, Tom Robles, Mickey Cunningham, Glen Dangleis, and coach Oscar Gallegos; (second row) Robert Carrillo, Ray Escovedo, Fred Scott, and Nick Shubin. Robles, Figueroa, and Dangleis were All-City players at Garfield, and the three later signed with the Pittsburgh Pirates. Scott was All-League shortstop at East Los Angeles Junior College and All-League and College World Series shortstop at the University of Southern California (USC). Miranda played third base for Garfield. (Courtesy of Fred Scott.)

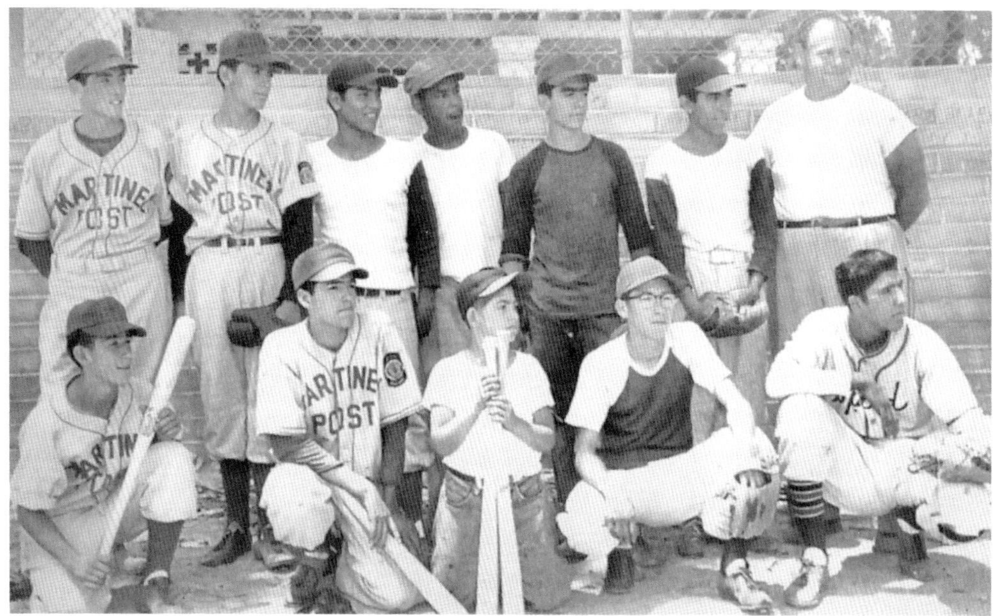


Sponsored by the American Legion in the 1940s, the José P. Martínez Post No. 623 included three sets of brothers: Conrad (second row, far left) and Joe Muñatones (first row, second from left), Ernie (first row, far left) and Rubén Rodríguez (second row, second from left), and Gilbert (first row, far right) and Tony Gamez (batboy, first row center). José P. Martínez, a farm laborer from New Mexico, was the first Mexican American to be awarded the Congressional Medal of Honor during World War II. Martínez received the award posthumously. (Courtesy of Gilbert and Alma Gamez.)

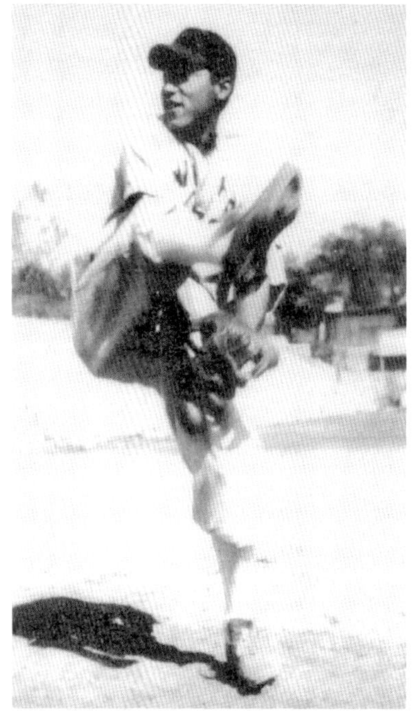

Richard Peña was born in 1930 in East Los Angeles. His father, William, was an outstanding player during the first decade of the 20th century. Richard is the second youngest of nine Peña brothers coached by their father. He is shown here at 16 playing for an American Legion team. Peña played at Roosevelt High School, for several East Los Angeles community teams, and professionally in the United States and Mexico. He said he learned his love of and respect for the game from his father and that it was important for him to continue that legacy. Following his playing days, Peña coached several Little League teams in East Los Angeles and Montebello. Among those he coached were future Dodger standout Willie Davis, and future USC and NFL star Mike Garrett. Peña especially enjoyed coaching young players from the same neighborhood where he grew up learning to play ball. (Courtesy of Richard Peña.)

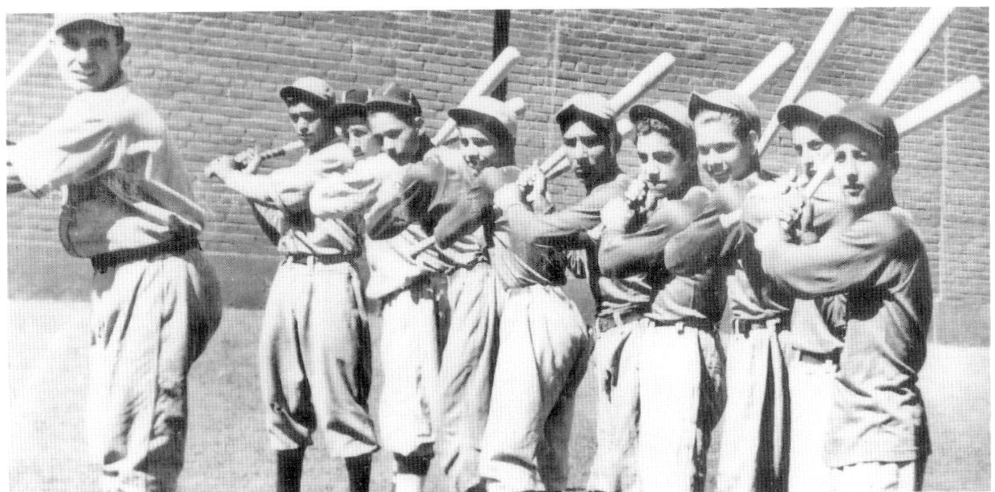

Ray Alderete was born in 1921 and started playing baseball at an early age. His future father-in-law, Joe J. Macias, coached the Los Angeles Cardinals in the early 1930s. Macias invited teams from Mexico to play in East Los Angeles at a field near Medick and Brooklyn Avenues, where Belvedere Park is now located. This photograph was taken in 1940 at Wrigley Field in Los Angeles. From left to right are coach Charlie Root, Mel Salinas, Victor Peña, Frank Salazar, Sal Toledo, Ray Puentes, Joe Hernández, Chuck Valenzuela, Ernie Sierra, and Ray Alderete. (Courtesy of Ray Alderete.)

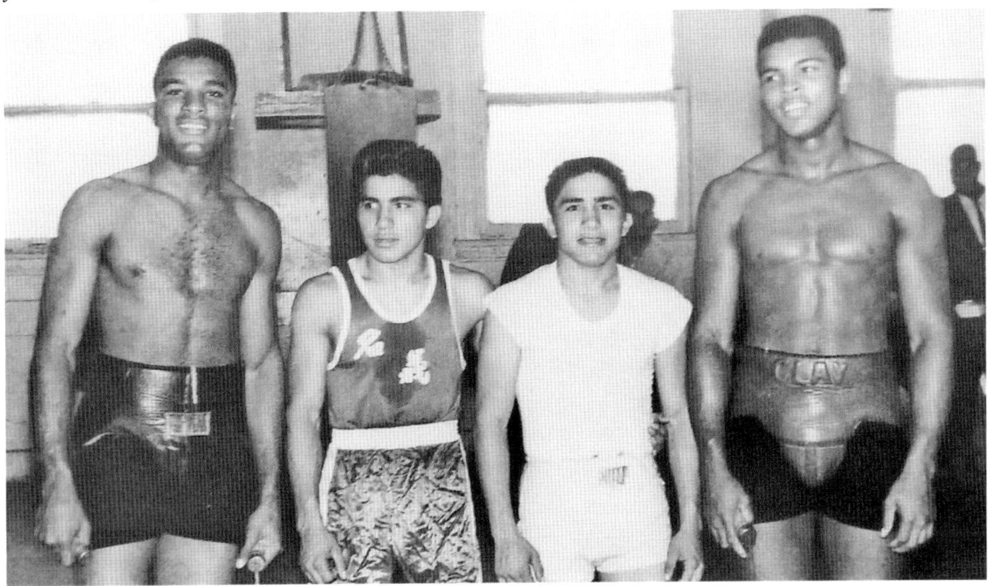

Twins Joe Luís (second from left) and Jesús Pimentel (second from right) are seen here with Muhammad Ali (right) and his younger brother Rahman Ali (left). The Pimentel brothers played youth ball at Belvedere Park with teams sponsored by the Brooklyn Ford Market and Ramírez Mortuary. Both later became outstanding boxers. Joe was known as "Big Poison" and Jesús as "Little Poison." They fought at the Olympic Auditorium, Los Angeles Sports Arena, and the Forum. Both are in the International Boxing Hall of Fame. Joe Luís and another brother, William, served in the military. (Courtesy of Victor Pimentel.)

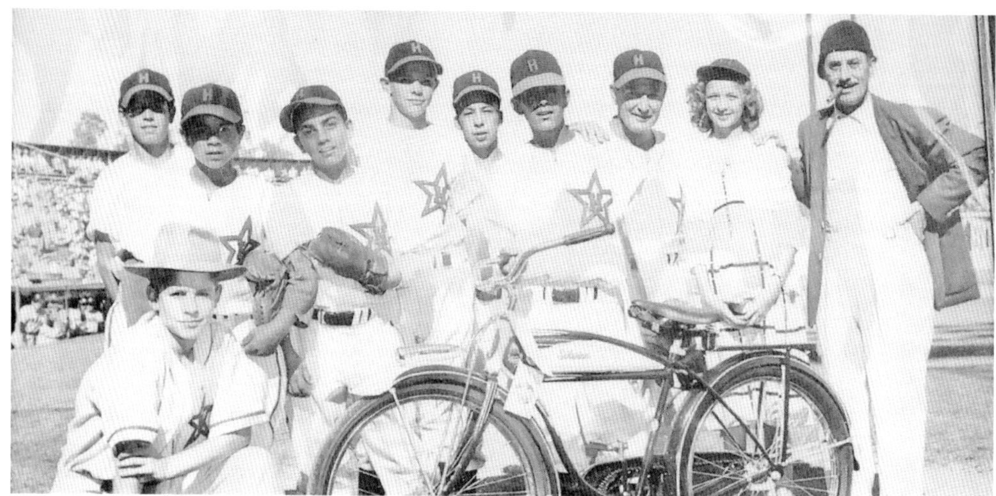

The Hollywood Stars sponsored the Infield of the Future, where neighborhood teams were invited to take infield practice at Gilmore Field. Fresno and Evergreen Parks from East Angeles participated around 1950. The players wore borrowed youth Stars uniforms. From left to right are Bobby Recendez, Tom Robles, Richard Casares, Donald Dangleis, Joe Gaitan, Fernando Farfán, Fred Haney, Haney's niece, and Groucho Marx. The kneeling batboy is wearing Groucho's hat. Farfán won the bike. Coach Joe Castañeda (not pictured) knew Billy Martin and Casey Stengal and arranged for Eastside teams to be invited. (Courtesy of Bobby Recendez.)

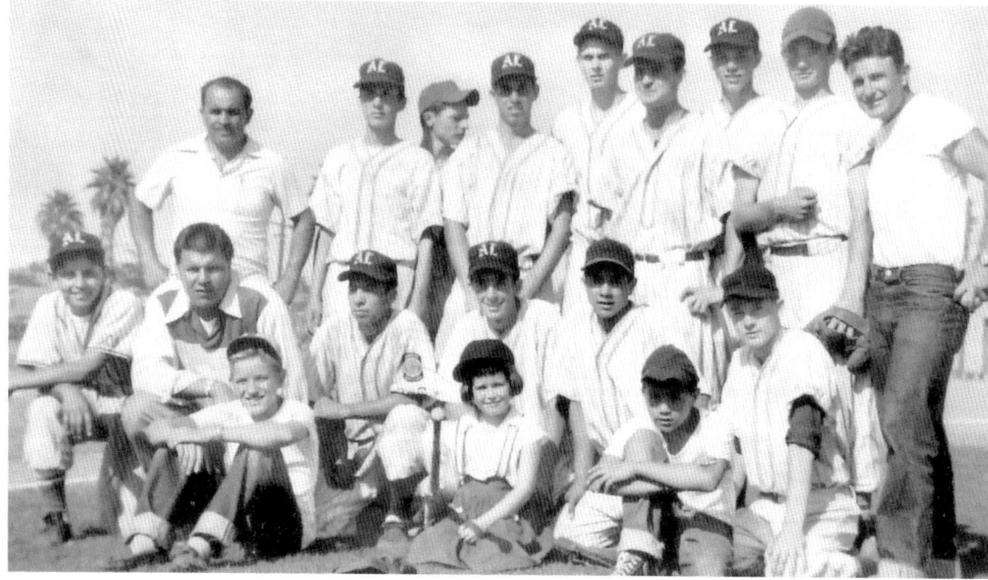

The 1952 American Legion Post No. 508 team was coached by Garfield High School coach Bob Holmes (standing, far right). Joe Gaitan (kneeling third from left), Tom Robles (kneeling, second from right) and Pete Ortega (standing, second from left) were outstanding players for Holmes. East Los Angeles American Legion teams played an annual tournament at La Palma Park in Anaheim. Gordon Moreno owned a produce market and drove the players to the tournament in the back of his truck filled with fruits and vegetables. Moreno's two sons were batboys. (Courtesy of Joe Gaitan.)

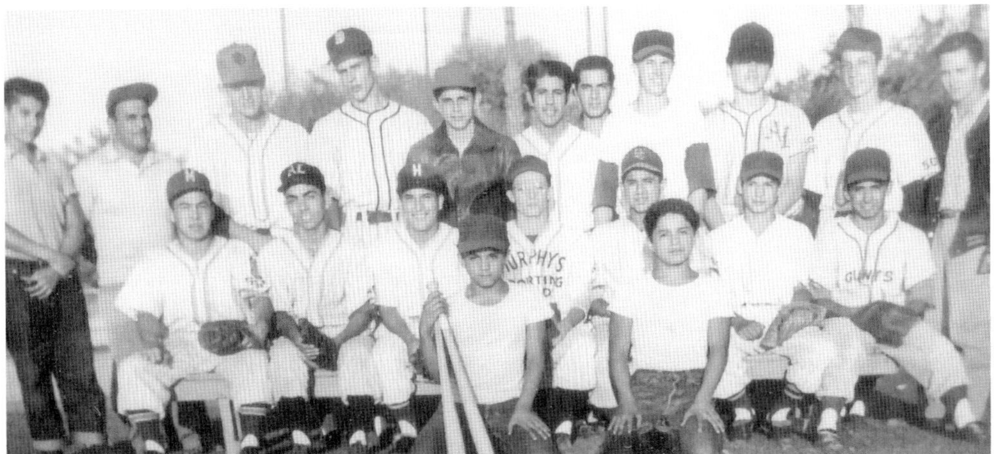

The 1953 American Legion Post No. 508 team featured several outstanding Mexican American players, including Joe Gaitan (first row, far left), Richard Casares (first row, second from left), Ángel Figueroa (first row, third from left), Tom Robles (first row, third from right), Ernest Negrete (first row, second from right), Lawrence Govea (first row, far right), and Pete Ortega (second row, second from right). Most of these players were on the Garfield High School team. Robles and Ortega signed professional contracts with Pittsburgh. Robles later played ball in Mexico City. (Courtesy of Joe Gaitan.)

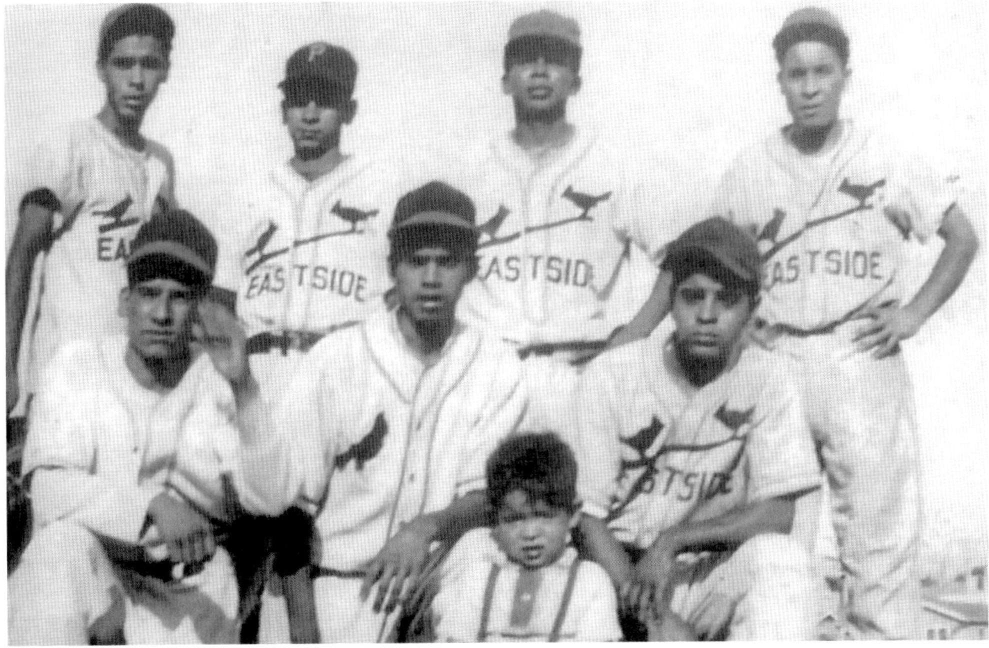

This East Los Angeles team played at Evergreen Park in 1953. Cousins George and Sal Saiza had fathers who played on a 1917 Los Angeles team. The batboy is five-year-old Alfonso Olmos, who played ball at East Los Angeles College. He was drafted by both the San Francisco Giants and the US Army. His brother David recalled that he was proud Alfonso had seen him play in La Puente before being shipped overseas. Alfonso was killed in Vietnam; David named his son Alfonso after his brother. (Courtesy of David Olmos.)

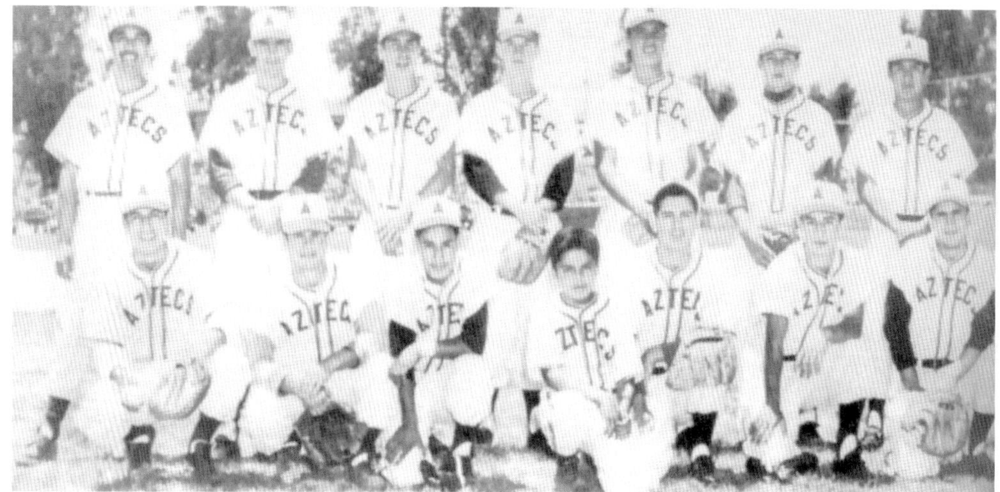

The Corral Aztecs team played in the Rio Hondo League and was comprised of 16- to 18-year-old players. This 1953 team highlights several players from different high schools, including Roosevelt, El Rancho, and Wilson. From left to right are (first row) Adolfo García, Joe Pomo, Art Lagunas, batboy Art Corral, John Mitchell, Bob Lagunas, and Jack Latona; (second row) manager Manuel Moreno, Nick Pomo, Robert Moreno, Vince Zeimis, Willie García, Mel Gonzáles, and Danny Holguín. Not shown are Ronald V. Butcher, Conrad Muñatones, and James Blanda. (Courtesy of Art and Bob Lagunas.)

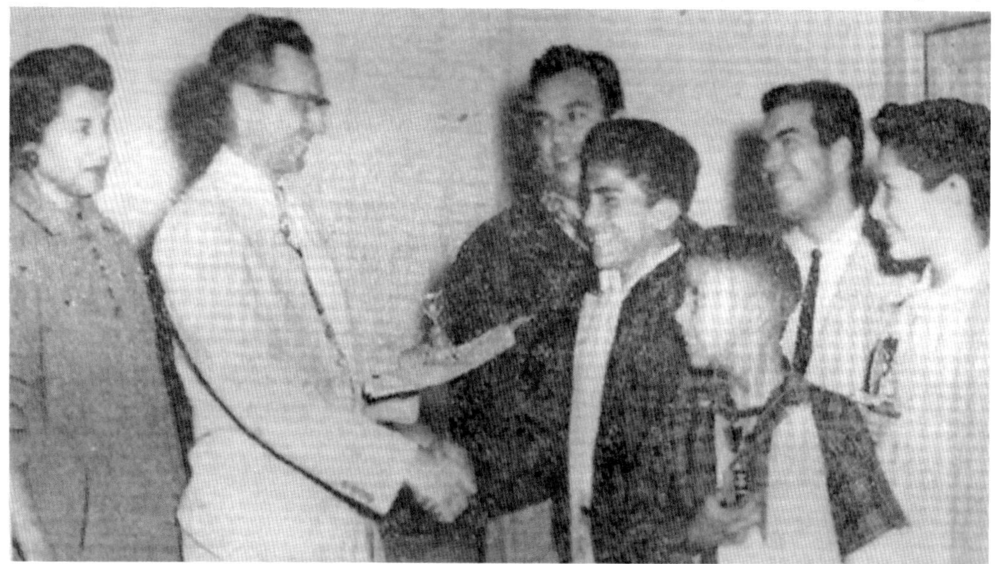

Three local softball teams, the Midgets, Juniors, and Peewees, participated in a 1955 sportsmanship award presentation at Laguna Park (now Rubén Salazar Park) with certificates and trophies. From left to right are Josephine Escarciga, Mel Heller, George Peña, Jesús Pimental, Robert Chávez, Roy Alba, and David Escarciga. Another local team, the Eastside Boys' Club, won the North's Little League Championship. Their manager was 16-year-old Billy Lujan. The league included the Evergreen Angels, Hollenbeck Stars, Wabash Seals, Evergreen Padres, and Variety Boys' Club. (Courtesy of David Escarciga.)

Monte (right) and Steve Pérez (left) loved baseball. They attended Harrison Elementary School, Belvedere Junior High School, and Garfield High School. Both played varsity baseball at Garfield. As youths, Monte played for the Laguna Park Giants while Steve was the batboy. Steve was later an outstanding pitcher for the City Terrace Stars, for whom he tossed a no-hitter. Monte later played shortstop for the City Terrace Stars. His teammates included Richard Télles and Joe Ronquillo. Steve became a plumber and had three daughters, while Monte became a college administrator. Steve passed away in 2015. (Courtesy of Monte Pérez.)

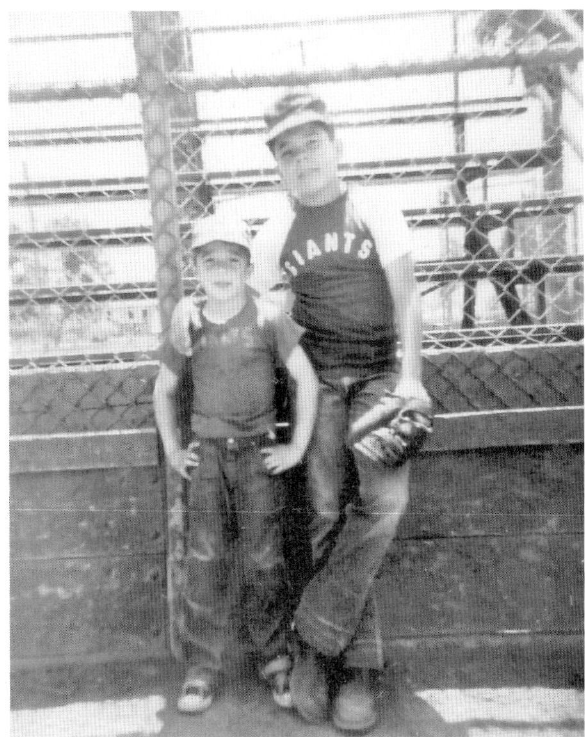


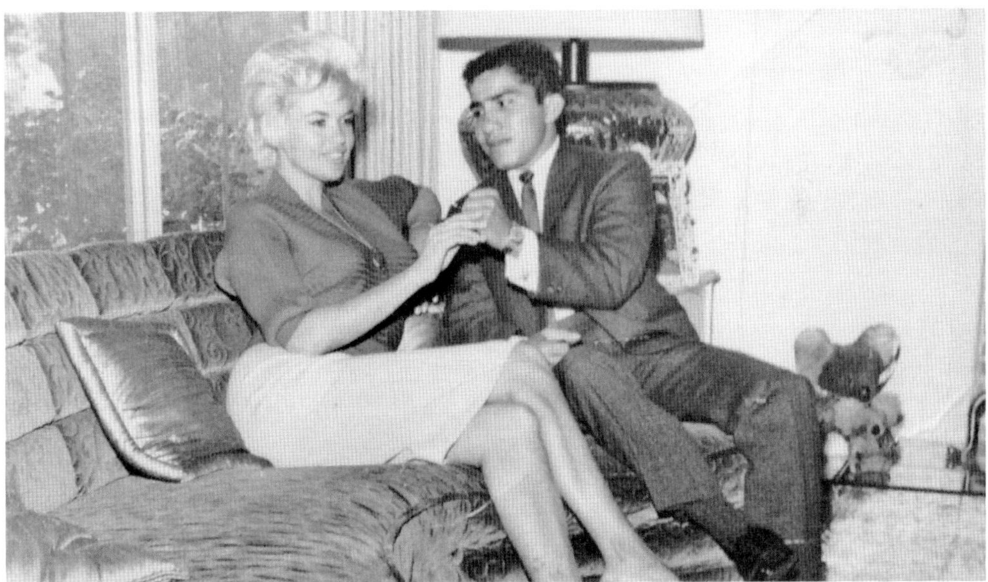

Belvedere Park produced several outstanding teams in the 1950s and 1960s, especially the Midgets and the Juniors. Both had several sets of brothers, including Joe Luis and Jesús Pimentel. Another brother, William, also played youth baseball. All three could have been baseball stars, but two of them, José Luis and Jesús, decided to become boxers. Jesús is seen here with Jane Mansfield in Hollywood. He currently lives in North Hills in the San Fernando Valley. He married Maria Elena Torres, and they had four children. (Courtesy of Victor Pimentel.)

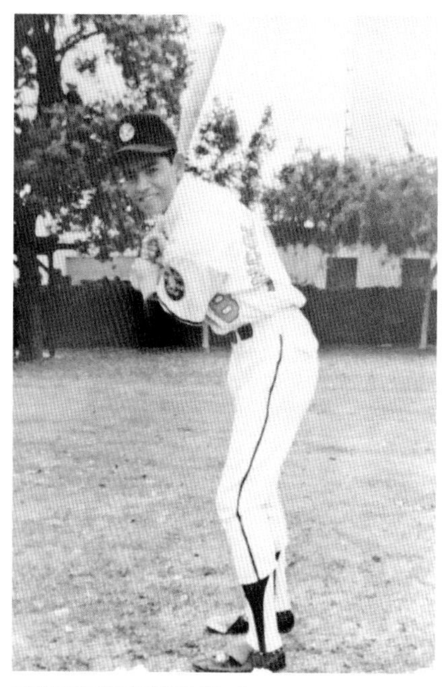

Alfonso Olmos's family settled in East Los Angeles but moved to both Watts and Compton, where Alfonso played ball at Edison Junior High School and Huntington Park High School. He played organized youth ball and travel ball with his uncle Remi Álvarez and played for East Los Angeles Community College. His father, Raúl, coached Alfonso and his teammates Reggie Smith and Kenny Landreaux, both of whom played for the Dodgers. Alfonso's mother, Theresa, and her sisters played ball too. Alfonso's brothers David and Eddie also played ball. Alfonso played baseball in the military and sadly, was killed in Vietnam in 1969. His three uncles, Remi, Richard, and Art, all brothers, played military baseball. (Courtesy of Rosemary Olmos Esquievel.)

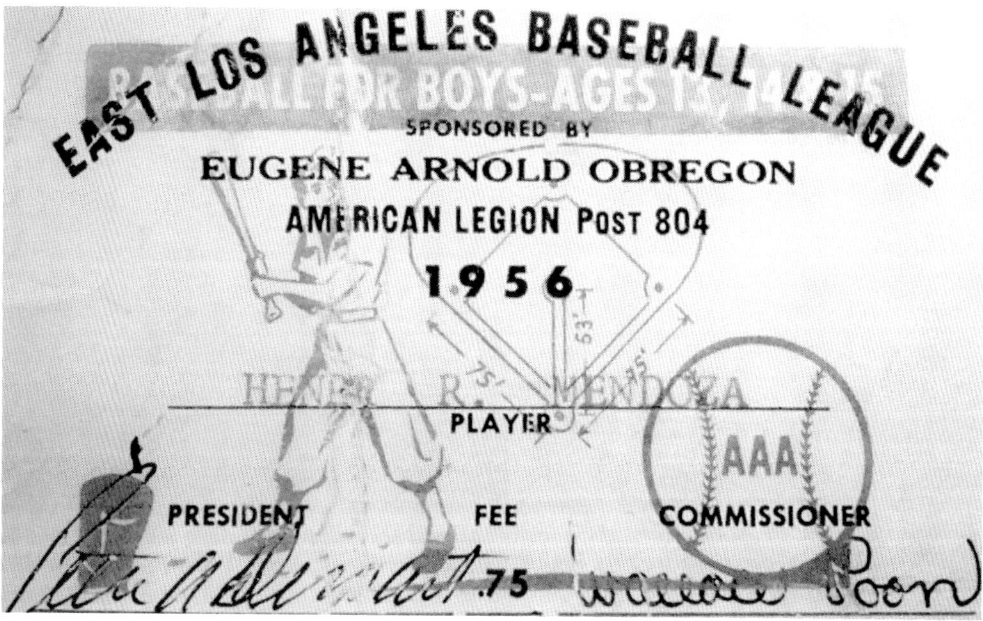

EAST LOS ANGELES BASEBALL LEAGUE
SPONSORED BY
EUGENE ARNOLD OBREGON
AMERICAN LEGION POST 804
1956
HENRY R. MENDOZA
PLAYER
AAA
PRESIDENT
FEE
.75
COMMISSIONER

The East Los Angeles Baseball League was sponsored by the American Legion Eugene Arnold Obregón Post No. 804. This card was issued to Henry R. Mendoza in 1956. The post was named after Roosevelt student Obregón, killed in action in Korea and posthumously awarded the Congressional Medal of Honor. Obregón enjoyed playing baseball in the community and in school. Obregón Park on First Street and a section of the 10 freeway near Soto Street are named after him. Commissioner Wally Poon had an illustrious baseball career as one of the few non-Mexican Americans to play in East Los Angeles. Chinese American Poon attended East Los Angeles Junior College. (Courtesy of Henry R. Mendoza.)

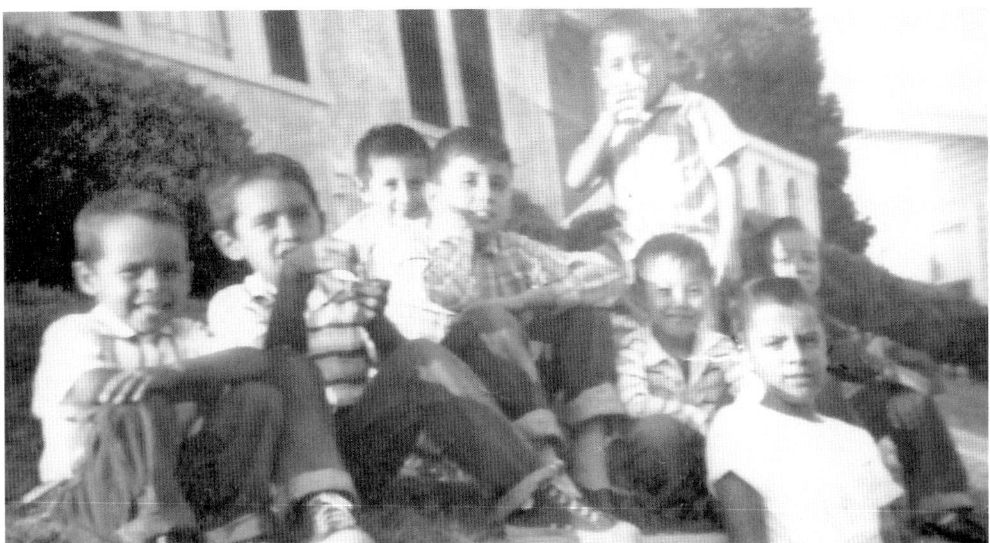

Tomas J. Benítez grew up in East Los Angeles and started playing neighborhood ball at an early age. The boys called themselves the Evergreen Comets after their local park. They played ball in the park and in the streets after school until dark. The team was comprised of Mexican, Jewish, and Japanese kids united in a game they loved and bonded by their desire to become Americans. Players in the late 1950s and early 1960s included Little Ricky, Big Ricky, Doc, Sonny, Chuck from New Orleans, Yoshi, Luciano, Larry, and Steve. (Courtesy of Tomas J. Benítez.)

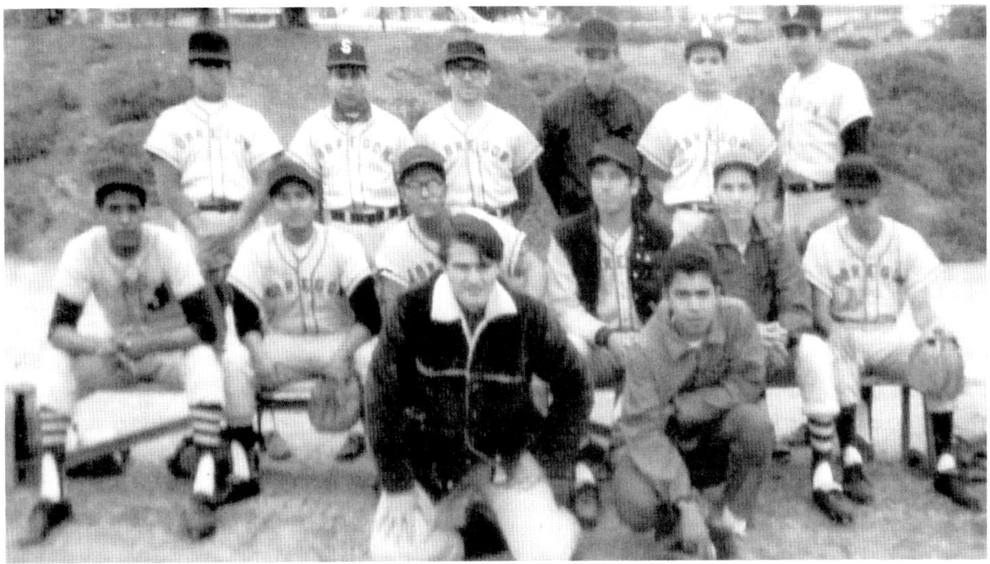

This 1960s Obregón team played at East Los Angeles College. The coach was Mexican American Jess Hunter. The team played against Southgate, Los Angeles, Huntington Park, Lynwood, Montebello, and Alhambra. The club included Sergio Hernández (first row, second from left), Richard López, John Baca, ? Guerrero, and James Retana. Hernández, a renowned artist, cofounded *Con Safos* magazine in the late 1960s. His father and two uncles fought in World War II. He is named after one of his uncles, who died at the Battle of the Bulge. (Courtesy of Sally Hernández.)

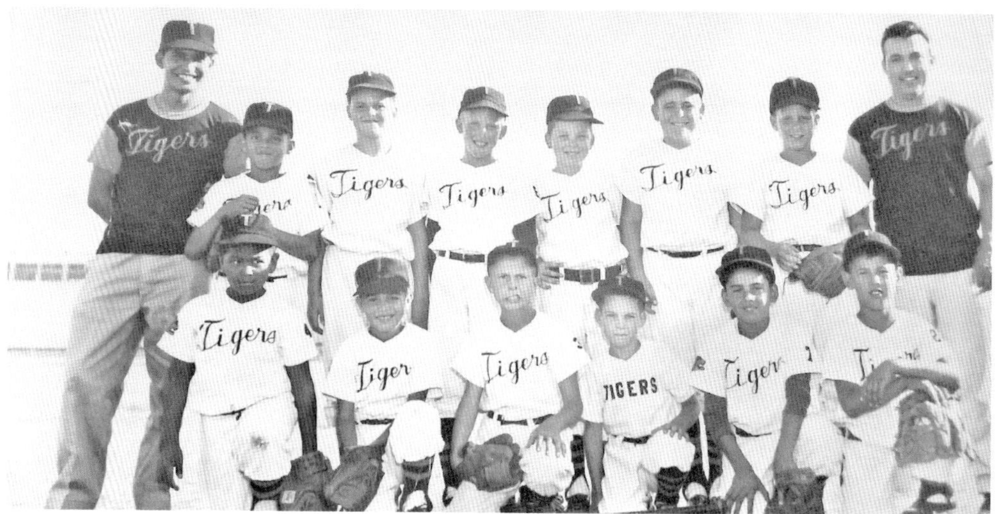

The 1956 East Los Angeles Little League Tigers were the city champions. Manager Richard Peña (second row, far right) and coach Art Carrasco (second row, far left) coached various teams for six years. Carrasco was married to Ana Maria, the daughter of Mario López, owner of Carmelita Provision Company. López asked Peña to recruit his son-in-law to coach. Tragically, Carrasco and his younger brother were killed in an industrial accident. The Carmelita Provision Company logo is a pig wearing a baseball cap and holding a bat. Peña claims that his daughter Linda drew it, but López disagreed. (Courtesy of Richard Peña.)

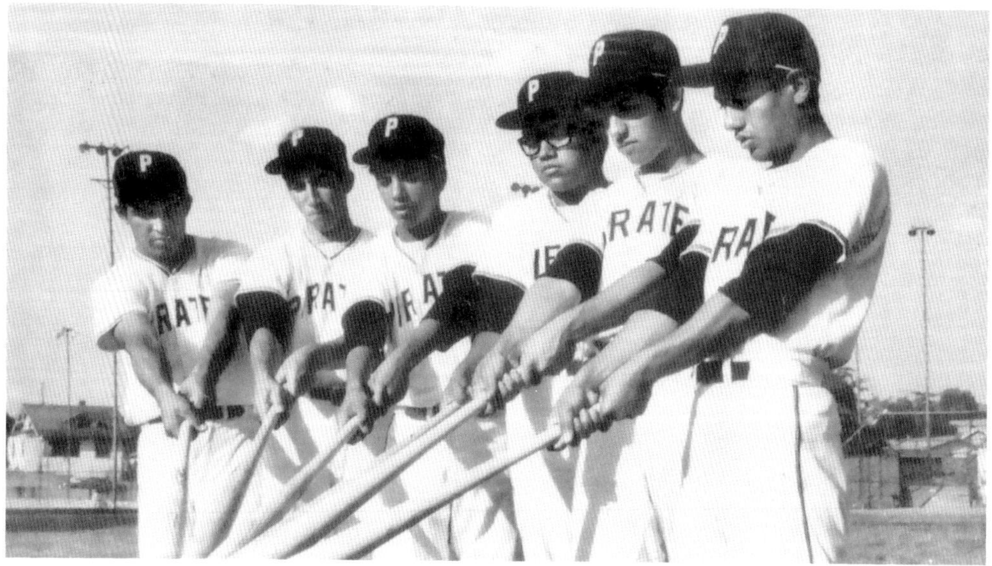

The 1968 Pirates played at Evergreen Park in the Boyle Heights section of East Los Angeles. The manager was Jesús Paz. From left to right to right are Myron Tinsley, Anthony Lara, Joel Palomares, Victor Orona, James Roberts, and Ray Murillo. Palomares and Murillo later played at Garfield High School, while the others played at Roosevelt. Roberts was scouted by the Pittsburgh Pirates. Palomares played at East Los Angeles College and with the East Los Angeles Monarchs. Orona also played with the Monarchs. (Courtesy of Al De La Rosa.)

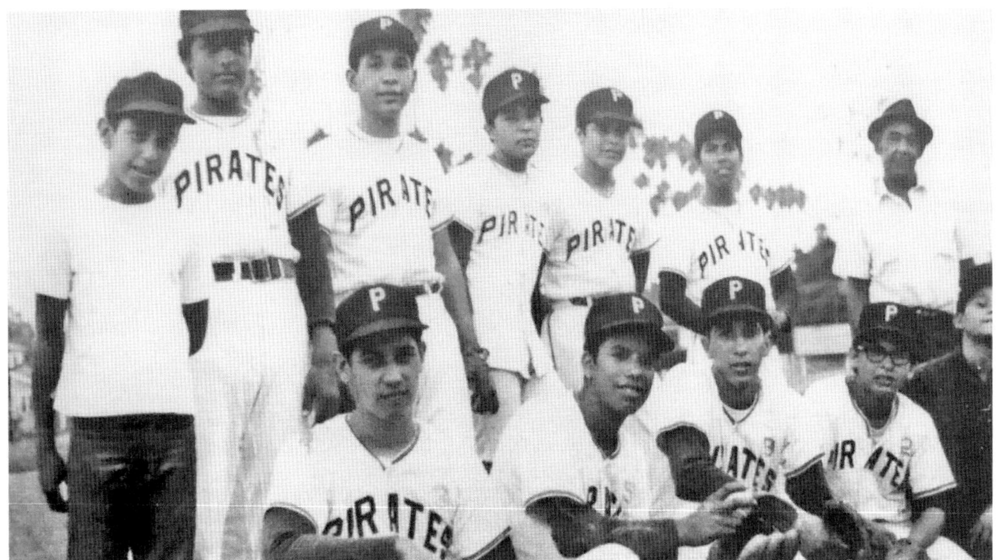


The 1969 Pirates are, from left to right (first row) Steve Paz, Mike Estrada, Joel Palomares, and Tony Sánchez; (second row) Randy Paz, Jimmy Reza, Eddie López, Ray Soto, Ray Murillo, Jesse Estrada, and manager Jesús Paz. Steve Paz went on to play third base for Cal State Los Angeles, while Mike Estrada and Palomares played for East Los Angeles College as infielders. Jesse Estrada coached at Evergreen Park when Jesús Paz retired. Estrada later attended UCLA and became a school police officer. He passed away in 2014. (Courtesy of Kelvin Paz.)

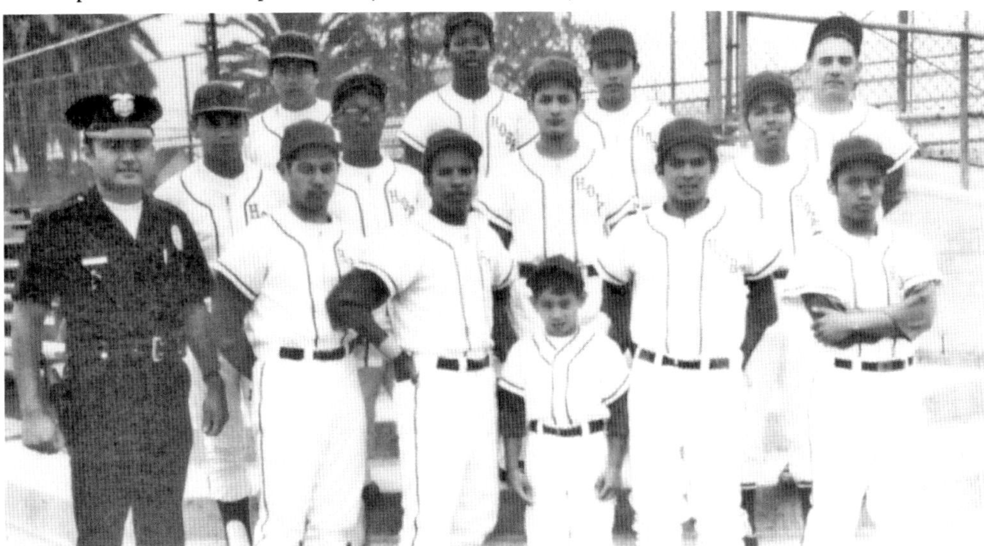

In 1969, the Los Angeles Police Department sponsored teams including the Hollenbeck Division in Boyle Heights. At far left is officer Bob Acosta. From left to right are (first row) Steve Paz, Mike Estrada, Kelvin Paz, unidentified, and Al De La Rosa; (second row) Billy Téllez, James Roberts, Tony Lara, and Jesse Estrada; (third row) Jimmie Reza, Melvin Tinsley, Frank Ortiz, and manager Jesús Paz. Jesse Estrada later became a Los Angeles police officer. Not shown is Victor Orona. (Courtesy of Al De La Rosa.)

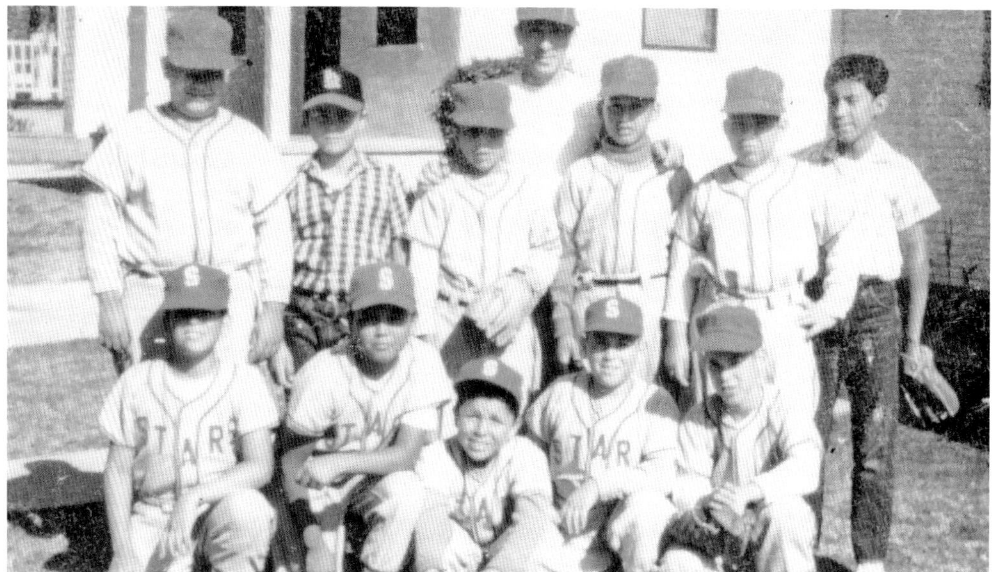

The 1960 City Terrace Stars played their games at City Terrace and Belvedere Parks. Ray Molina Sr. (standing in back) coached the team while his son Ray Jr. (first row, center) was the catcher. Ray Sr. coached his son for 10 years in East Los Angeles, Monterey Park, Summer Leagues, and at Cantwell High School with the junior varsity baseball team. Ray Jr. played ball in East Los Angeles, Monterey Park, Cantwell High School, and at East Los Angeles College. His mother, Molly, washed and sewed uniforms for all the boys in addition to feeding them. (Courtesy of the Molina family.)

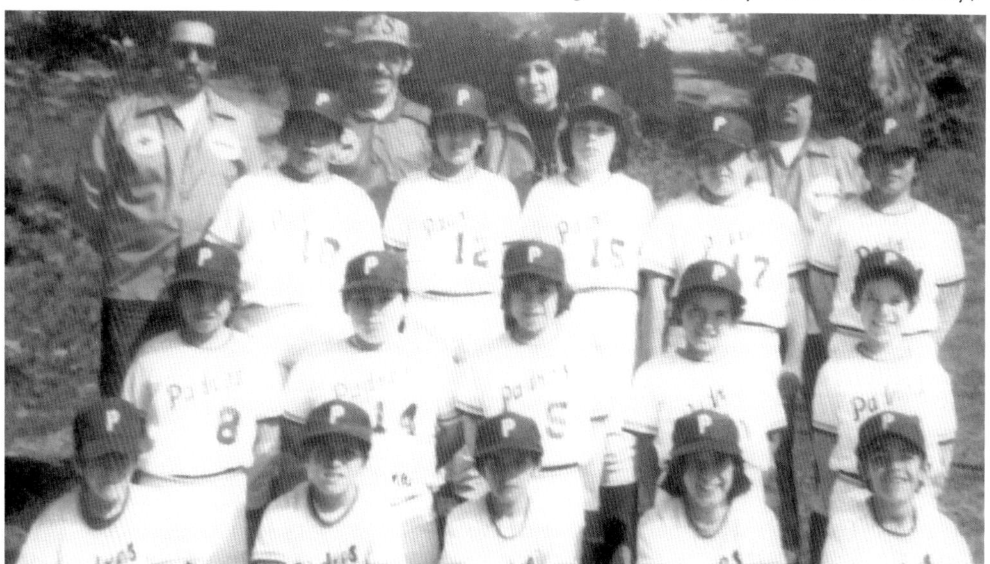

The 1975 El Sereno Padres were division league champions. From left to right are (first row) Albie Enriguez, Martin Rodríguez, Felipe De La Riva, Mike Loya, and Jerry Olivas; (second row) Jaime Longoria, Richard Escalante, Richard Robles, Armando Lucero, and Frank Vargas; (third row) Channing Estrada Jr., Ricky Quinonez, Armando Molina, unidentified, and Paul Renteria; (fourth row) Channing Estrada Sr., Richard Quinonez, Mrs. Quinonez, and ? Loya. (Courtesy of Jaime Longoria.)

Pictured in 1915 are Simons Brickyard players Maggie Montijo (left) and 17-year-old Mary Cano. The Latino Baseball History Project has published nearly 150 women's baseball and softball photographs. This is the earliest one discovered to date. The majority are from the 1930s through the 1950s. Baseball and softball fields provided one of the many spaces where young Mexican American girls could flourish as women and contributing members of a bicultural community. Mexicanas were able to shatter both racial and gender sterotypes. The lessons learned on the field helped these women regarding progressive political involvement, business opportunities, economic independence, and cultural enhancement. The girls marched onto the diamond like queens in feminine uniforms but played like warriors. They have served as role models for generations of Mexican American girls who continue to play with the same energy, spirit, and *corazon*. (Courtesy of Virginia Ruiz Durazo and Theresa Tresierras Durazo.)

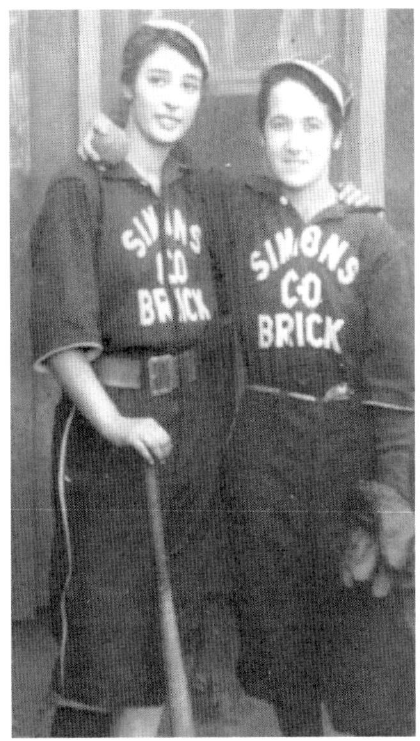


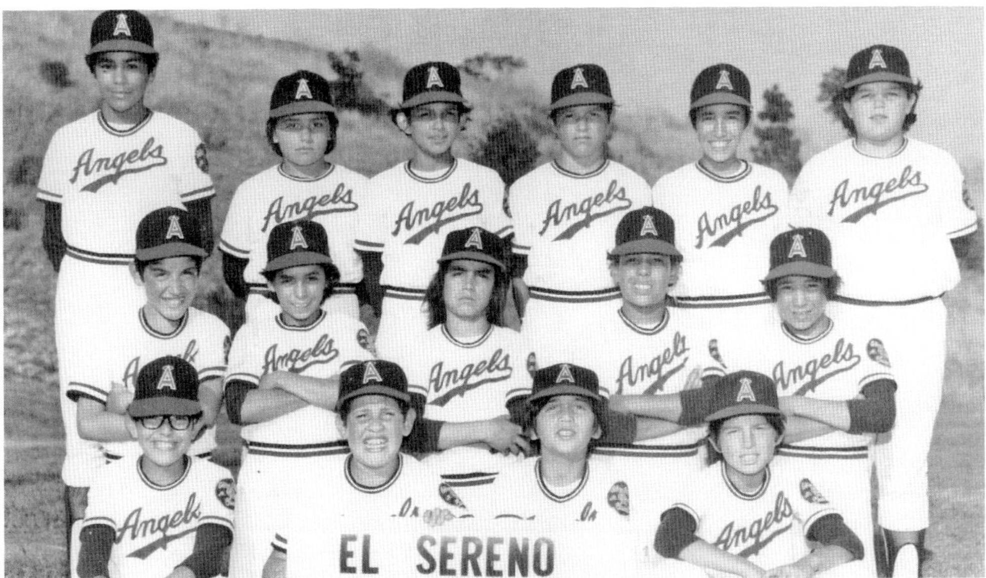


The 1973 El Sereno Angels played in the Golden State Baseball League and in Pop Warner football. Most played various sports at Wilson High School including baseball, football, basketball, tennis, and wrestling. In football, Wilson's record from 1975 through 1978 was 50-1. From left to right are (first row) Richard Duarte, Eppie ?, Birdy Perales, and Manuel Villa; (second row) unidentified, Victor Ascencio, Mark Flores, Eddie Gómez, and Eddie Martínez; (third row) Louis Aguilar, Ángel ?, Steve Martínez, Santi Cuevas, Anthony Luna, and Raúl Pedroza. (Courtesy of Anthony Luna.)

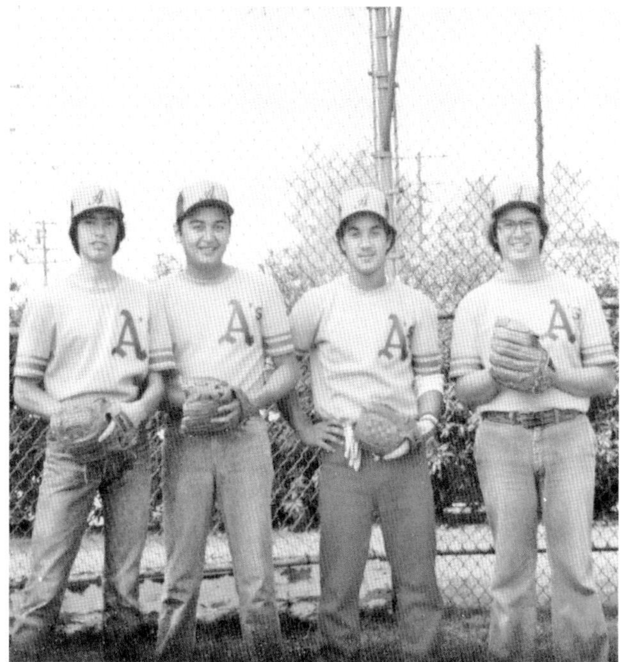

The A's were a fast-pitch softball team from Boyle Heights that played in the Pecan Men's Softball League at Pecan Park. Leading the A's to second place in 1978 were, from left to right, Ramiro Caro (outfield), Gene Aguilera (second base), Richard Vásquez (shortstop), and Leo Gutiérrez (third base and coach). Childhood friends since 1962, Aguilera and Gutiérrez grew up playing endless sandlot baseball at Evergreen Park with brothers Ernesto and David Acosta. Gutiérrez has served as director of the East Los Angeles Youth Baseball Association since 1997. (Courtesy of Gene Aguilera.)

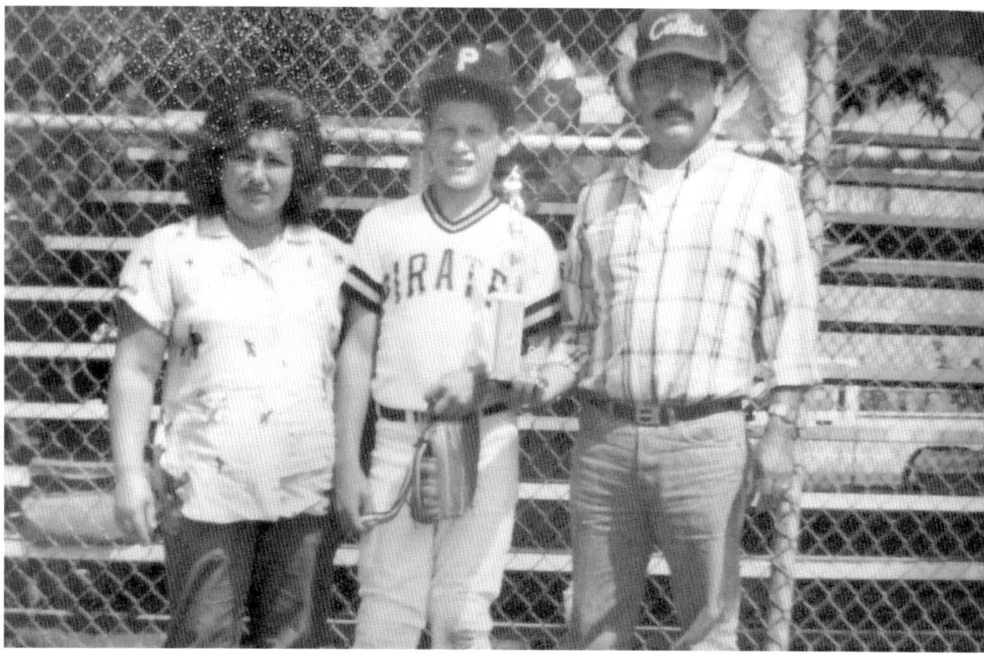

Ray Ruiz (center) has played and coached in East Los Angeles for many years. His parents, Ramón and Guadalupe Ruiz, were from Jalisco, Mexico. Guadalupe was from La Laja, and Ramón was from Mascota. They both migrated to Los Angeles in 1969 and met there in 1970. They married and moved to Boyle Heights, where Ray was born and raised. Ray started playing baseball at Costello Park in Estrada Courts. His mother saw his passion for the game and always made sure that he had the right equipment and was on time for practice and games. (Courtesy of Ray Ruiz.)

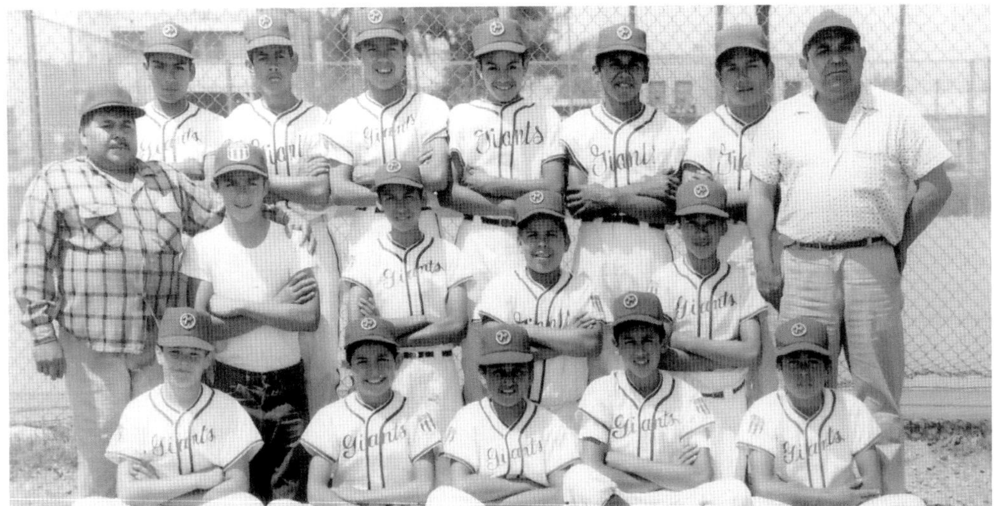

This is the 1963 Laguna Park Giants of the 325 Sportsman League. From left to right are (first row) Nicky Escamilla, Richard Morales, Ernie Paderez, Nefty Navarro, and unidentified; (second row) manager Joe Gonzáles, Ray ?, Joe Velasco, R. Martínez, and unidentified; (third row) Ray Velásquez, two unidentified, Andy Zamarripa, Alfred Lara, Jimmy Valenzuéla, and coach Manuel ? Joe Gonzáles coached several teams in East Los Angeles including American Legion, Our Lady of Lourdes, and the Monterey Park Firebirds. His son, Richard, had a tryout with the Cincinnati Reds in 1970 and hit the outstanding batter Tony Pérez with a pitch. (Courtesy of Richard Gonzáles.)

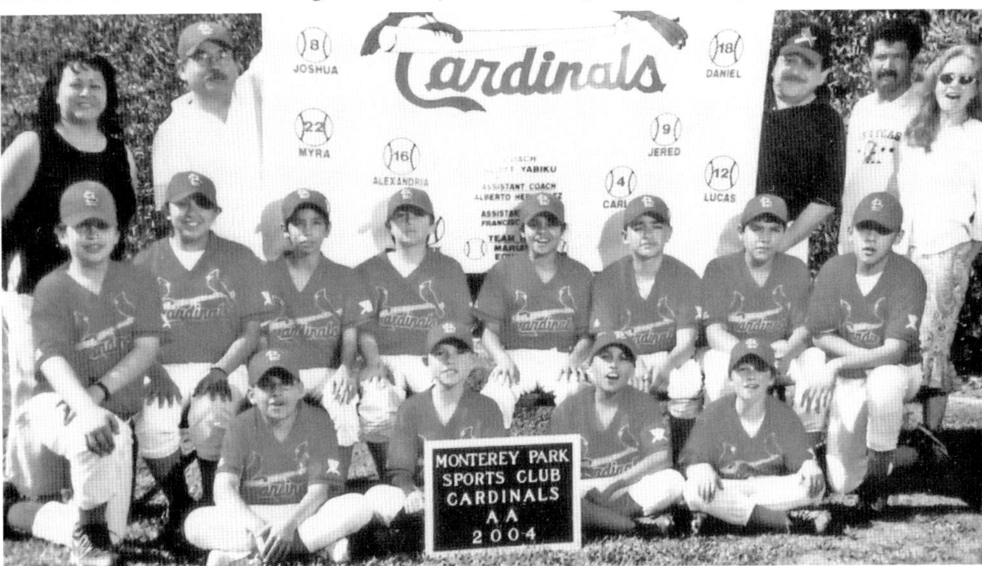


Tomas J. Benítez (standing third from right) grew up in the Evergreen section of East Los Angeles. As a young man, he played neighborhood ball. He coached pitchers and catchers with the 2004 Cardinals in nearby Monterey Park. His son, Lucas (second row, fourth from left), played second base. For more than 150 years, fathers have played an important role in managing and coaching the young men in the Mexican American community. For Tomas, there is nothing like the bond of baseball between a father and his son. (Courtesy of Tomas J. Benítez.)

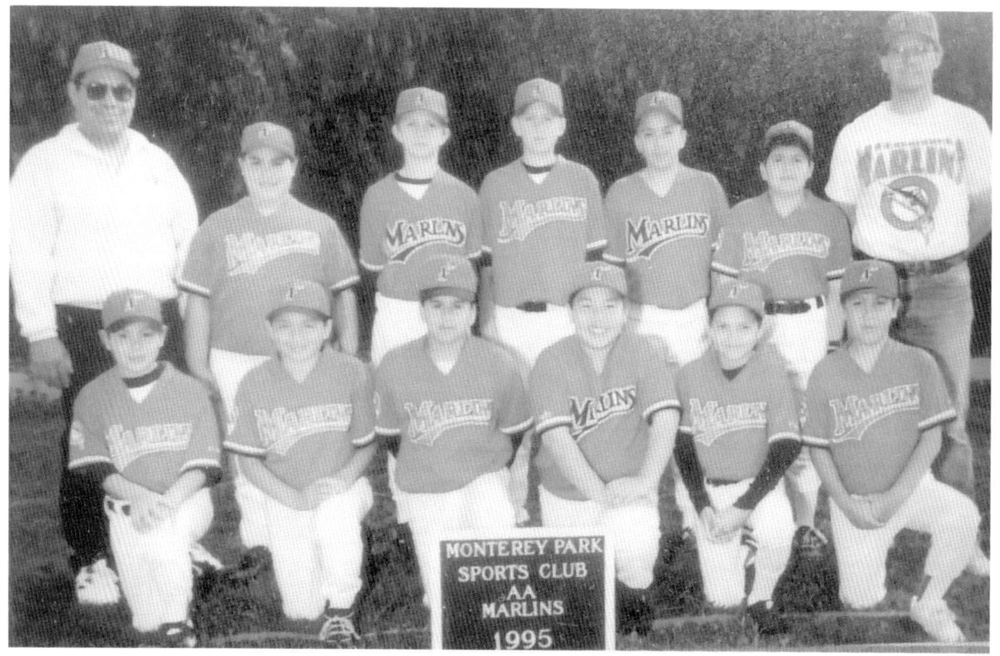


Frank De La Rosa is a longtime player and coach in East Los Angeles. He also coached in neighboring Monterey Park. Frank (second row, far left) coached the 1995 Marlins at La Loma Park. His son Daniel (first row, far right) played second base and outfield. Frank also coached Daniel with the Monterey Park Cubs and Reds and in San Gabriel. Daniel played three years as a catcher for Don Bosco Tech High School in Rosemead. Frank was president of the high school booster club. (Courtesy of Frank De La Rosa.)

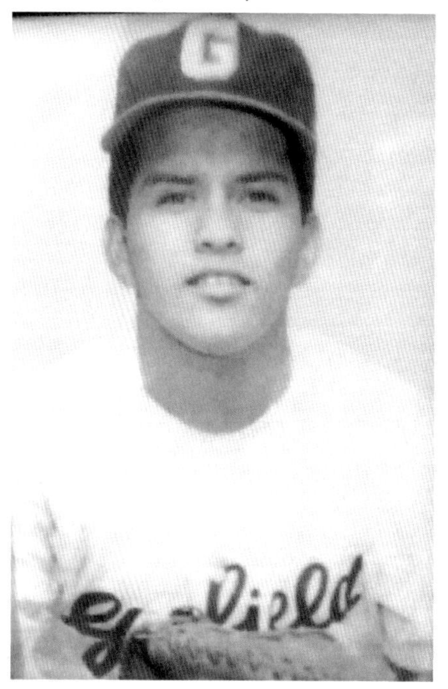

Gil Pérez is the son of Manuel "Shorty" Pérez, the legendary manager from East Los Angeles. Gil recalled being the batboy for the Carmelita Chorizeros and arriving early to help his father chalk the field. Gil saw games that his dad managed at Belvedere, El Sereno, Evergreen, and Hazard Parks. His dad would give him a bag of quarters to give to the kids who retrieved foul balls. Gil played Little League at Belvedere Park, where his father coached him for many years. Gil fondly remembers hitting a home run—his proudest baseball moment. He played ball briefly at Garfield High School before hurting his arm. He served in Vietnam. (Courtesy of Gil Pérez.)

# 2

# High School and College

There are four major public high schools in the greater East Los Angeles region, all named after US presidents: Theodore Roosevelt (Roughriders), James Garfield (Bulldogs), Woodrow Wilson (Mules), and Abraham Lincoln (Tigers). A fifth school, for troubled boys, was Andrew Jackson High School (the girls had Ramona High School). There is one community college, originally known as East Los Angeles Junior College (Huskies), established in 1945 by the Los Angeles School Board and offering classes to 117 students at Garfield High School.

The Los Angeles Board of Education purchased 82 acres of farmland where the present East Los Angeles Community College (ELAC) offers courses to over 40,000 students. The first classrooms were in wooden bungalows from the Santa Ana army base in Orange County. Many Mexican American veterans used their GI Bill after World War II, Korea, and Vietnam to attend ELAC. The nearby Maravilla housing project initially housed many of these veterans and their families. Today, ELAC is going through a building initiative, transforming and modernizing the entire campus.

Just a few miles away from ELAC is California State University at Los Angeles (Golden Eagles), established in 1947. Old-time alumni remember their alma mater as Cal State LA or LA State, and the team then was the Diablos (the Devils). All of these high schools, ELAC, and Cal State Los Angeles continue to produce celebrated baseball and softball teams, upright players, and nitty-gritty coaches.

Baseball and softball helped keep some young men from being juvenile delinquents, and for others, the sport served as an incentive to stay in school and graduate. Baseball gave several talented players a once-in-a-lifetime opportunity to attend college with baseball scholarships. So many of these blue-chip players themselves later became gung-ho managers and coaches for several generations of players. Coaches have had a colossal impact on countless young lives. Youth, high school, and college ball established unshakable relationships between players and their coaches. Their legacy will live on as long as young boys and girls play ball in East Los Angeles.

These athletes, during the springtime of their lives, played endless games without a care in the world, monkeyed around with boyhood pals, played good-natured pranks, roughhoused, and gave each other affectionately unflattering nicknames. These happy-go-lucky vagabonds established an extraordinary kinship and camaraderie that endured long after they hung up their gloves. When all is said and done, these old fogies still keep in touch with each other to relive their long ago laugh-a-minute days, and still to horseplay and wisecrack.

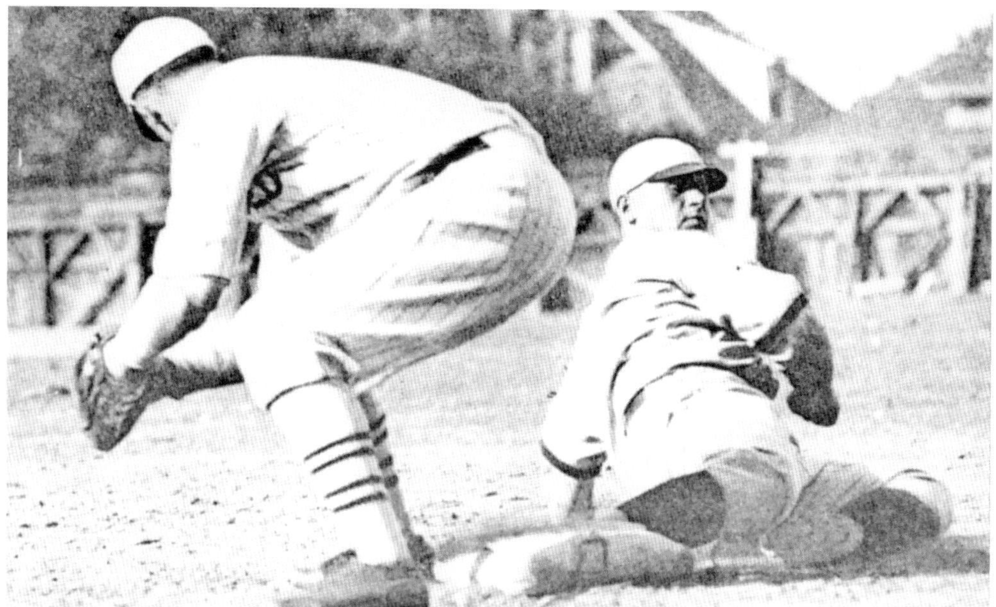

Charles "Coney" Galindo was raised in San Diego, where he played high school baseball. He was awarded a baseball scholarship to USC as a second baseman. He is seen here sliding into base as a Trojan in 1925. He majored in education, gaining a teaching credential. For his entire teaching career, students were his most precious individuals. His first teaching job was at Roosevelt High School. In 1932, he became the varsity coach at the school. (Courtesy of Al Padilla.)

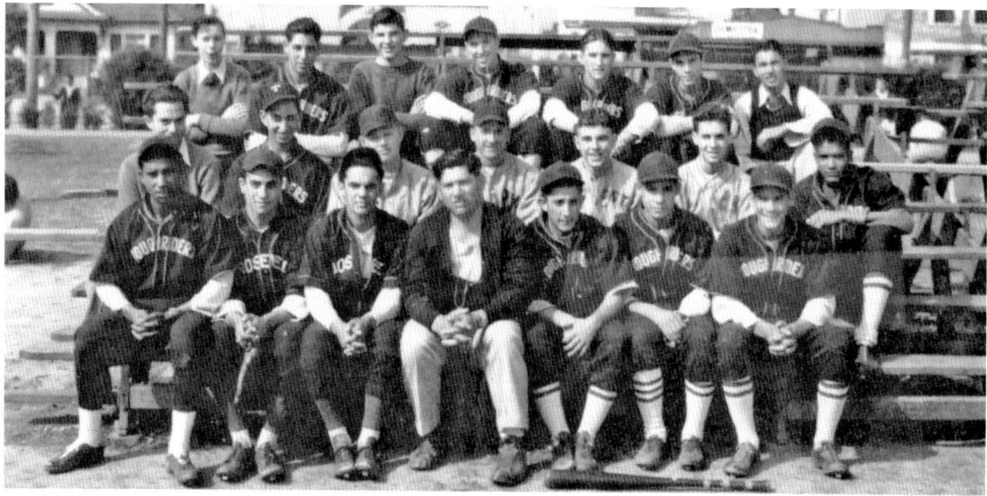

In 1932, Charles "Coney" Galindo (first row, center) was the varsity baseball coach at Theodore Roosevelt High School in Boyle Heights, where he had a profound influence on countless Roughriders, including brothers Joe (first row, far right) and Candido Madrid Gonzáles (first row, second from right). Both Joe and Candido received baseball scholarships to USC. Candido decided that his brother Joe should go on to USC, since one of them had to financially care for their parents and younger siblings during the Great Depression. Candido continued to play community ball at Evergreen and Belvedere Parks. (Courtesy of Christine Gonzáles Gillett.)

At Roosevelt High School, Coach Charles "Coney" Galindo mentored countless young men to be athletes and upright citizens. One of his protégés was Joe Gonzáles, who went on to pitch for the Boston Red Sox before enlisting at the start of World War II. Gonzáles returned to coach at Roosevelt High School and, like Galindo, influenced a generation of young men. Galindo later taught at John Adams Junior High School and became an umpire. He was considered one of the best umpires in Los Angeles city baseball. (Courtesy of Al Padilla.)

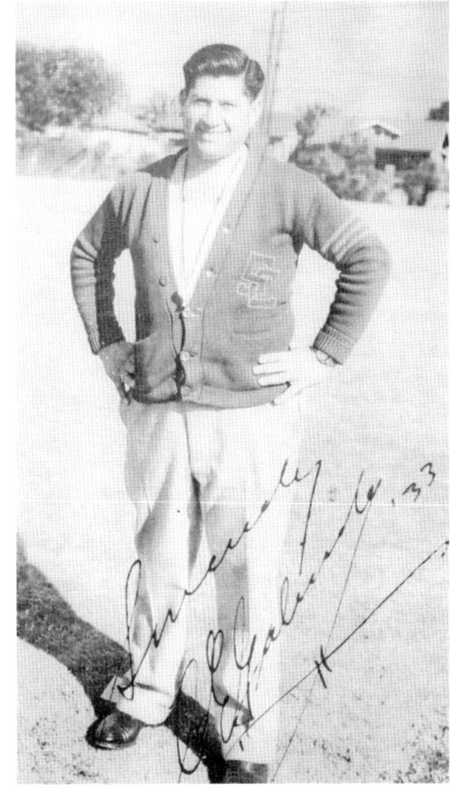

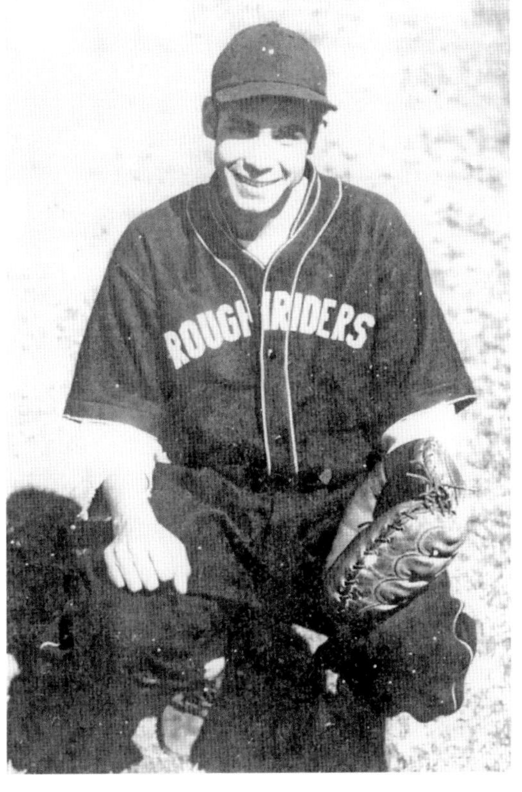


Candido Madrid González was born in 1913 in the mining town of Sutter Creek, California, the oldest of eight children. His father, Candido Sr., moved around a lot, looking for work for his big family. They eventually settled in Boyle Heights. At nine, Candido sold newspapers and shined shoes, helping the family financially. Any free time was devoted to baseball with his brothers Joe and Freddie. In retirement, he loved Dodger dogs and cold beer at Dodger Stadium and rarely missed a game on TV with his wife, Margaret. He passed away in 1987. His daughter Christina was born at White Memorial Hospital and attended East Los Angeles College and Cal State Los Angeles. She retired after working 36 years at Cal State Los Angeles. (Courtesy of Christina González Gillett.)

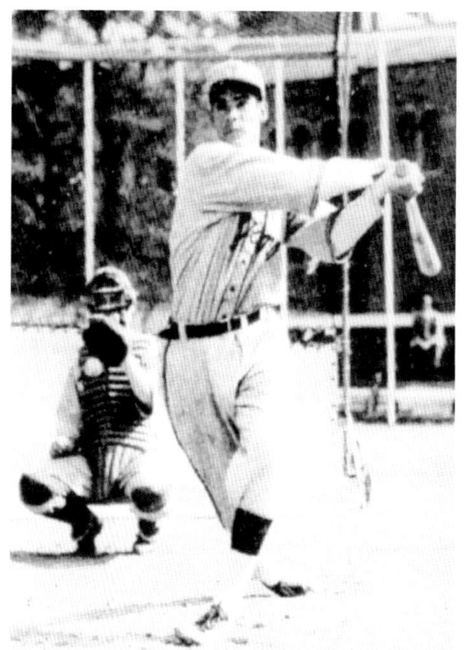

Joe Gonzáles is born in San Francisco in 1915 and later attended Roosevelt High School in Boyle Heights, where he learned to pitch from Charles "Coney" Gallindo. He made his professional baseball debut with the Boston Red Sox as a right handed pitcher in 1937. Joe DiMaggio hit a home run off him. Gonzáles earned All-City honors and received a scholarship to the University of Southern California. He is seen here batting in a game at USC in 1935. He was undefeated as a USC pitcher his last two years. He toured Japan with an All-American baseball team for the American Baseball Congress. Gonzáles has been inducted into both the Roosevelt and USC halls of fame. He served in World War II and taught and coached for 30 years, winning six high school baseball championships. (Courtesy of Al Padilla.)

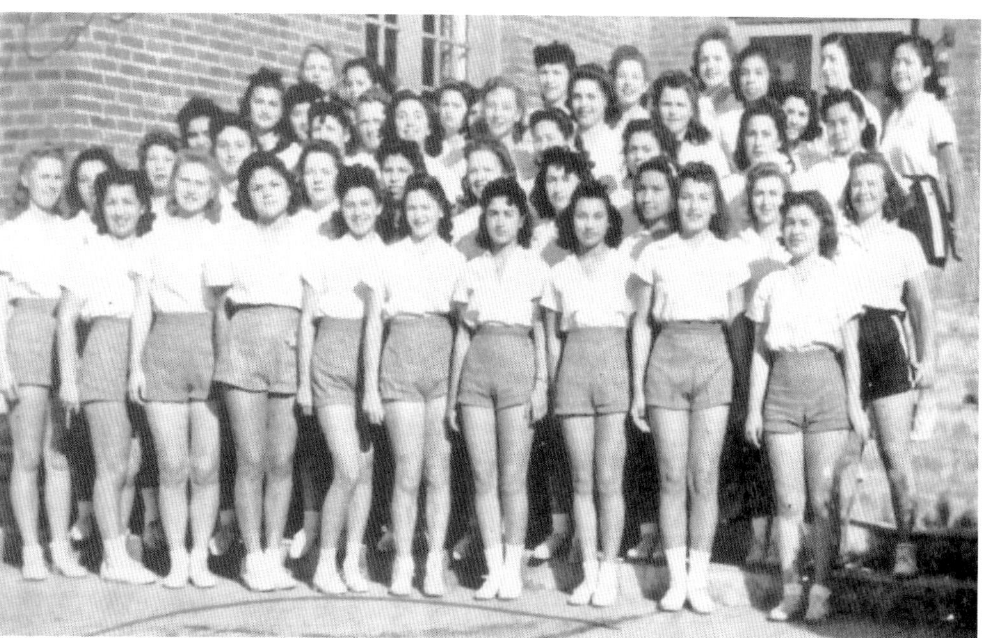

The 1941 Girl's Athletic Association (GAA) at Roosevelt High School played several sports, including softball, tennis, basketball, shuffleboard, and volleyball. The GAA started at Roosevelt in 1923 with 30 girls, and by 1941, there were over 200 members. The aim of the GAA was to further interest in sports and aid girls' physical and emotional development. Like the boys, the girls earned sports letters and wore their letter sweaters on campus. Several Mexican Americans were active with the GAA, including Gloria Rodríguez, Olivia Correa, Pauline García, and Mary Camarillo. (Courtesy of Carlos V. Santillán.)

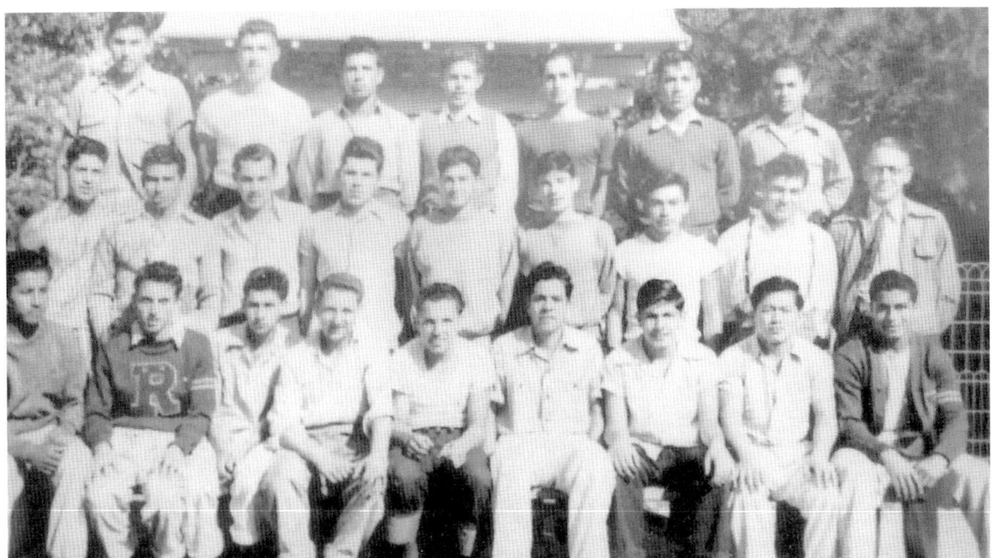

In 1943, Roosevelt High School started a softball team, since nearly all the baseball players had enlisted for World War II. From left to right are (first row) Lorezizo Santa Maria, Ernie Sierra, Albert Casillas, Dave Manwaring, Manuel Ocampo, Rubén Cardona, Tons Sakalis, Hideo Ishimine, and Raúl Rejalado; (second row) Henry Santoya, Ángel Chávez, Alex Obeso, Eddie Pérez, Marvin Annenberg, Morris Class, Tony Serrato, Ray Gonzáles, and Coach Tom Denny; (third row) Dominic Arcuri, John Brajkovich, Eddie Bonillo, Harold Taubman, Roy Atinksy, George Peña, and Ángel Bañuelos. (Courtesy of Carlos V. Santillán.)

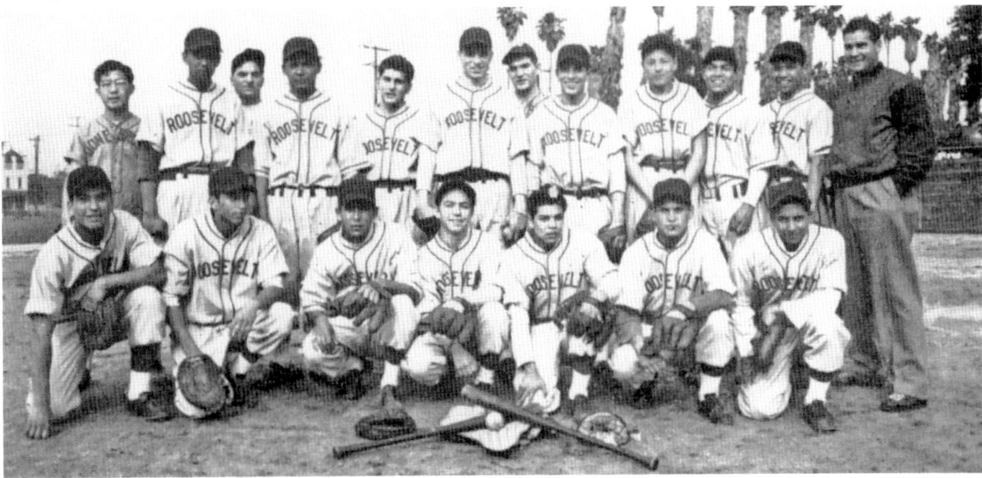

The 1946 Roosevelt club was the first baseball team after the war. From left to right are (first row) Bill Cota, Charlie Sierra, Pat Molina, Simón Trujillo, Louie Gómez, Dick Duran, and Roberto Ontiveros; (second row) Frank Yamamoto, Tamoe Rodríguez, Dominic Salgarolo, Manuel Flores, Nick Sadd, Richard La Carra, Charlie Chávez, Robert Ortiz, Henry Hinojoso, Johnny Peña, Al Padilla, and coach Joe Gonzáles. Padilla and Peña were the pitching battery for years in East Los Angeles. Coach Gonzáles had pitched for the Red Sox organization before enlisting in World War II. (Courtesy of Al Padilla.)

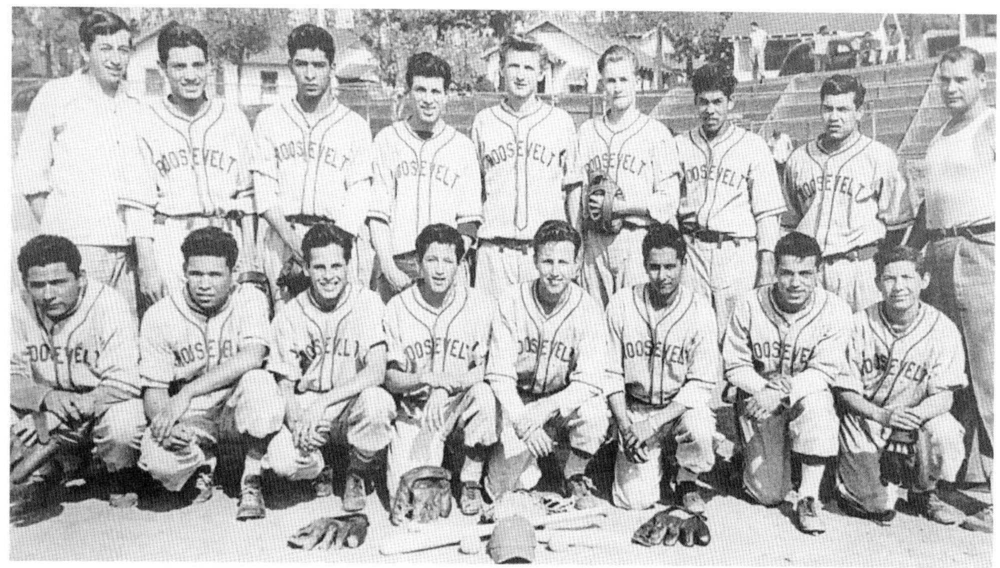


The 1947 Roosevelt team had several outstanding players. From left to right are (first row) Manuel Flores, Al Padilla, Richard Duran, Fermín Magaña, Jim Miller, Robert Ontiveros, Richard Peña, and Benny López; (second row) manager Bernard Wilson, Preciliano Recendez, Robert Lugo, Robert Ortiz, Jim Slevcove, Jim Williams, Arnold Hernández, Johnny Peña, and coach Joe Gonzáles. Gonzáles served in the Navy during World War II, and four brothers also served in the military: James, Ernest, Freddy, and John. Ernest was killed in action; John was wounded. (Courtesy of Al Padilla.)

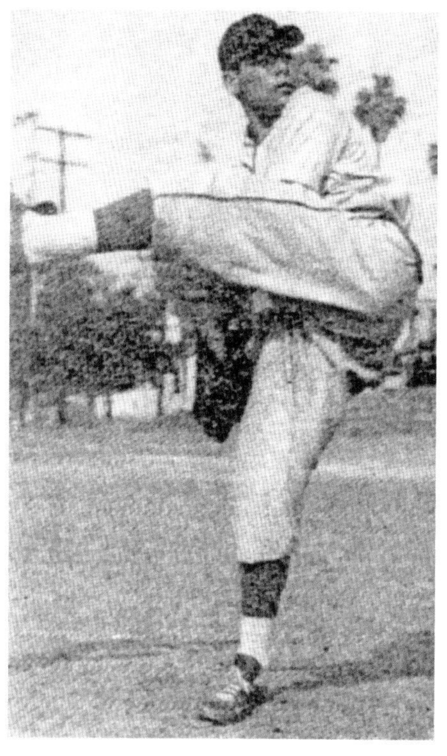

Al Padilla was an outstanding pitcher in the late 1940s at Roosevelt High School and is seen here winding up for the curveball. He pitched in 1946 and 1947. His catcher was Johnny Peña, who also played centerfield. Both Al and Johnny were also teammates on the football team. Roosevelt won the Los Angeles city championship Division II with Padilla as the winning pitcher. He coached at Roosevelt and Garfield high schools and took the 1974 East Los Angeles Junior College football team to the state championship. At Roosevelt High School, he coached several outstanding players who became football stars at USC. An inductee to the Occidental College football and baseball halls of fame, he retired after 43 years of coaching in East Los Angeles but continues to remain active with youth sports. He is one of the founders of the Latino Baseball History Project. (Courtesy of Al Padilla.)

Tony Lugo (batting) grew up in East Los Angeles near Our Lady of Lourdes Church. The entire neighborhood was later uprooted for the construction of the Pomona Freeway. As a young boy, Brooklyn Dodger great Duke Snider had an aunt and grandmother who lived near Tony in East Los Angeles. Even though Snider was older, they became summer friends. Tony wore No. 4 or a variation of it for all his teams as a tribute to Snider. When Snider learned that Tony was very ill in 2009, he sent him two autographed balls. (Courtesy of Richard Lugo.)

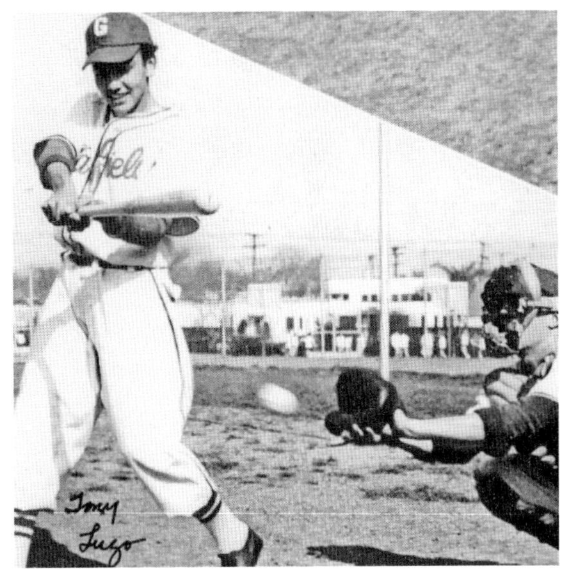


Eastern League Championship

Class A G 1949

This is to certify that Tony Lugo

was a member of the James A. Garfield High School

Eastern League Championship Baseball team.

Given in recognition of services rendered.

Raymond Brothers
Principal

Bob Holmes
Coach

B.A.A. Commissioner

Los Angeles, California
June 17, 1949

This is Tony Lugo's certificate that he had lettered in baseball at Garfield in 1949. Tony was not able to share this great news with his father, Antonio, who served in the Navy during World War II and was killed in the hard-fought battle on Saipan against the Japanese. Tony also played for semipro teams throughout the greater Los Angeles area. While raising his family, he played for business-sponsored teams like Helms Bakery and Wilson Meats. (Courtesy of Richard Lugo.)

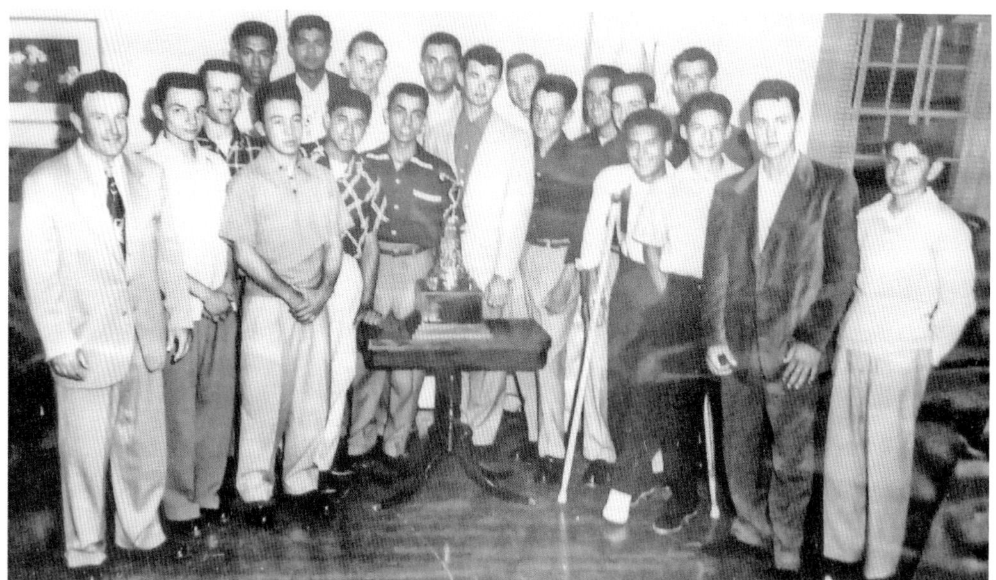

The 1952 Garfield High School team won the Los Angeles city championship. The players are seen at a school banquet celebrating their achievement. Among those pictured are coach Bob Holmes, Joe Gaitan, Tom Robles, Richard Cazares, Peter Ortega, Ernest Negrete, Ángel Figueroa, Benny García, and his cousin Ray García. The city baseball championship was the first one by any high school in the East Los Angeles area, which included Bell, South Gate, Roosevelt, Huntington Park, Wilson, and Lincoln High Schools. (Courtesy of Joe Gaitan.)

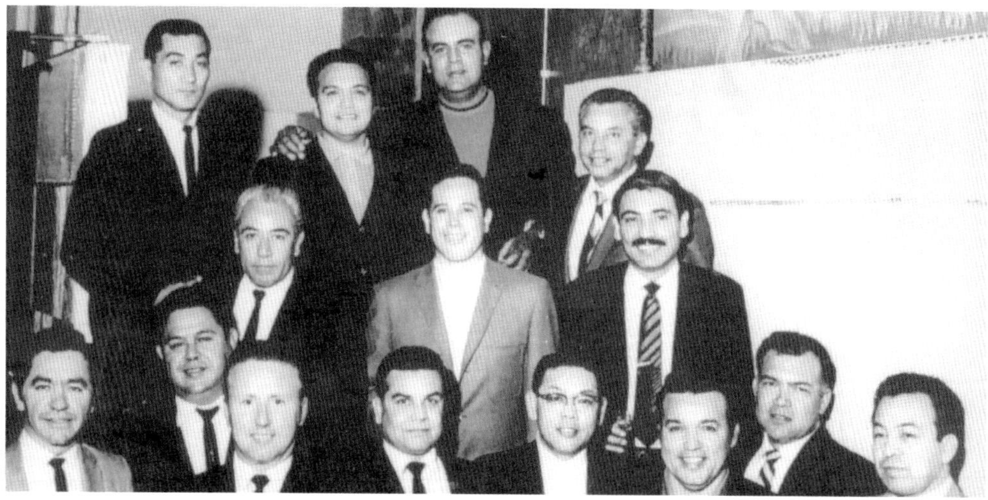

This photograph was taken around 1960 at Patriotic Hall in downtown Los Angeles. The retirement event was for longtime East Los Angeles coach Louis Lunetta (not pictured), who had coached these men as youngsters at Fresno, State, Hazard and many other local playgrounds. From left to right are (first row) Simon Trujillo, Frank Oblea, Jim Miller, Louis Gómes, Wally Poon, Richard and Johnny Peña, and Joe Gaitan; (second row) Phil Beltran, Bobby Recendez, and Percy Recendez; (third row) James Yoshishtake, Gabriel Peña, Henry García, and Charlie Sierra. (Courtesy of Bobby Recendez.)

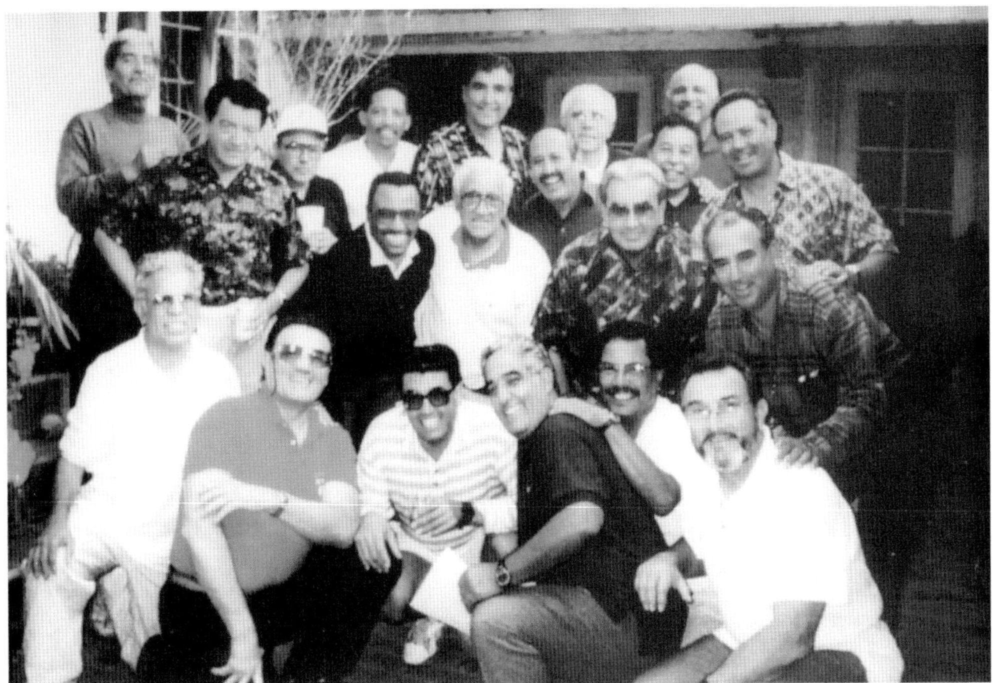

This 1997 event was held at the home of Neno Félix in Pico Rivera, California, to honor legendary coach Dominck Campollo (center with white sweater). In no particular order are Conrad and Joe Muñatones, Art Velarde, Rubén Rodríguez, Donald Watson, Louie González, Gil Farias, Bobby Recendez, Henry Ronquillo, Armando Pérez, Gil Gamez, Fernando Farfán, Floyd Jeter, Ray Delgado, and Ralph ? All of these men were outstanding players from youth to professional levels. Many of them later dedicated themselves to coaching. (Courtesy of Bobby Recendez.)

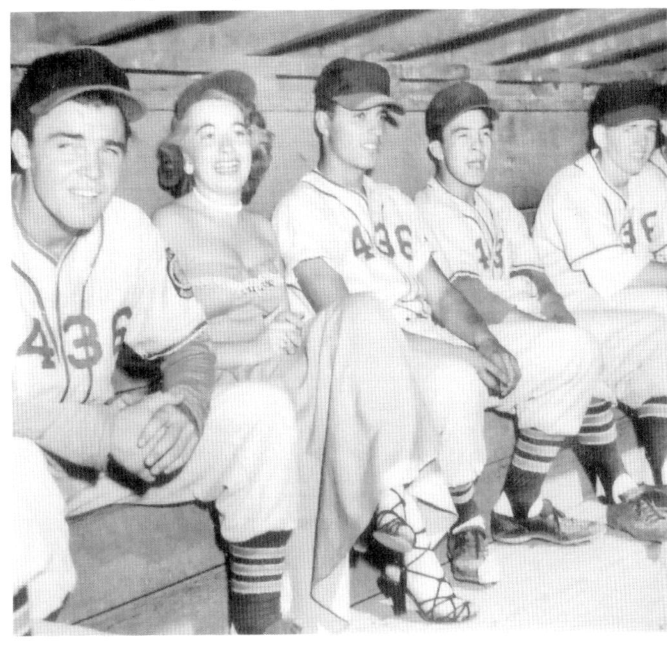

Joe Gaitan (fourth from left) and Willie García (third from left) are seen in the Bay Area during a game. García pitched for Wilson High School in El Sereno. This El Sereno American Legion team had a few players who went on to play collegiate baseball. Garry Mason and Louis Baltz played at USC, Joe Gaitan played at Fresno State, and Bill Lunetta played at UCLA. After this double header, the players were treated to a banquet at a nice restaurant. (Courtesy of Joe Gaitan.)

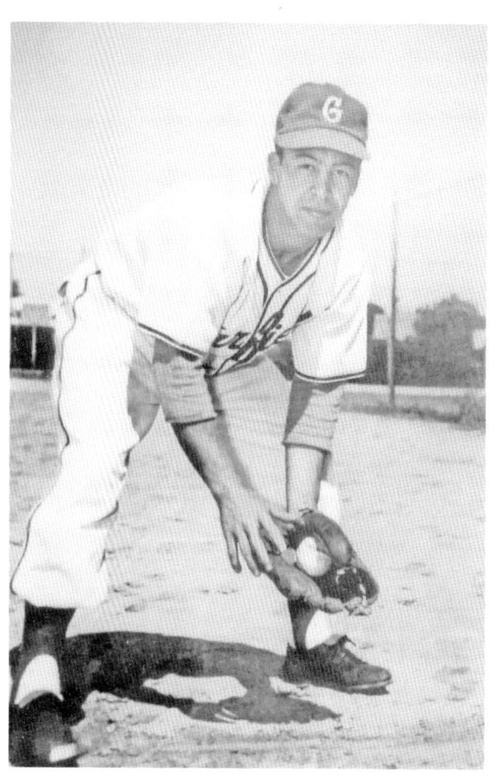

Joe Gaitan takes infield practice before a 1952 game against Washington High School at Garfield High School. Garfield was in the Southern League, considered the strongest division in the city. The league was made up of Fremont, Washington, Jefferson, Roosevelt, Manuel Arts, and Garfield. Garfield won the Southern League championship in 1951, 1952, and 1953. The 1952 team also won the city championship. Two outstanding Bulldogs were Don Dangleis and Benny García. Dangleis signed a professional contract with the Pittsburgh Pirates, and García continued his star-studded athletic career at ELAC in baseball and football. (Courtesy of Joe Gaitan.)

★ High School Hall of Fame

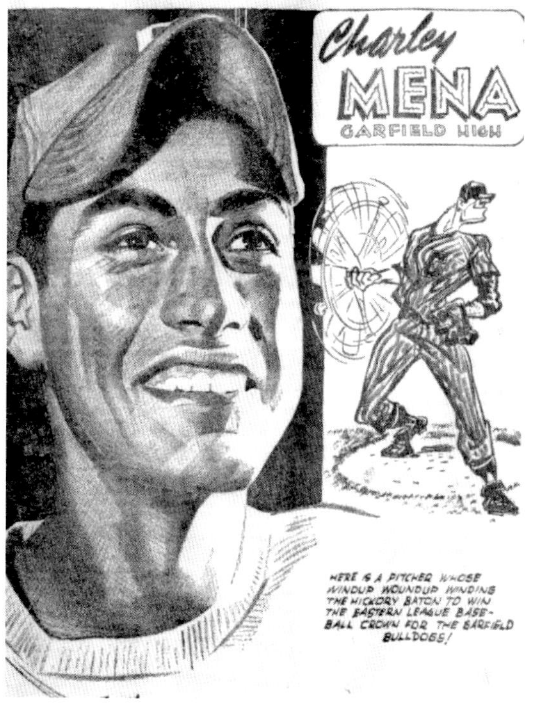


Charlie Mena was born in East Los Angeles. His father, Victor II, was from Mexico and had married Delia Carpio from El Paso, Texas. Victor II worked at the Malboro Lamp Factory in downtown Los Angeles. Charlie attended Belvedere Elementary, Belvedere Junior High, and Garfield High School. He was an outstanding left-handed pitcher in 1955, with a wicked curveball and fastball. The Bulldogs played against Huntington Park, Bell, Jordan, Roosevelt, and other surrounding schools. Charlie's brother, Victor III, played basketball for Garfield. After high school, Charlie received a baseball scholarship to USC. He received his PhD in education from the University of Colorado at Boulder in 1977. (Courtesy of Charlie Mena.)

Benny García was outstanding in baseball and basketball at Garfield High School, making All-League and All-Conference in both sports. He was over six feet tall and weighed over 200 pounds. He also played American Legion ball for a few seasons and became a baseball and football star at ELAC, where he was an outstanding receiver and punter. He was a terrific softball player in the recreational leagues during the 1950s and 1960s. Benny had enough talent to play professionally, but he gave up sports to pursue a career in business. Two cousins, Ray and Eddie García, also played both baseball and football. (Courtesy of Ray Gaitan.)

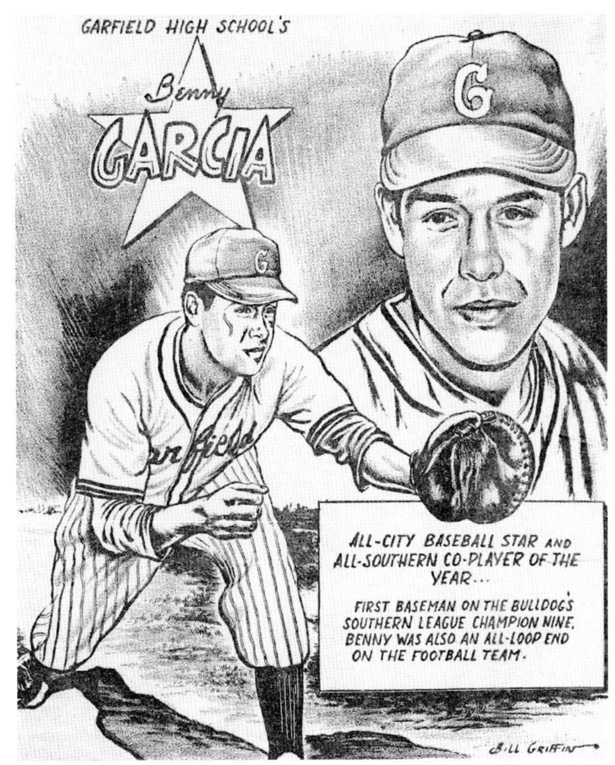


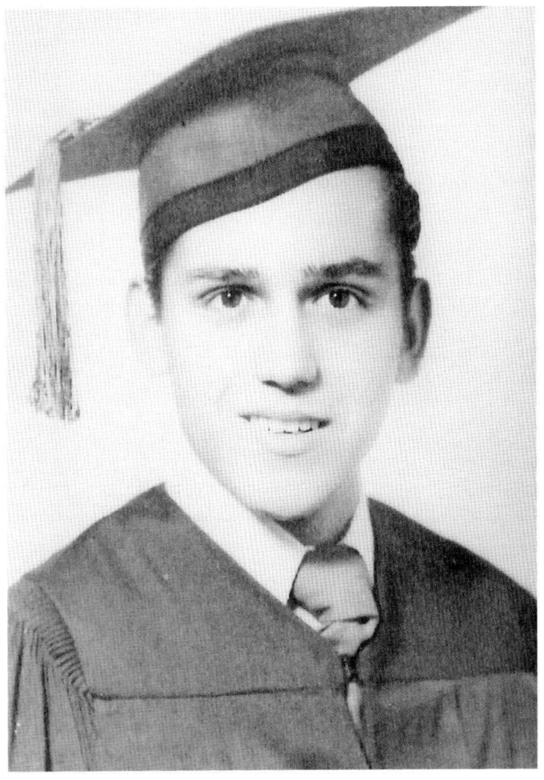

Tommy Benítez was born and raised in El Paso, Texas. After his mother died in 1942, his family moved to the Maravilla section of East Los Angeles when Tommy was 13 years old. The change of venue and playing baseball with the neighborhood boys helped him deal with the loss of his mother. He attended Roosevelt High School and was selected student body president in 1948. He played on the basketball team, but the baseball team had too many outstanding players for him to make the roster. Tommy took his son, Tomas Jr., to his first Dodger game—the fourth game of the 1963 World Series. The Dodgers swept the heavily favored Bronx Bombers. (Courtesy of Tomas Benítez.)

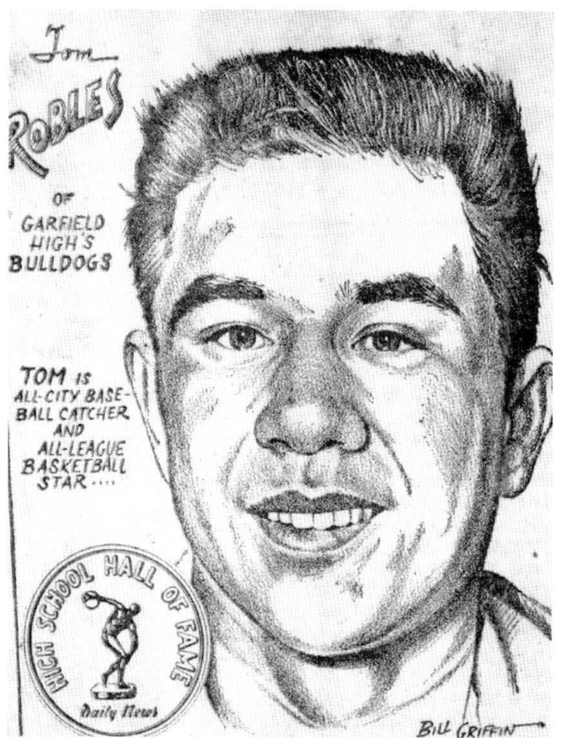


Tom Robles was born and raised in East Los Angeles. His idol as a boy was Joe DiMaggio of the New York Yankees. From an early age, Tom loved to play catcher, regardless of the fact that his equipment was secondhand. His older brother John was his biggest supporter and bought Tom his first glove. Tom played at local parks, including Fresno, Evergreen, and Hazard. He played ball at both Lorena Elementary School and Stevenson Junior High School. Besides a great baseball career at Garfield High School, Tom was the senior class president. His brother John was a football and baseball star at Roosevelt and was a teammate of the legendary Al Padilla. (Courtesy of Mary Robles.)

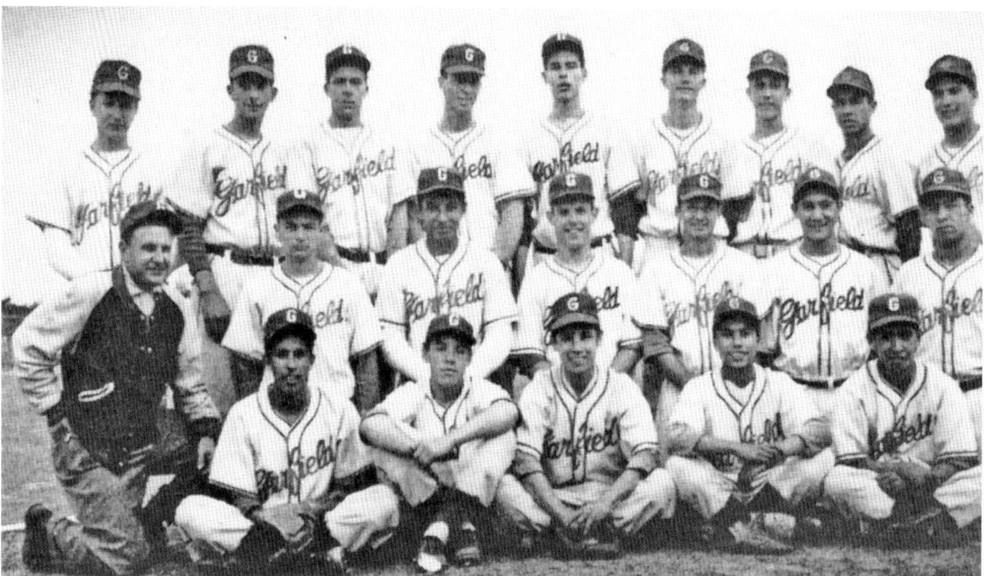

The legendary Bob Holmes coached the 1953 Garfield baseball team, which included Joe Gaitan; Tom Robles, All–Southern League Player of the Year; Ángel Figueroa, first-team All-City; and Clarence Saavedra and Glenn Dangleis, second-team All-City. Ángel Figueroa, Tom Robles, and Pete Ortega all played for the Pittsburgh Pirates minor-league system. Fred Scott played at ELAC and USC and signed with the Baltimore Orioles, playing on their minor league teams. (Courtesy of Fred Scott.)

Bobby Recendez is shown here pitching against Wilson High School in 1952. After high school, he went on to pitch and win many games for several East Los Angeles teams, including Carmelita Provisions Company, Eastside Beer, and Lucky Lager. Bobby also pitched for the Baltimore Orioles Winter League semipro team, where he befriended Chet Brewer, who is now in the Baseball Hall of Fame in Cooperstown, New York. Recendez is in the Roosevelt High School Hall of Fame. Besides baseball, Recendez is considered one of the foremost experts on the history of Los Angeles boxing and the Olympic Auditorium, where matches were held. (Courtesy of Bobby Recendez.)

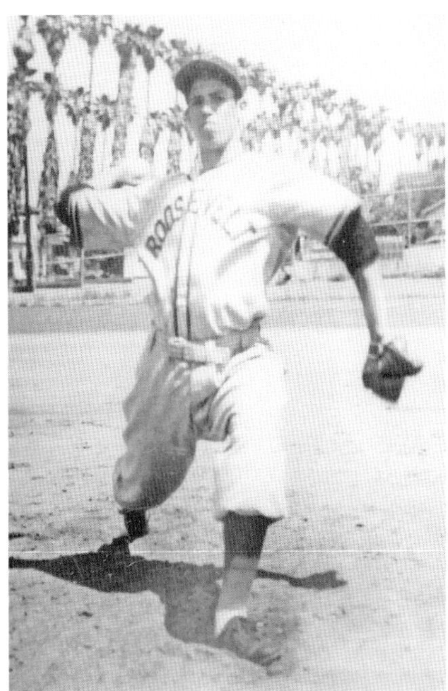

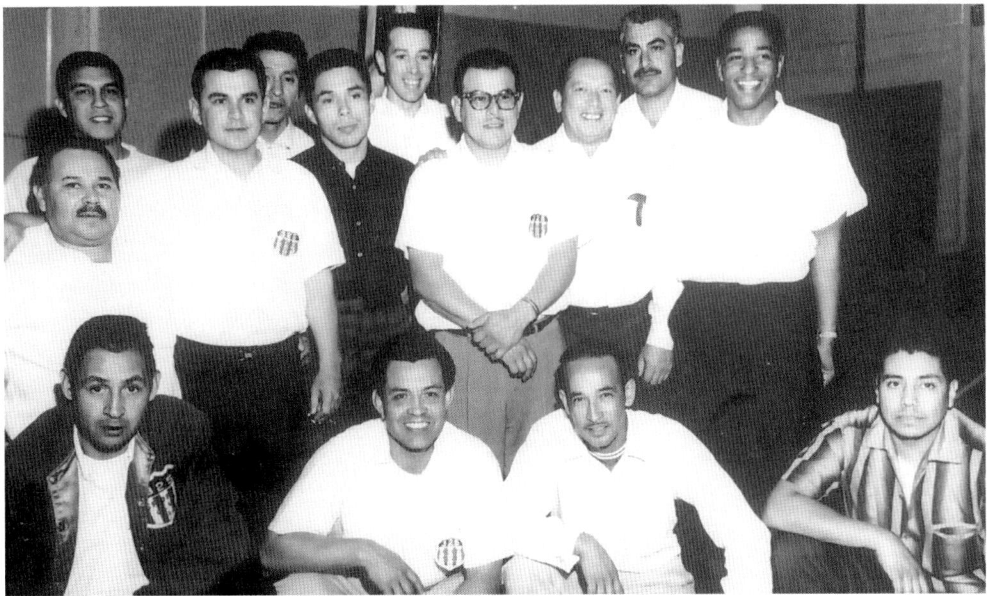

Baseball players were mentored by outstanding coaches at Laguna Park in the 1960s. From left to right are (first row) Tom Sánchez, Jesus "Chuy" Salazar, Bob Tellez, and Octovio ?; (second row) Joe Gonzáles, Armando Rojas, Jess Flores, Manny Rojas, Steve Romero, unidentified, and Ray Sánchez; (third row) park director Bob Villagrama, unidentified, and Joe Escalante. Laguna Park was the site of a violent confrontation between law enforcement and anti-war protestors on August 29, 1970. The park was renamed Ruben Salazar Park in memory of the *Los Angeles Times* reporter and Spanish television commentator who was killed by a Los Angeles sheriff's deputy. (Courtesy of Richard Gonzáles.)

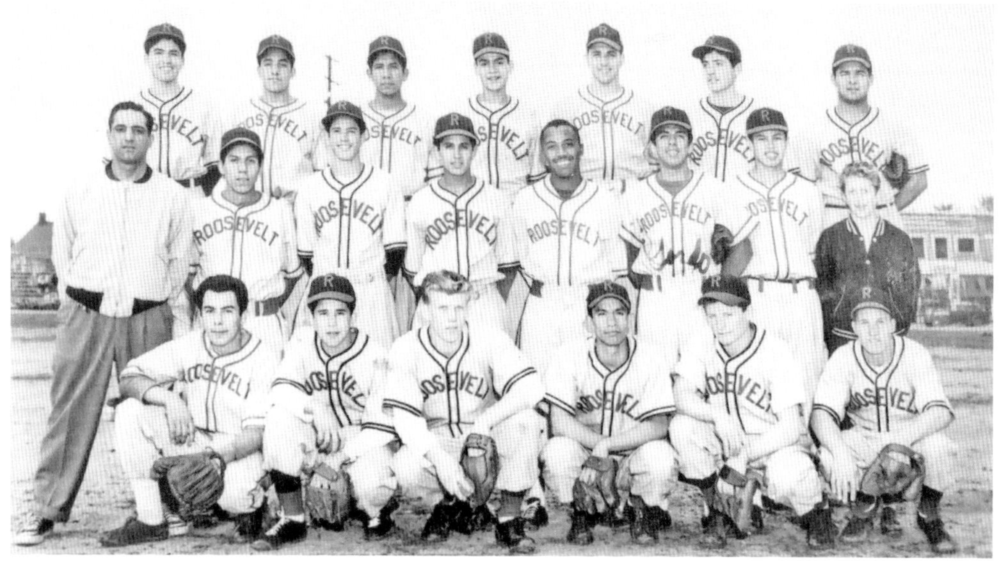

The 1953 Roosevelt High School Roughriders played their home games at Evergreen Park, two blocks away from the campus. This team had lost several stars to graduation and was rebuilding. From left to right are (first row) Bob Morales, Tommy Martínez, Louie Mills, Manny Arellanos, and Bill and Alex Novakoff; (second row) coach Dominck Campallo, Art Melanez, Bobby Recendez, Fernando Farfán, Donald Watson, Joe Herrera, Juan Porras, and ? Miller; (third row) Joe Muñatones, Art Velarde, Tinker De La Rosa, Ray Terrones, ? Miller, Conrad Muñatones, and Mark Urquiti. (Courtesy of Bobby Recendez.)

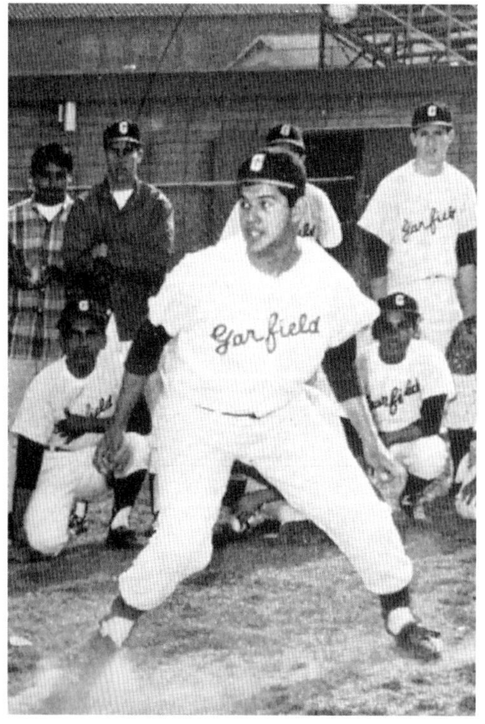


Richard Gonzáles was born in a Chinese hospital near Roosevelt High School in Boyle Heights. He attended Belvedere Elementary and Belvedere Junior High Schools, Our Lady of Lourdes, and Garfield High School. He played softball and basketball at Lourdes. His father coached him at Laguna Park with the Little League Tigers and Pirates. Richard played both pitcher and catcher. One of his teammates was Nicky Escamilla. At Garfield, Gonzáles pitched for the varsity team in 1966 and 1968. He had a wicked curve and outstanding slider. He struck out 16 Lincoln Tigers in a playoff game. During the summers, he played Connie Mack and American Legion ball. He later played two seasons at East Los Angeles College and with several community teams including the Monterey Park Firebirds. He had a tryout with the Cincinnati Reds in 1970. (Courtesy of Richard Gonzáles.)

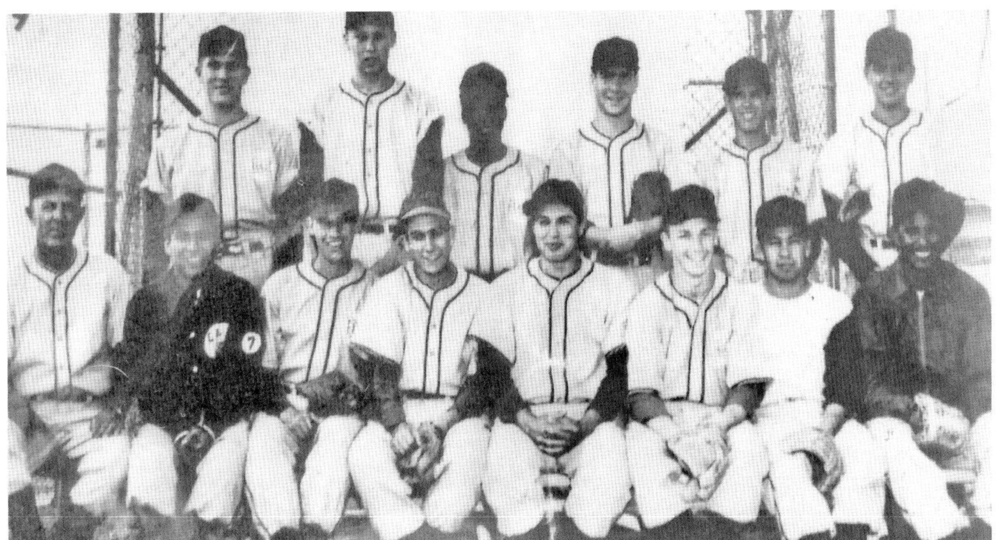

The 1953–1954 East Los Angeles Junior College team included several players from Roosevelt and Garfield High Schools, including Marcelino Saucedo (first row, third from left), Joe Gaitan (first row, second from right), Bobby García (first row, far right), Bobby Recendez (second row, second from right) and manager Ching Duhm (first row, far left). During the off-season, Duhm drove a taxi on Catalina Island and was so impressed with Catalina High School star Saucedo that he recruited him to East Los Angeles Junior College. (Courtesy of Marcelino Saucedo.)

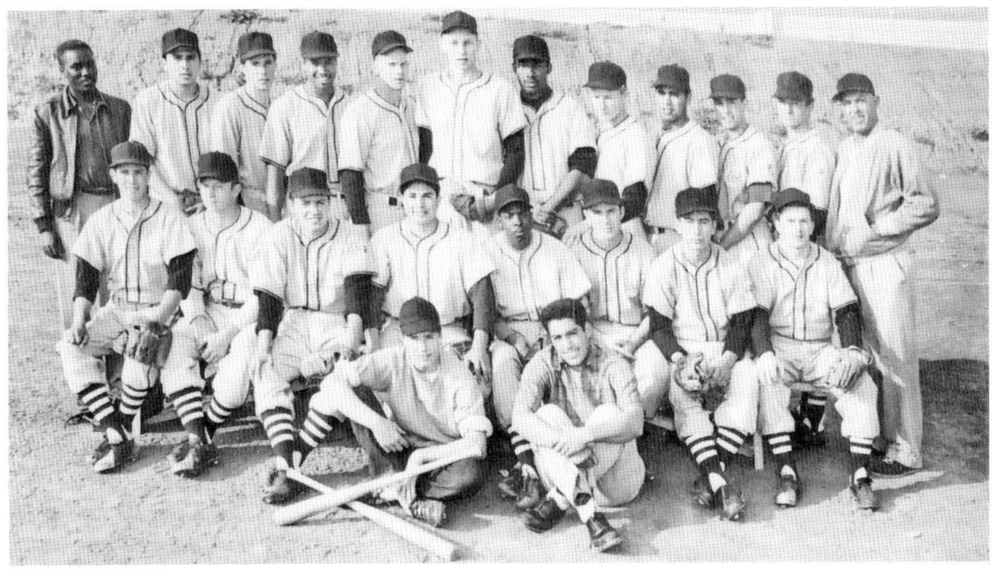

This is the 1955–1956 East Los Angeles Junior College team. Among the players were several who had played ball at local high schools. From left to right are (first row) equipment manger Mike Alridge and Art Velarde; (second row) Bobby Recendez, Jack Siebert, Ruben Rodríguez, Rudy Maldonado, Al Lang, Bill Jackson, Ernie Rodríguez and Jim Ruth; (third row) Earl Wilson, Armando Pérez, Carl Brio, unidentified, Dan Sarver, Ray De Lavallade, Tom Gaines, unidentified, Ray Gutierrez, Joe Munatones, Tom Bennett, and coach Ching Duhm. (Courtesy of Bobby Recendez.)

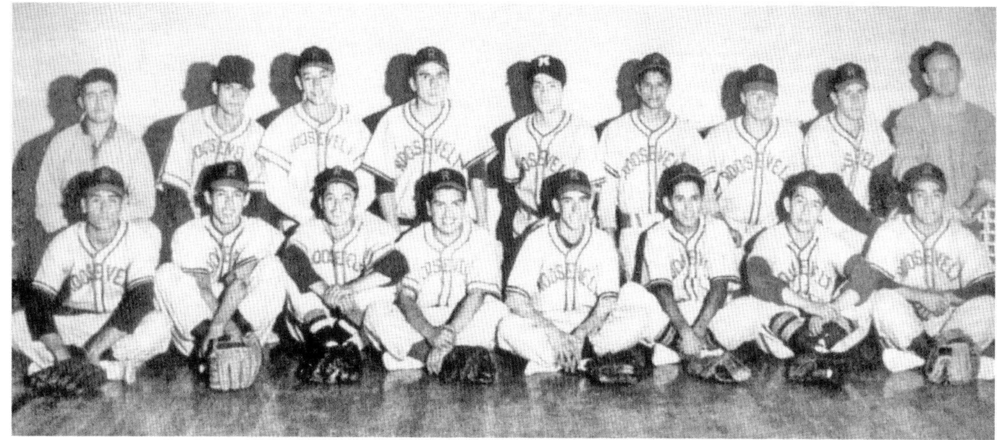

One of the greatest Roosevelt teams was the 1954 varsity squad. From left to right are (first row) Ray Delgado, Ernie Bustamante, Ernie Hunter, Luís Montes, Gil Farias, Fernando Farfán, Ernie Rodríguez, and Art Velarde; (second row) equipment manager Ron Paholsky, Tex Almedia, Joe Luskin, Armando Pérez, Conrad Muñatones, Tony Aguirre, Jim Wren, and Carl Brio. Rodríguez, Velarde, and Muñatones later played at UCLA. Rodríguez, Muñatones, and Pérez played professionally. (Courtesy of Art Velarde.)

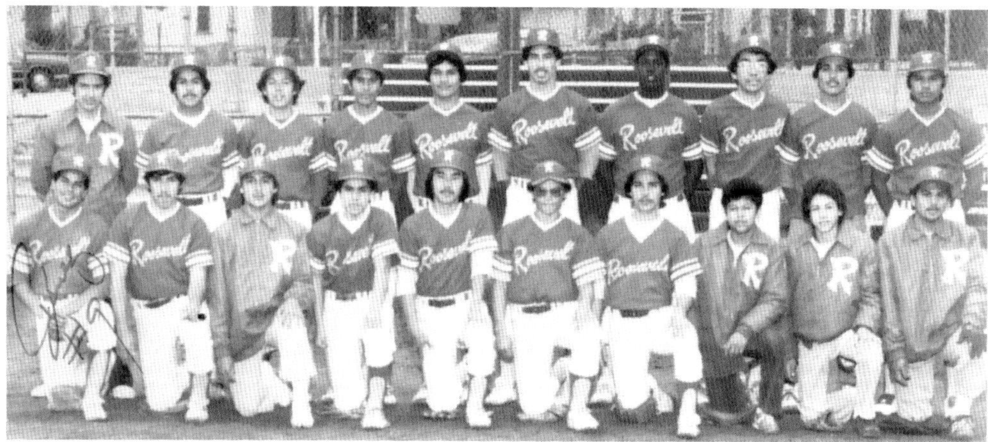

The 1979 Roosevelt High School team was a strong one, losing in the city playoffs to Crenshaw High School led by Darryl Strawberry. From left to right are (first row) Richard Sianez, Albert Orozco, Henry Bugarrin, Gilbert Rodríguez, Walter Konya, William Ortiz, Arturo Marin, Willford Rivas, Manuel Cruz, and Frank Hinajosa; (second row) Robert Argomaniz, Robert Maldonado, Manuel López, Angel Fonseca, Fernie Peña, Anthony Patterson, Toshio Miyamoto, Héctor González, and Jorge Moran. Sianez and his family were from El Paso, Texas, where Richard and his brother Greg played youth baseball. Richard also played football for Roosevelt along with his close friend Jose Arce. (Courtesy of Richard Sianez.)

Fred Scott (left) received a scholarship to play baseball at USC in 1959 at a time when the Trojans were a national powerhouse under coach Rod Dedeaux. Scott was recruited by Coach Dedeaux to start at shortstop. Dedeaux's teams won 11 national titles, including a record five straight from 1970 to 1974. His teams also won 28 conference championships. He was named the college coach of the century by *College Baseball* magazine. Dedeaux coached dozens of major-league players, including Tom Seaver, Dave Kingman, Fred Lynn, Mark McGwire, Randy Johnson, and Ron Fairly. (Courtesy of Fred Scott.)

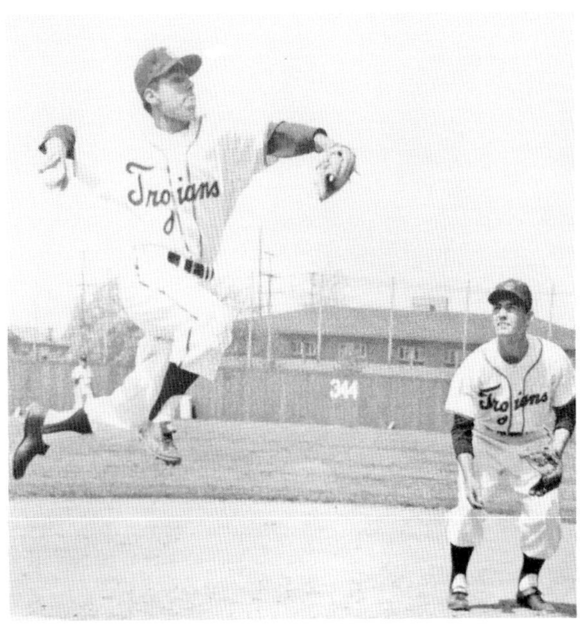


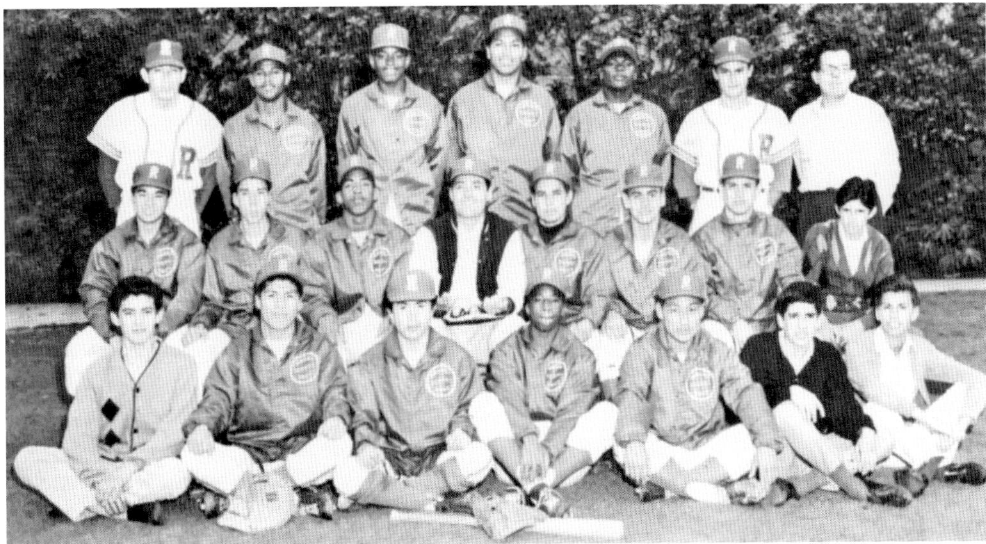

Roosevelt High School had an outstanding team in 1965. One of its better players was Richard Telles (second row, fourth from right) a left-handed pitcher. He served with the US Army in the Mekong Delta in Vietnam. He retired from the California Highway Patrol. To his right is coach Conrad Munatones, an outstanding high school and college player and coach. There have been countless outstanding community coaches including Sam Adachi, Ray Puente, Rudy Marin, Eppie González, Pat Molina, Vince Macias, Rudy Vieria, Larry Ochoa, Randy Olea, Ray Alderete, Roy Alba, Daniel Alessi, Joe Amaya, Sy Vernal, and Larry Silva. (Courtesy of Richard Telles.)

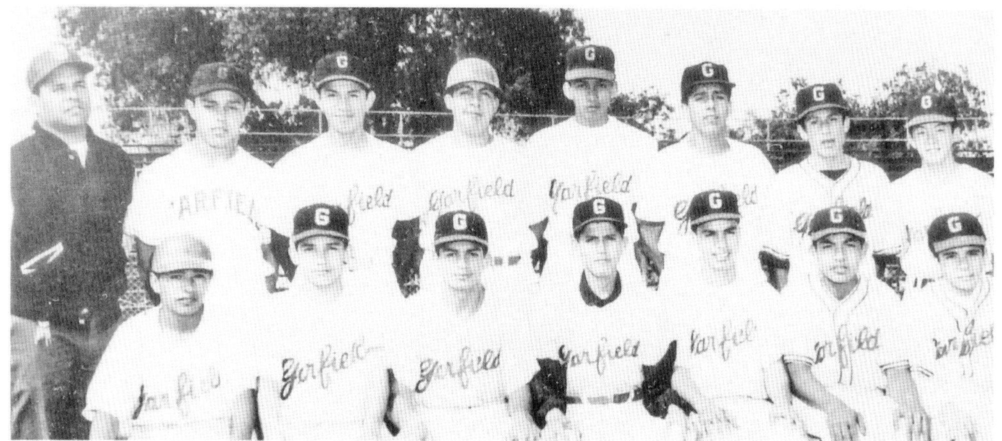

The 1966 Garfield High School junior varsity team won the Eastern League. The team was coached by Al Padilla (standing, far left). Some of the players were Pat Moya (first row, second from right), Alex Ochoa (first row, far right), Omar Cendejas (third row, second from right), and John Baca (third row, far right). (Courtesy of Al Padilla.)

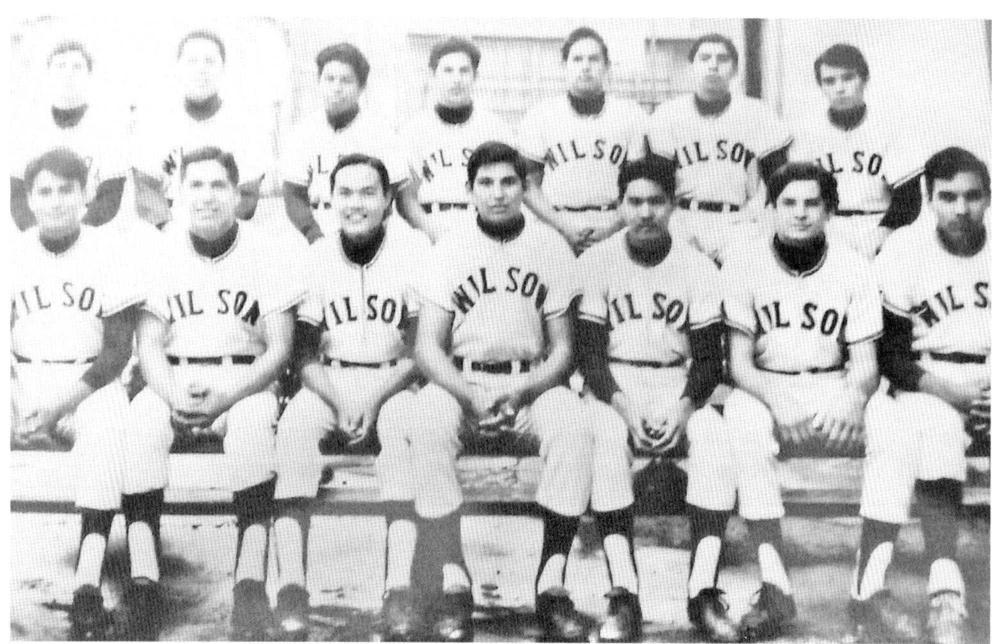

The Wilson High School teams during the 1960s had excellent players, many from the El Sereno region of East Los Angeles. From left to right are (first row) D. Hernández, L. Cabrera, F. Arakawa, J. Madrid, B. Arakawa, N. Escamilla, and E. Zepeda; (second row) R. Holoubek, S. Hernández, J. Rentería, D. Madrid, R. Murrietta, D. Rivera, and E. Porras. Holoubek was the quarterback on the football team and was Player of the Year. He went on to play at Pasadena Community College. He passed away in 2013. (Courtesy of Nicky Escamilla.)

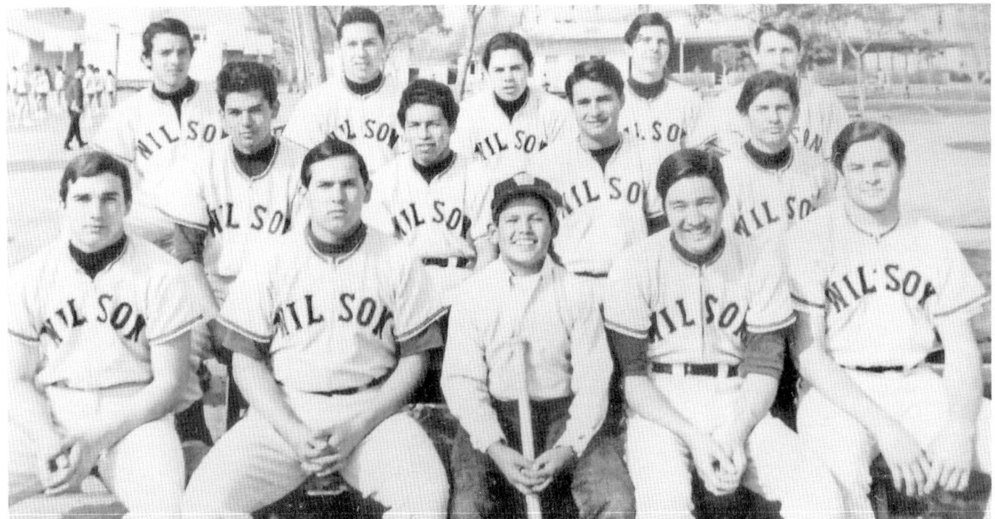


Wilson High School had excellent sports programs and produced powerhouse teams in football, basketball, baseball, softball, and tennis. From left to right are (first row) F. De Lilio, R. Murrietta, manager B. Arakawa, Ray Murrietta, and N. Escamilla; (second row) D. Gonzáles, J. Rentería, D. Hernández, and D. Madrid; (third row) V. Gamboa, S. Hernández, A. Mota, R. Holoubek, and V. Bernal. Murrietta lettered four years at third base and made the All-City team three seasons. In 1971, Wilson High School captured the city championship at Dodger Stadium. (Courtesy of Nicky Escamilla.)

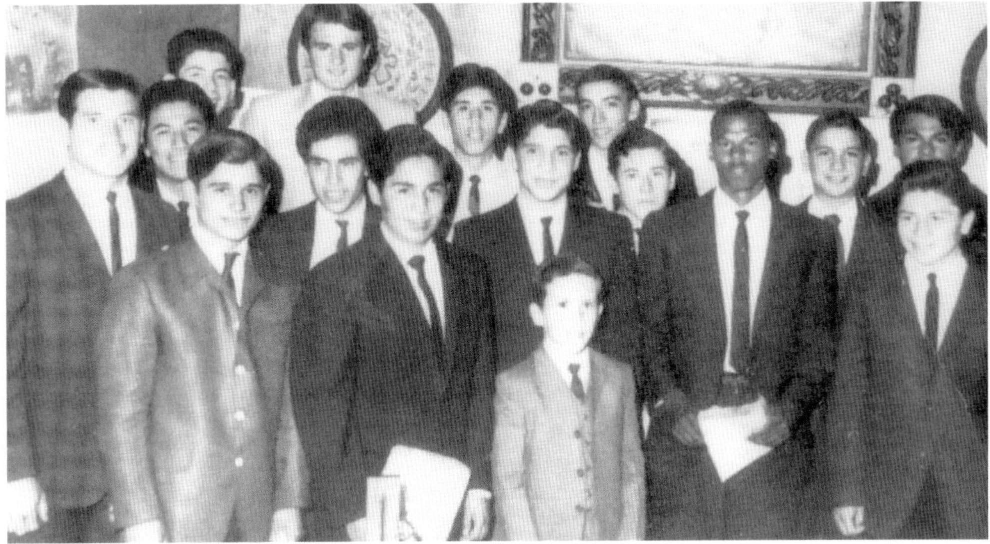

The 1967 Lincoln High School Tigers won the Northern League title. The team was honored at the Golindrina Restaurant on Olvera Street. Those shown are, in no particular order, David Vidaurrazaga, Gilbert Baltazar, Héctor Chaidez, Gus Martínez, Teddy Peacot, Jack Arenas, George Fernández, Robert Duran, Roberto Lavato, Louis Ramírez, Paul Franco, Ray Lara, Melvin Pride, Victor Morales, and Rodolfo Martinez, along with coach Dave Chávez. Coach Chávez, a graduate from Garfield High School, was an outstanding baseball mentor for years. (Courtesy of Rodolfo Martínez.)

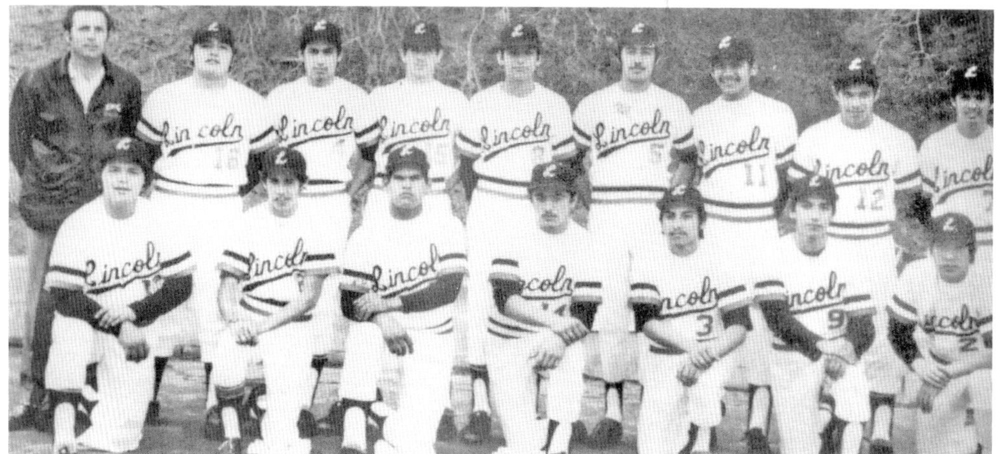

During the 1960s and 1970s, the Lincoln High School Tigers fielded several outstanding teams, including this one with Bobby Castillo. He had an excellent major-league career with the Dodgers and Twins. He passed away in 2014. From left to right are (first row) Simón Ortega, Elizar Lozano, Ray Murieta, Bobby Castillo, Felipe Vásquez, Manuel Hernández, and Yip Quan; (second row) coach Carl Brío, Frank Martínez, Richard González, Greg Broomis, David Duran, George Balles, Robert Alcarez, Robert Guzmán, and Daniel López. (Courtesy of Al Padilla.)

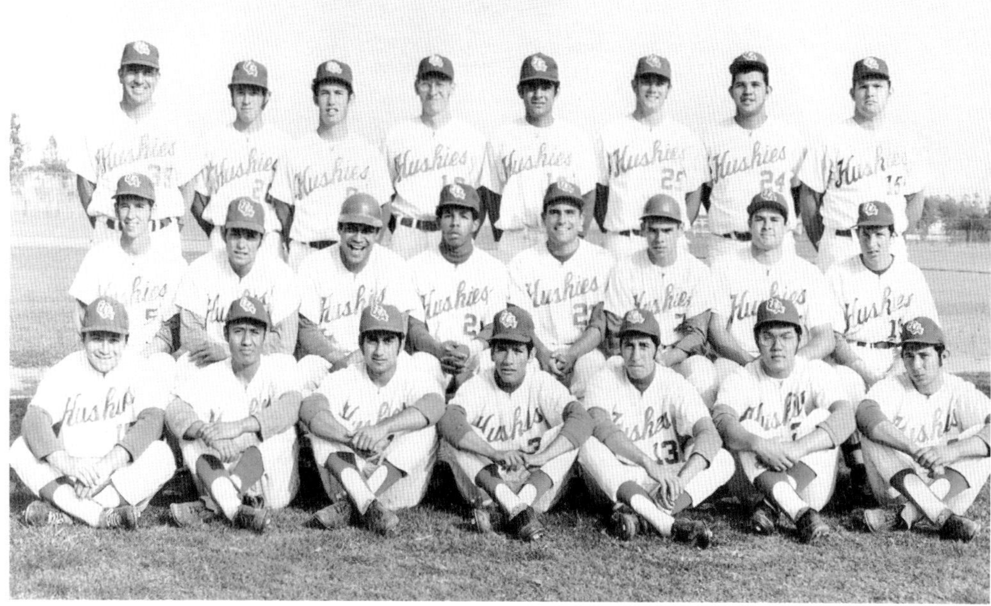

Bob Hertel (third row, fourth from left) managed the 1970 East Los Angeles Junior College Huskies and coached for 27 years. He played at USC and with the New York Yankees in 1952. The Huskies team was comprised of Mexican Americans representing several high schools, including Alhambra, Bell, Cathedral, Garfield, Lincoln, Montebello, Mark Keppel, Roosevelt, San Gabriel, Wilson, and South Gate. The players included Jack Arenas, Al De La Rosa, Marty Provéncio, Nick Medrano, Joel Palomares, Raúl Morales, Alex Santana, Rick Apodaca, Nicky Escamilla, Steve Romero, Randy Chávez, and Richard Gonzáles. (Courtesy of Jackie Arenas.)

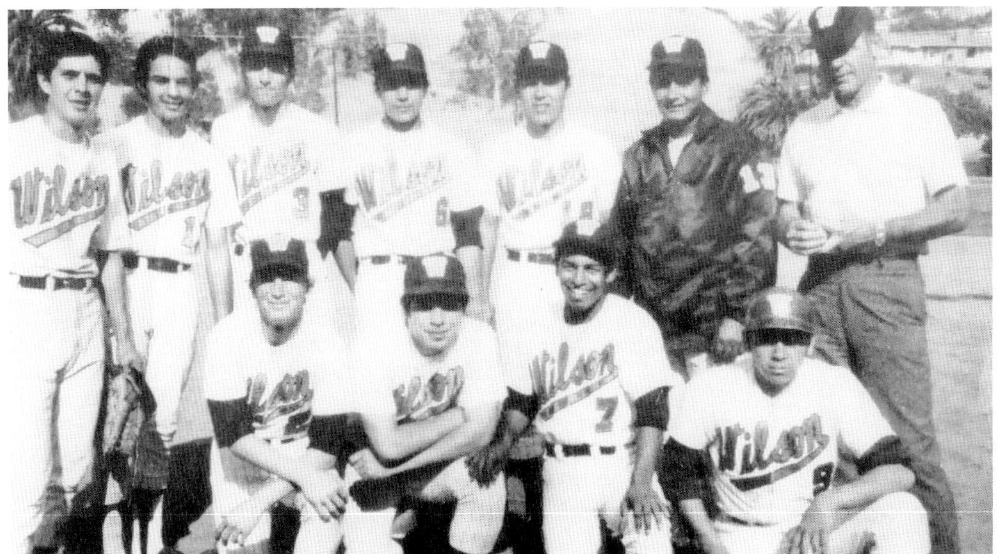

The 1970 Wilson High School team were California Interscholastic Federation (CIF) champions. Victor Gamboa (standing, second from left) played second base. He tried out with the Los Angeles Dodgers when Walter Alston was manager and was later part of an American Vancouver baseball team that won the Olympic Sports Festival bronze medal in Baton Rouge, Louisiana. Other Mexican Americans on this Wilson team included Al Moto, Jess Rentería, Mike Robles, Victor Bernal, Steve Hernández, Ric Holoubek, and Dan Hernández. Several players were drafted by the A's, Padres, and Angels. Hernández was the High School Player of the Year. Bernal, standing third from left, played for the San Diego Padres. (Courtesy of Victor Gamboa.)

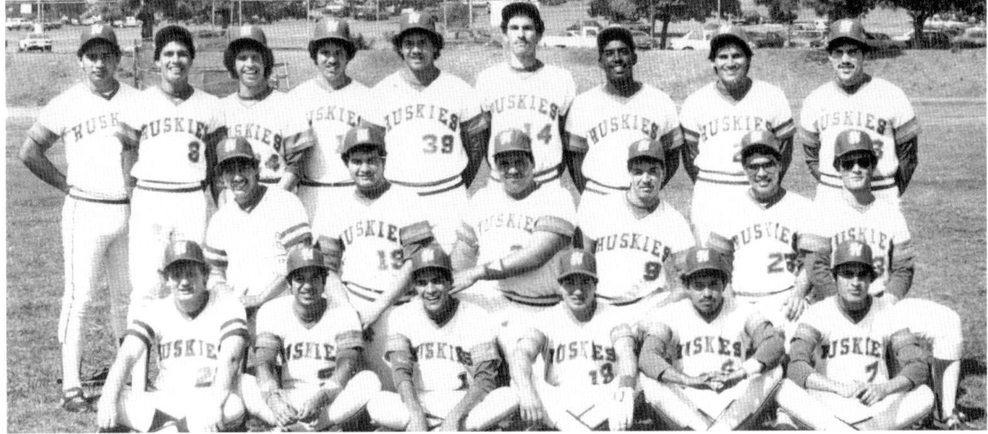

The 1985 ELAC Huskies were coached by Al Padilla and Ernie Rodríguez (neither pictured). Both had been outstanding players in high school and college. Rodríguez was later signed by the Los Angeles Dodgers. From left to right are (first row) Don Fite, Mike Macias, Elías Flores, Roland Meléndez, Pablo López, and Miguel Lifrenas; (second row) Anthony Chávez, Louie Placencia, Joe Aranda, Joe Zermeno, Tom Ochoa, and Marco Armenta; (third row) Oscar Duran, Henry Corona, Jess Pedroza, Ken Gutiérrez, Billy Bonds, Leo Ramírez, Pat Campbell, Ken Vega, and Mando Verdugo. (Courtesy of Al Padilla.)

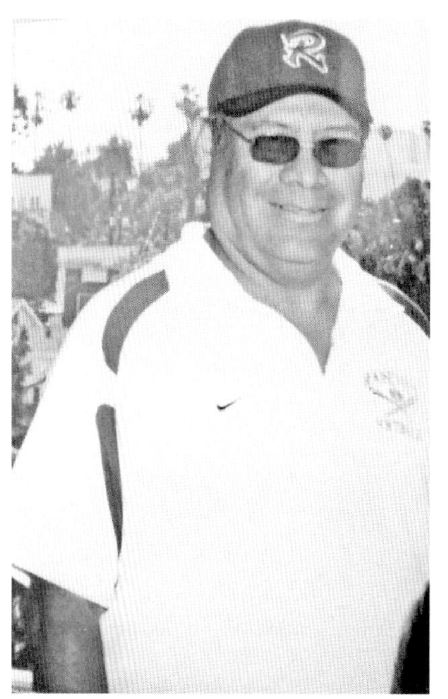

Frank De La Rosa was born in Anapra, New Mexico, and the family moved to East Los Angeles in 1957. He played ball at Soto Street Elementary School, Little League at Fresno Park in Boyle Heights, and three years at Roosevelt High School, making first-team All-League in 1972. During the summers, Frank played for Joe Carmona with a Connie Mack team, Jesús Paz with the Evergreen A's, Armando Pérez with the Montebello Stars, Jess Hunter with a semipro team, and with Los Indios. Since the late 1970s, he has volunteered as a coach to boys' and girls' teams, including Roosevelt High School, St. Thomas Aquinas, and youth baseball in Montebello, Monterey Park, and Alhambra. (Courtesy of Frank De La Rosa.)

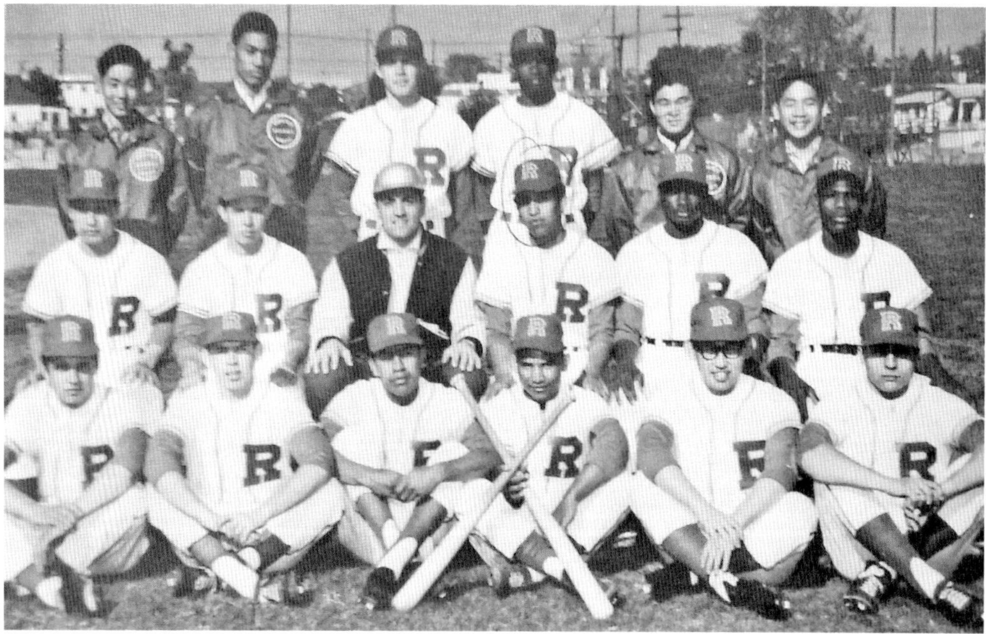

The 1966 Roosevelt team had solid pitching and defense. From left to right are (first row) A. Gutiérrez, A. Martínez, E. De La Rosa, L. Adams, M. Hirata, and A. Gomes; (second row) W. Shiota, R. Pérez, coach Conrad Muñatones, O. Araisa, J. Shingleton, and E. Knight; (third row) manager K. Nakatsui, T. Ioane, C. Pinedo, R. Cain, L. Akasaka, and manager P. Chan. De La Rosa, Gomes, and Pinedo served in Vietnam, where De La Rosa earned the Bronze Star. Muñatones was the first Los Angeles–born Mexican American to be signed by the Dodgers in 1958. (Courtesy of Frank and Al De La Rosa.)

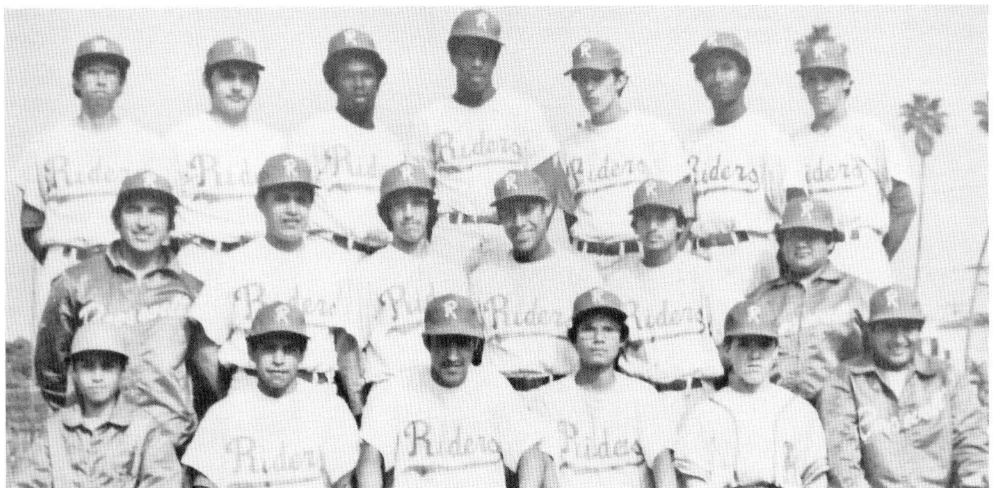

The 1972 Roosevelt High School team was managed by Ernie Rodríguez. From left to right are (first row) T. Chávez, R. Domínguez, F. Sandoval, J. Saldivar, S. McBain, and A. Aguilar; (second row) Coach Rodríguez, R. Hernández, R. Paz, F. De La Rosa, D. Sánchez, and M. Sánchez; (third row) G. Rendón, J. Díaz, A. Green, D. Wyrick, T. Chevelek, G. Evans, and M. Velarde. Ernie Rodríguez played at Roosevelt, ELAC, and UCLA. He was signed by the Los Angeles Dodgers. After his professional career, he coached at Roosevelt for 35 years. (Courtesy of Frank De La Rosa.)

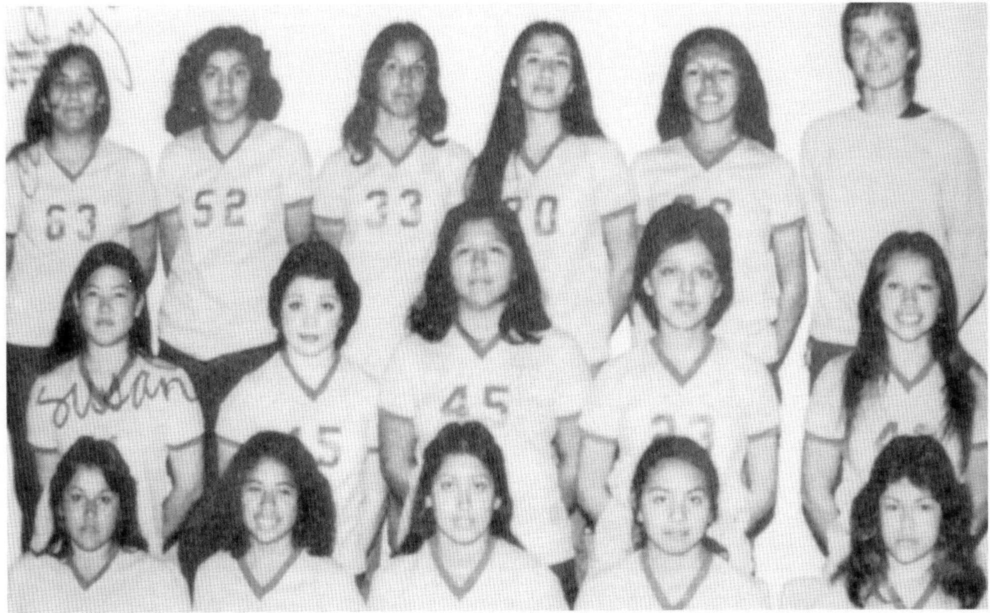

The 1975 Roosevelt High School girls' varsity team included, from left to right, (first row) Liz Quesada, Adraine Guerrero, Liz Baltierra, Dora Najera, and Alice Triana; (second row) Susan Shirakawa, Carmen Valdez, Jenny Perea, Celia Celaya, and Tillie Wiley; (third row) Elena Carvajal, Marina Robles, Juanita González, Laura Vélez, Jossie Duran, and coach Barbara Colwell. Dora Najera (Perez) was on the softball, basketball, volleyball, and track teams. At Cal State Los Angeles, she played varsity volleyball. She coaches softball and basketball at Roosevelt. (Courtesy of Frank De La Rosa.)

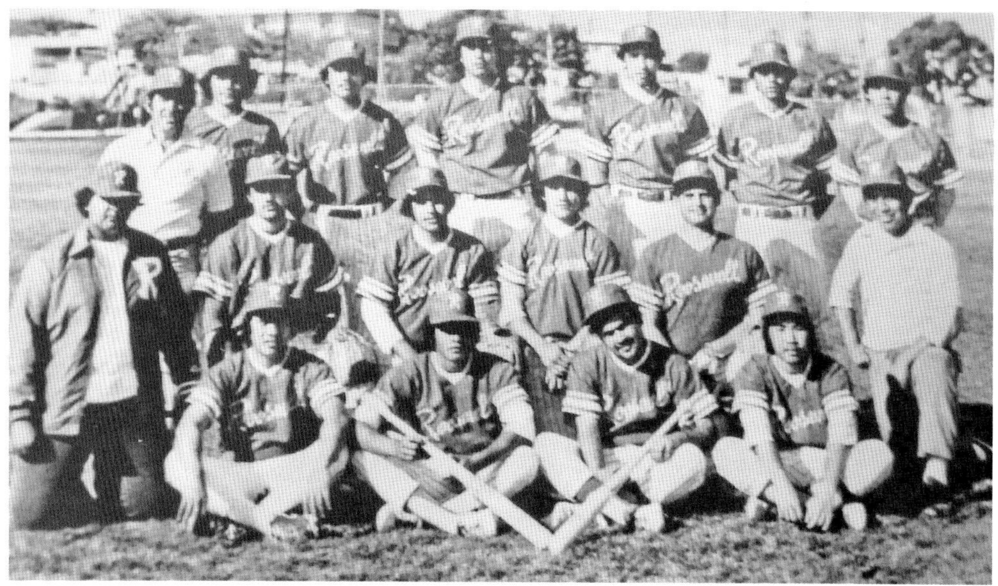

The 1977 Roosevelt team included, from left to right, (first row) coach Al De La Rosa, Javier Castillo, Domingo Flores, and Walter Konya; (second row) George Seriano, Sergio Flores, Robert Argomaniz, Javier Gonzáles, Carlos Valenzuela, and coach Frank De La Rosa; (third row) coach Ernie Rodríguez, Ángel Fonseca, Héctor Gonzáles, Gil Marín, Fernie Peña, Eddie ?, and unidentified. Al De La Rosa played flag football and softball at Marianna and Soto Elementary Schools. At Hollenback Junior High School, he played four sports and was named Athlete of the Year in 1966. (Courtesy of Frank De La Rosa.)

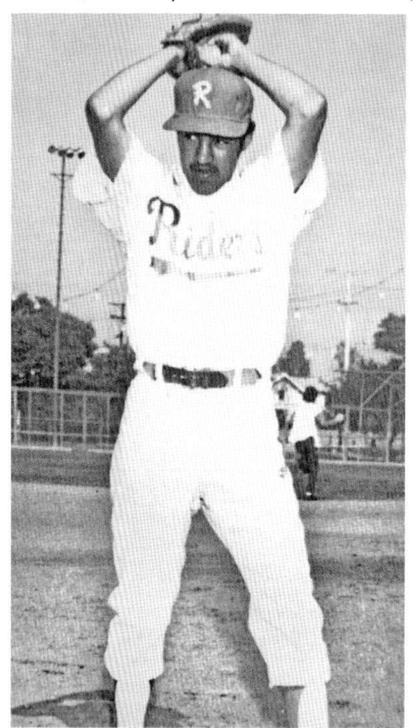

Frankie Sandoval was born in East Los Angeles in 1954 and played Little League at Evergreen Park and with the Variety Boys Club as a pitcher and outfielder. He was an outstanding player at Roosevelt under Ernie Rodríguez. Frankie played three years of varsity ball along with his brother Johnnie. Frankie recalled that baseball saved his life due to all the gangs in the area. He gives Coach Rodríguez credit for his success on the field and in life. Rodríguez played Triple-A ball for the Dodgers. Frankie became the practice pitcher for the Dodgers for 11 years, including when the Dodgers won the 1981 and 1988 World Series. He wears his 1988 World Series ring with much pride. (Courtesy of Frankie Sandoval.)

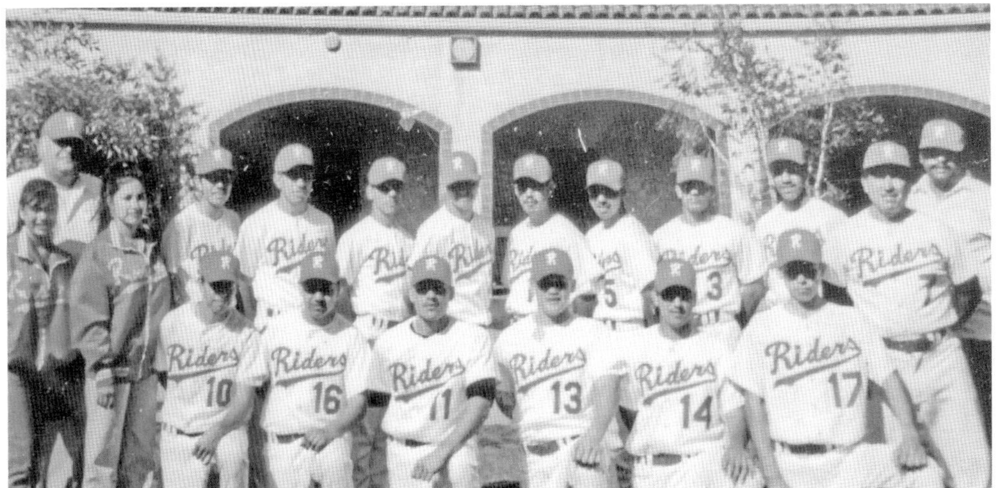


Ray Ruiz (No. 13) was an outstanding player at Roosevelt. His coach was Ernie Rodríguez, the first former pro Ray ever met. Ernie was an excellent mentor and showed Ray what it took to make it to the professional leagues. More important, Ernie instilled in Ray the confidence to serve as team captain. Ray made many longtime friends and mentors during his three years and still keeps in touch with Ernie, since Ray is now the coach at Roosevelt High School. (Courtesy of Ray Ruiz.)

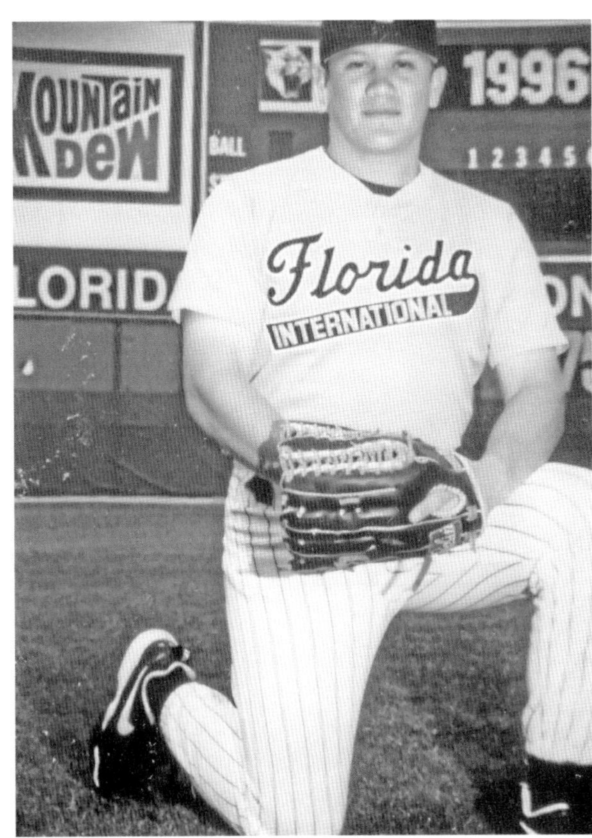


Ray Ruiz played at ELAC after graduating from Roosevelt. His proudest accomplishment was receiving an athletic scholarship from Florida International University—he had promised his mother, Guadalupe Ruiz, that one day he would make her proud by receiving a college scholarship. He remembers his mother crying at the airport as he left for Miami. She passed away in 2014. His parents sacrificed for Ray to acquire a quality education and a better life. Ray and his wife, Teresa Reteguin, try to give their daughter, Juliet Ruiz, opportunities just like his parents gave him. (Courtesy of Ray Ruiz.)

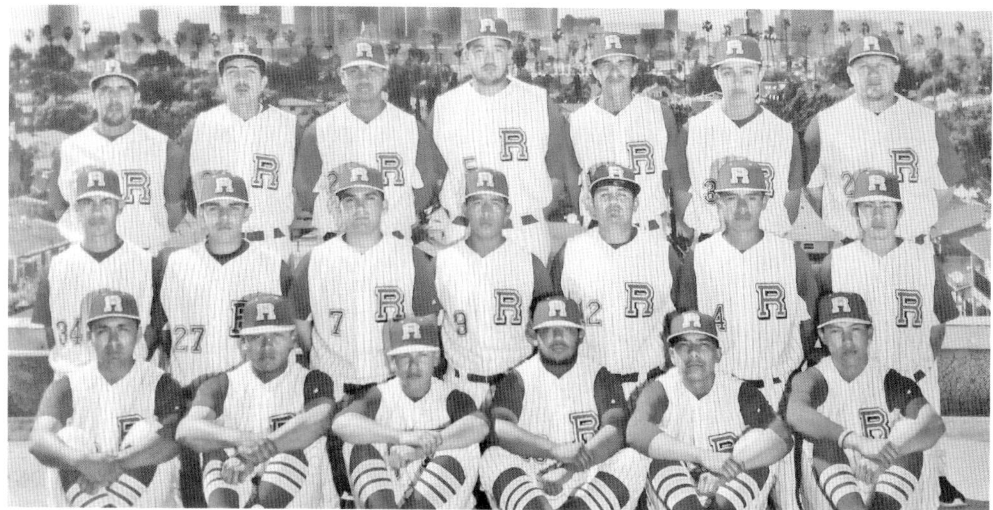

Ray Ruiz (third row, far right) returned to Roosevelt as a teacher and coach. Nearly half of the teachers are alumni. Ray wanted to give back to his beloved Boyle Heights community and show student athletes that there is much they can achieve in the world. He gives credit for his coaching success to his valuable assistant coach, Jaime Valle, who volunteered over 30 years of his life to Roosevelt High School and the community. Ray's coaching highlight was winning his first game against Wilson High School 11-3. He says it's been a great ride ever since. (Courtesy of Ray Ruiz.)

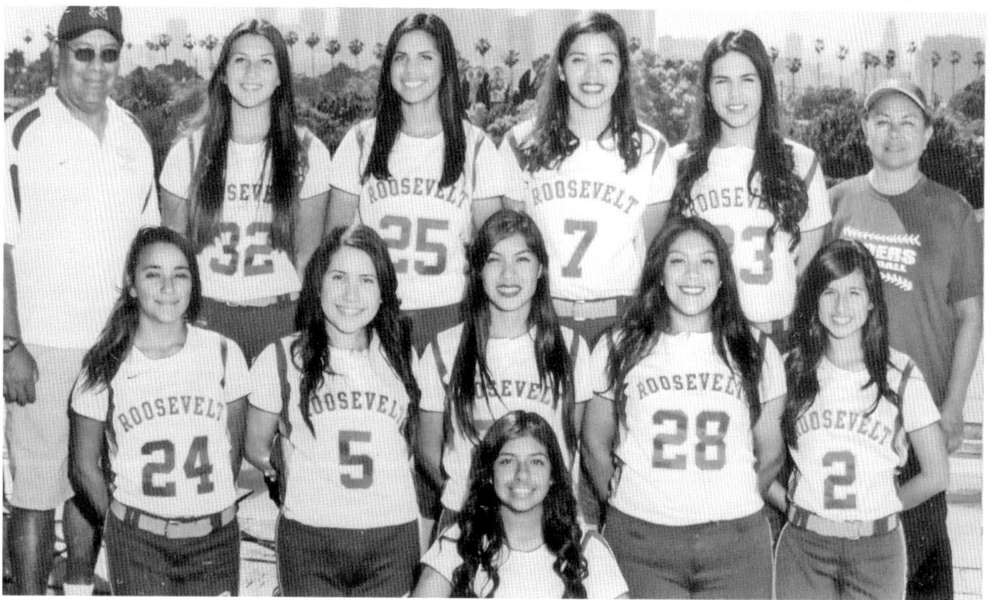


The 2015 Roosevelt softball team finished tied for third in the Eastern League. In the Division II playoffs, Roosevelt lost to Chavez High School, the eventual champions. The Roosevelt program has been in 10 of the last 11 city playoff tournaments. From left to right are (first row) J. Ulloa; (second row) B. Osuna, E. De La Cruz, V. Alejandre, A.J. Cetz, and D. Sosa; (third row) coach Frank De La Rosa, B. Godoy, P. García, A. Gonzáles, J. Helguera, and coach Dora Najera Pérez. (Courtesy of Frank De La Rosa.)

Alfonso Aguilar started playing Little League at El Sereno Park when he was nine. He was a pitcher and second baseman. He played youth ball until he enrolled at Wilson High School and made the B team. In his senior year, Alfonso made varsity at third base wearing the number 19. After high school, he played in the Mike Brito League for years. His grandfather was an outstanding player in the El Paso–Juarez region during the 1920s. (Courtesy of Alfonso Aguilar.)

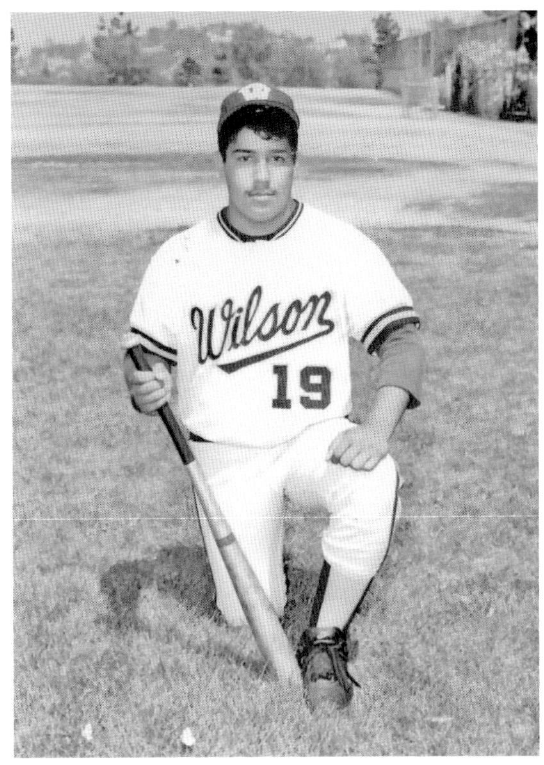


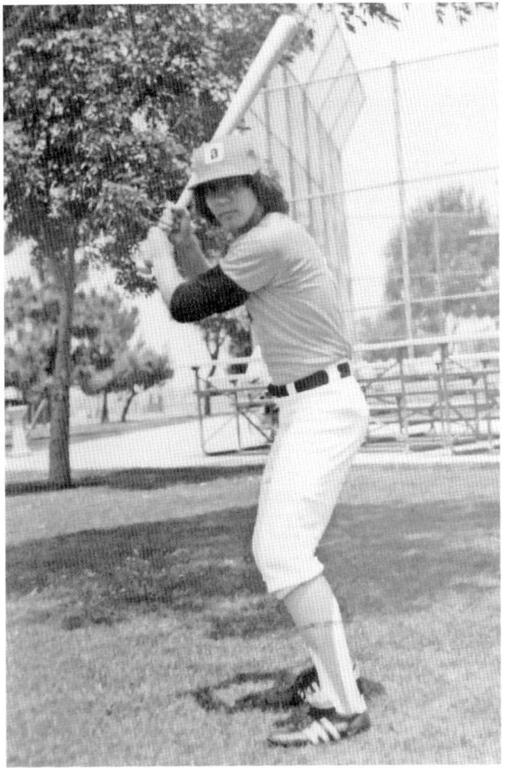

Richie Campos grew up in Boyle Heights, where he played several sports at Fresno Park. He started playing organized ball at 14 at Laguna Park in the summer of 1973. Ray Guzmán was his first coach for the Laguna Park Angels. At Roosevelt, under Ernie Rodríguez, Richie moved from third to second base. He made All-League three years and was the Eastern League Co-Player of the Year and on the All-City team. He was scouted by several top universities and selected nearby Cal State Los Angeles. In 1977, the team, coached by Jack Deutsch, made it to the final four at the College World Series. Richie later played for the Evergreen Yankees, coached by Jesse Estrada, in the Mike Brito League. (Courtesy of Richie Campos.)

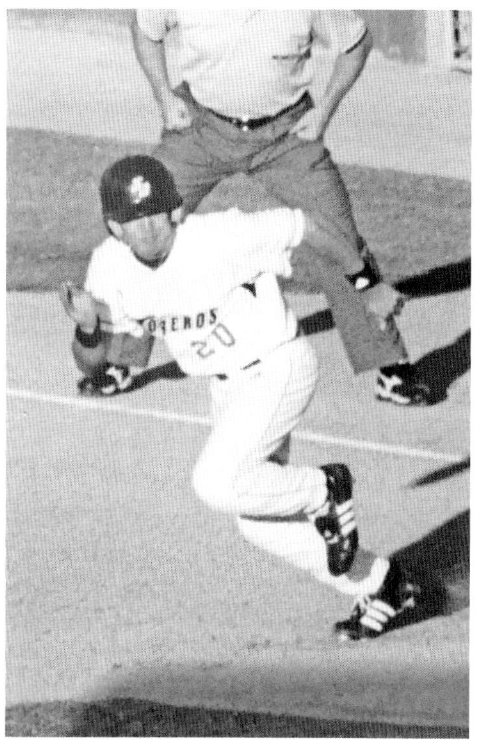

Michael Lugo, born in Los Angeles, represents the third generation of Lugos from East Los Angeles. Michael follows in the baseball footsteps of his father, Raymond Lugo, and grandfather Tony Lugo. Michael was also inspired to play by his older brother Anthony, who had great success on the field at Bishop Amat Catholic High School for four years. Michael played second base at the same school and earned an athletic scholarship to the University of San Diego. In 2006, the USD Torreros beat the University of Texas, who at the time were national champions. Like his father and uncle Richard, he went into law enforcement with the Los Angeles County Sheriff's Department. In 2002, the Bishop Amat baseball team were state champions and were ranked as national high school champions. Michael's older brother Anthony was on this 2002 team. (Courtesy of Richard Lugo.)

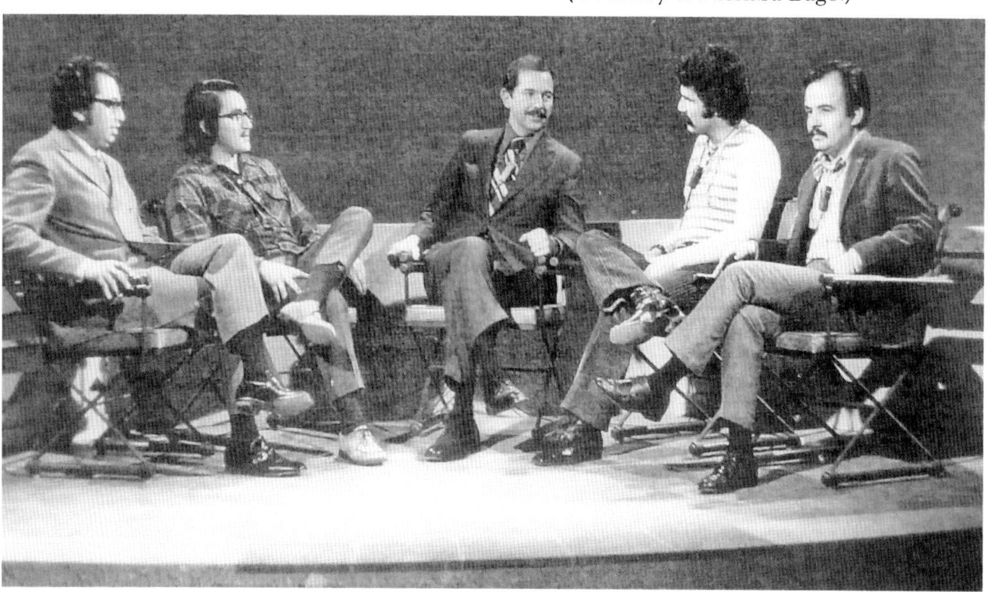

Ray Andrade was born in East Los Angeles. He was expelled three times and was finally sent to Jackson High School for nonconforming boys. Jackson had a ragtag team, and Ray was the pitcher. He later boxed professionally before being drafted and was wounded in Vietnam. Ray became one of the leaders of the Chicano movement and founded *Justicia* to confront Hollywood's negative depictions of Mexican Americans. He is seen here with other activists. From left to right are Herman Sillas, Rosalio Muñoz, Manuel Aragón, Andrade, and Raúl Ruiz. (Courtesy of Ray Andrade.)

# 3

# Catholic School

The five major Catholic high schools in the general East Los Angeles area are Cathedral (Phantoms), Sacred Heart of Jesus (Comets), John J. Cantwell (Cardinals), Salesian (Mustangs), and Sacred Heart of Mary (Scooters). Cantwell and Sacred Heart of Mary merged into one coed high school in 1991. In addition, there are several Catholic grammar schools, including Our Lady of Talpa, Resurrection, Soledad, Assumption, Our Lady of Lourdes, All Saints, Our Lady of Guadalupe (two of them), Dolores Mission, Our Lady of Immaculate Medal, Santa Teresita, Sacred Heart of Jesús, Santa Isabella, Our Lady of Help of Christians, St. Thomas More, St. Thomas Aquinas, St. Mary, St. Isabel, and St. Alphonsus.

Catholic schools, like their public counterparts, have produced well-trained teams, top-notch players, and phenomenal coaches. This chapter sings the praises of Catholic players and teams—their flair on the field, their high-octane hustle and bustle, their mastery of the nuts and bolts of the game, and their sensational home runs, breathtaking throws, and daring base running. Several of these parochial players went on to play at the college and professional levels, including the major leagues.

Catholic and public schools spiritually and physically overlapped at many levels. Public school students attended church on Sunday and celebrated baptisms, first communions, confirmations, weddings, funerals, passion plays, Ash Wednesday, Palm Sunday, *quinceañeras*, *las posadas*, *jaimicas*, *ferias*, *tardeadas*, and of course, the ever popular Saturday night dances at the parish halls.

Many public school students transferred to Catholic schools and vice versa. In high schools, there was dating between Catholic and public schools. Catholic and public school boys and girls played on the same Little League teams in the summer and traveling teams in the winter. Cantwell High School and Roosevelt High School often practiced against one another. Coaches from parochial schools coached at public schools and vice versa.

A deep-seated myth holds that Mexican Americans who attended Catholic schools were from wealthy families because they paid the expensive tuition as well as paying taxes for public schools. While this was absolutely true for some families, the majority of Catholic students were and are from working-class and immigrant backgrounds struggling against immense challenges and odds to become the first in their families to attend and graduate from college. Regardless of where they attended school, students were united by their unbeatable love for baseball and softball.

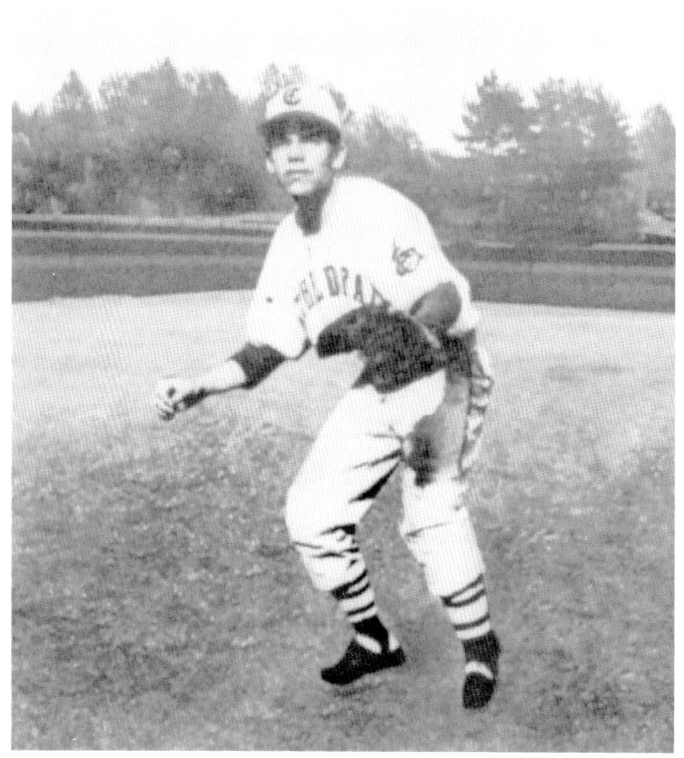

Rudy Castoreña played at Cathedral High School from 1957 through 1960 on a predominantly Mexican American team. Rudy was involved with baseball at an early age, playing for Resurrection Catholic Grammar School in East Los Angeles. Rudy's father, Pio, and uncles, Salvador and Porfirio, played during the 1920s and 1930s throughout San Bernardino and Riverside Counties. Rudy was a carpenter for 46 years. (Courtesy of Rudy Castoreña.)

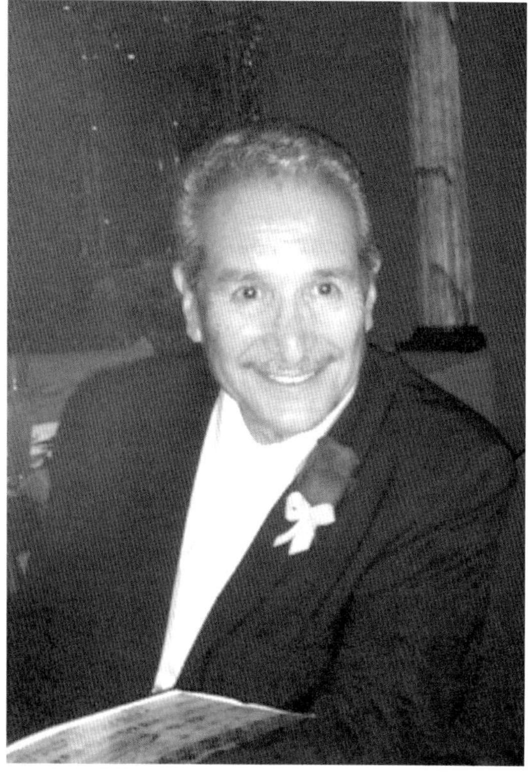

David Escarciga was born in Santa Monica in 1944. Both his parents worked in a factory that manufactured military products during World War II. In the early 1950s, the family moved to the City Terrace section of East Los Angeles. During the 1950s, he played for youth teams including Eastside Boys' Club; Brooklyn Avenue School; Belvedere, Laguna, Fresno, and Evergreen Parks; and with the Catholic Youth Organization (CYO) at Our Lady of Soledad School. At Cantwell High School, he was on the football, basketball, track, and baseball teams. He enlisted in the Army in 1966 and served in Vietnam. He retired from the County of Los Angeles in 1998. His greatest baseball thrill came in the 1990s, when he and his youngest son played outfield on the same team. (Courtesy of David Escarciga.)

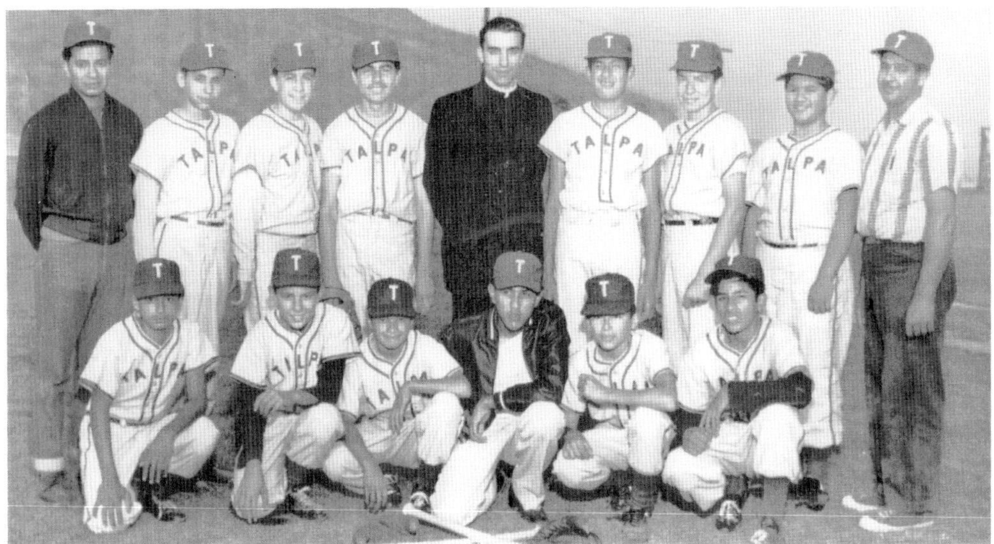


Fr. Hilario Liras (second row, center) came from Spain and quickly established a baseball team at Our Lady of Talpa in 1961. He promoted sports among the young people and took the kids to see the Dodgers and Angels at Dodger Stadium before the Angels moved to Orange County. Players include George Caro, Joe Santana, Frank Curiel, Joe Rivera, Art Sánchez, John Guerra, and ? Pacheco. Caro pitched for Salesian High School in 1963 and was the pitching coach for the school from 2004 to 2012. He served in the Army from 1963 to 1973. (Courtesy of George Caro.)

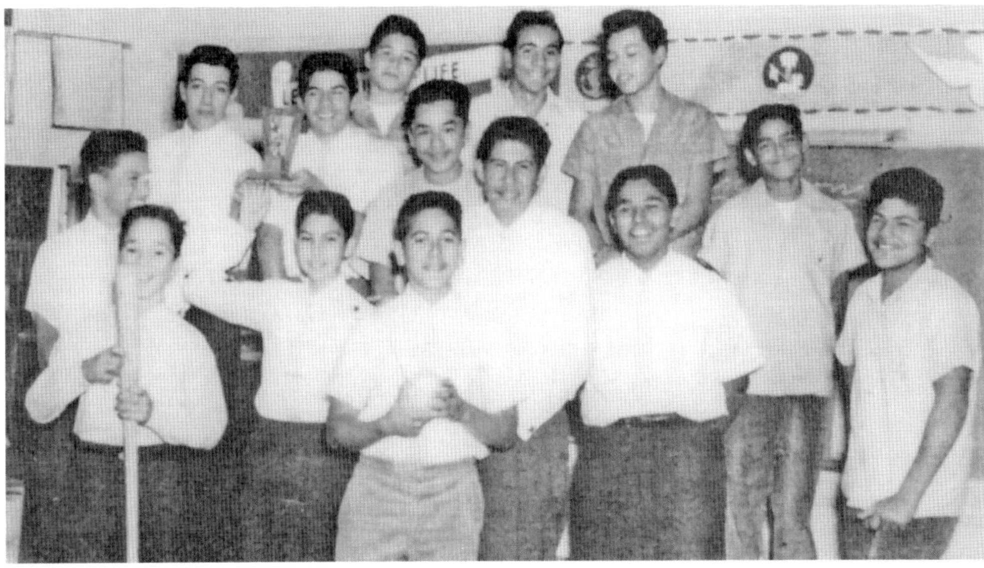

The Resurrection School team displays its 1961 CYO championship trophy. Rivals included Assumption, Our Lady of Lourdes, St. Isabel, St. Mary, Our Lady of Guadalupe, Dolores Mission, and Our Lady of Talpa. Team members included Joe García, Domingo García, Ron Baca, Joe Gras, Robert Basso, Louie Yánez, Danny Díaz, Paul De La Rosa, Manuel De La Rosa, Jerry Bilderrain, Ramiro Sandoval, Joe Montelongo, Richard Férrales, and Héctor Cuecuecha. The Garcías and De La Rosas were not related. (Courtesy of Ron Baca.)

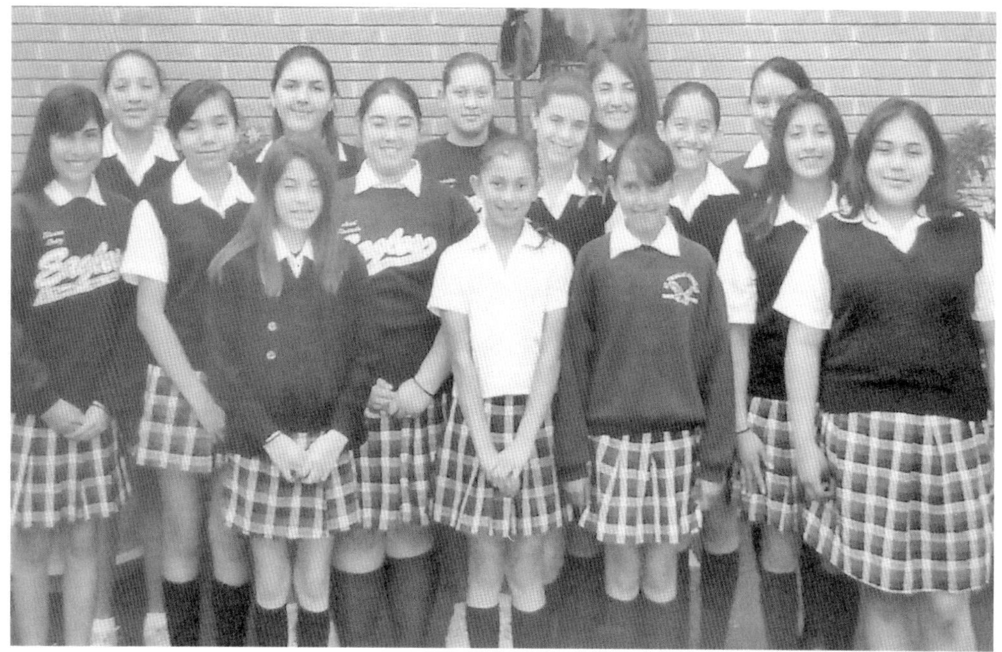

The 2006 St. Thomas Aquinas girls softball team was an outstanding team with excellent pitching, speed on the bases, and great defense. From left to right are (first row) A. Arana, S. Duran, M. Espinoza, and A. Feriben; (second row) E. Ortiz, C. Cruz, A. Pintado, I. Millace, C. Lara, and M. Mendizabal; (third row) F. Parga, J. Medina, D. Duran, C. Aguilar, and M. Torres. (Courtesy of St. Thomas Aquinas.)

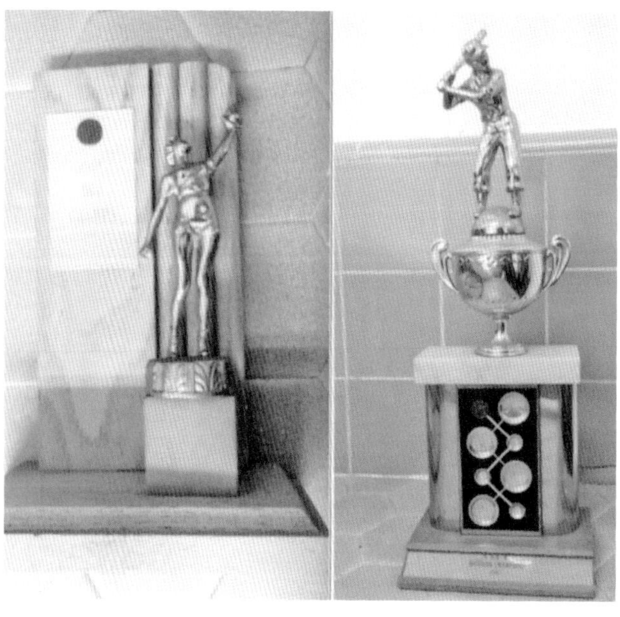

Our Lady of Lourdes has served the community since 1931. Lester G. Scherer, a Hollywood architect, incorporated numerous Art Deco elements into the Spanish Colonial Revival design, including the Latin-cross floor plan, central dome, bell tower, red tile roof, and smooth stucco surfaces. At left is a 1957 girls' team division championship trophy, and at right is a 1963 boys' trophy. The girls' trophy is the earliest one found so far for girls' parish softball in East Los Angeles. (Courtesy of Our Lady of Lourdes Church.)

Raising his family in East Los Angeles, Tony Lugo started the first summer parish Little League team at St. Alphonsus Parish in 1965, where he coached his two sons, Richard (right) and Raymond. The team played other third- and fourth-grade teams from Our Lady of Guadalupe, Our Lady of Soledad, Our Lady of Lourdes, and St. Marcellinus. The Lugo brothers continued in sports at Cantwell High School, where Raymond played football, baseball, and basketball and Richard was on the football and track teams. Raymond played football at ELAC. Raymond and Richard have a combined 75 years of law enforcement service. (Courtesy of Richard Lugo.)

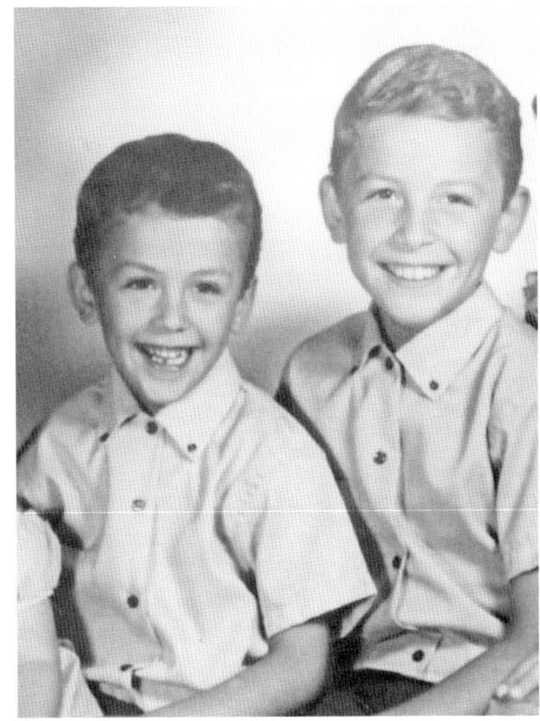

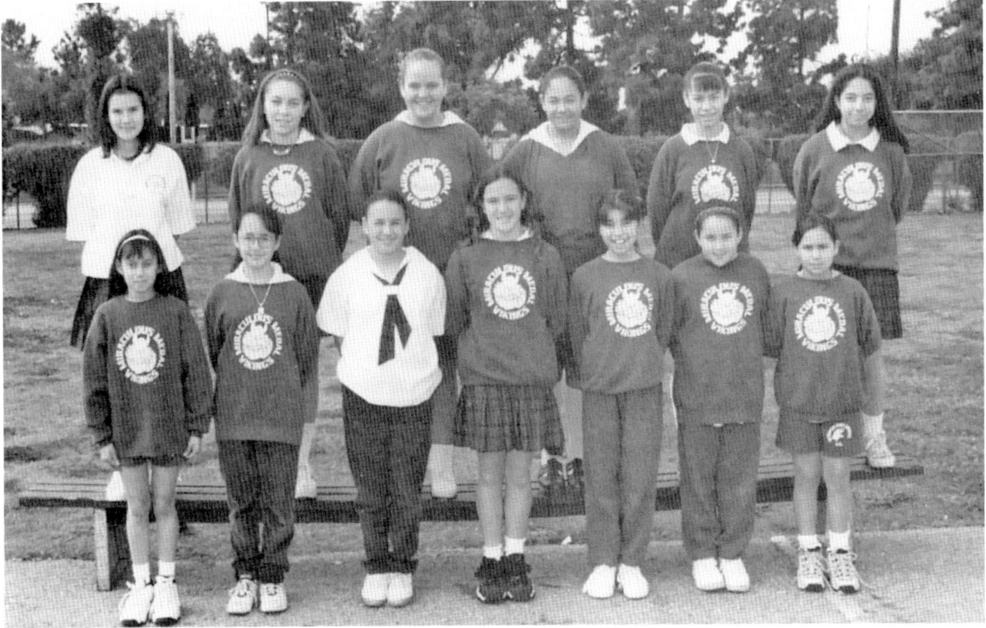

Miraculous Medal opened in 1954 through the leadership of the Daughters of Charity St. Vincent de Paul. The Daughters of Charity are an international community founded in Paris in 1633 by St. Vincent de Paul and St. Louise de Marillac. The Miraculous Medal was given to St. Catherine Laboure by the Blessed Mother through an apparition. Pictured is the 1998 Miraculous Medal Vikings girls' softball team. (Courtesy of Miraculous Medal School.)

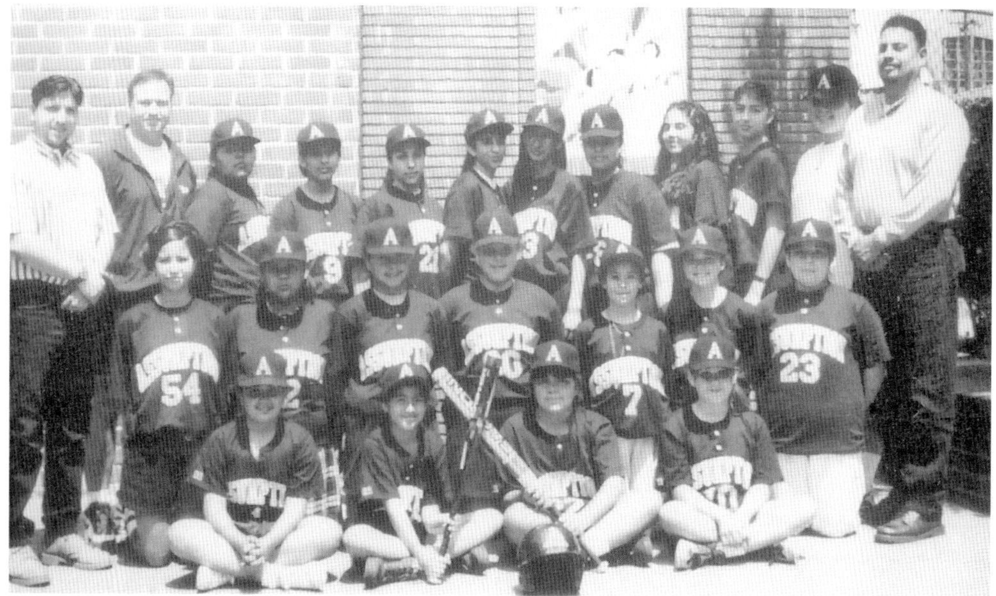

The 1995–1996 Assumption School Trojans had a solid softball team. From left to right are (first row) P. Mora, E. Román, J. Ramírez, and V. Armas; (second row) V. Ramos, J Pérez, J. Ortega, I. Sánchez, A. Hernández, M. Deszo, and C. Vásquez; (third row) Jaime Longoria, Ethan Buckhorn, C. Carrera, S. Jiménez, R. Cargboney, A. Gonzáles, C. Romero, M. Rentería, A. Colon, L. Rodríguez, A. Limón, and Frank Arvizu. (Courtesy of Jaime Longoria.)

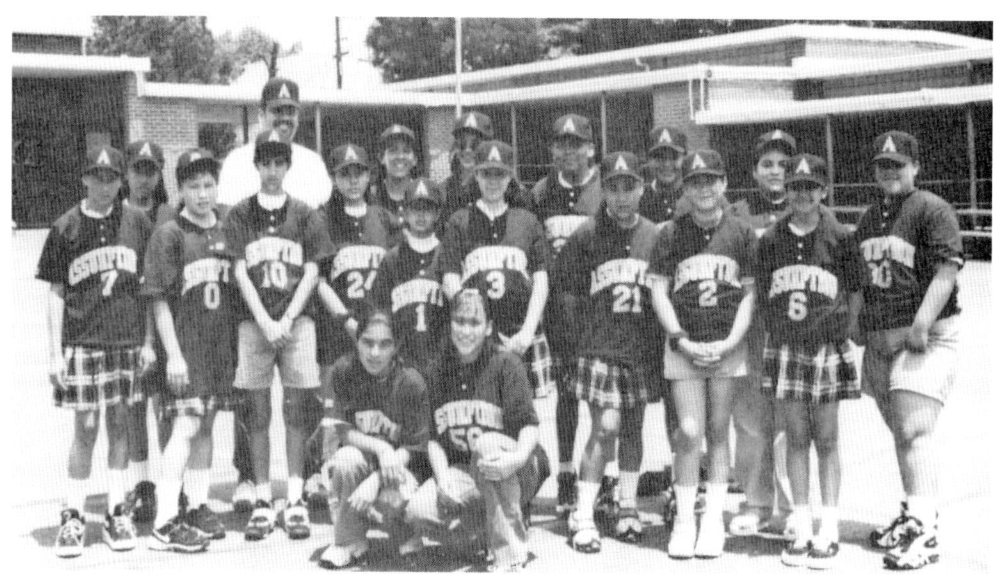

The 1996–1997 Assumption School Trojans had a very good season. In no particular order are Coach Frank Arvizu, S. Jiménez, C. Romero, C. Carrera, J. Jáuregui, M. Mercado, A. Guerrero, M. Hernández, A. Rosas, L. Álvarez, G. Jiménez, V. Armas, E. Román, I. Sánchez, L. Armendáriz, L. Pérez, Y. Castillo, J. Ortega, and E. Banales. (Courtesy of Jaime Longoria.)

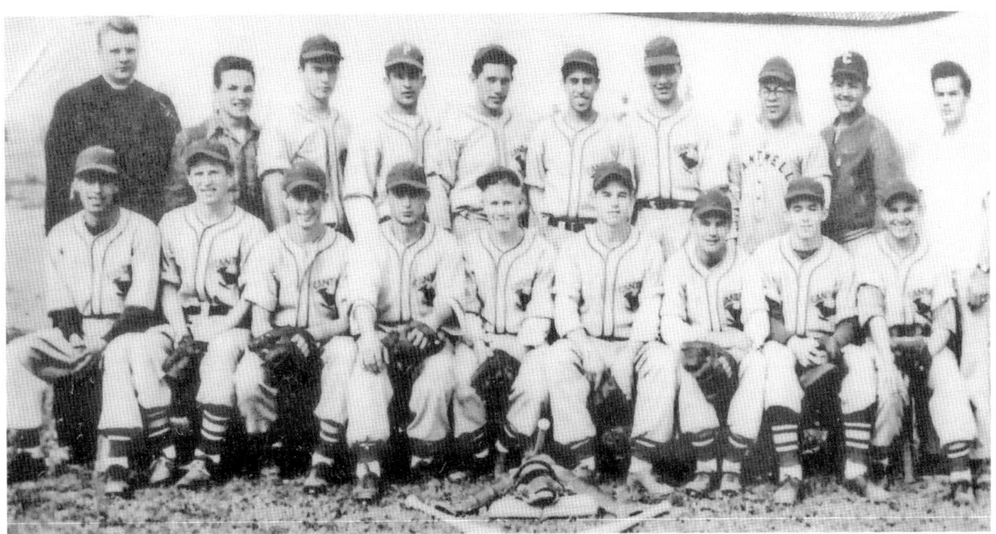

The 1950 Cantwell varsity team was the first baseball team in the school's history. The squad was talented enough to capture the first of two consecutive championships. They were led by Sal Reza and Ralph Rodríguez (both Cantwell Athletic Hall of Fame members) and Joe Villa. From left to right are (first row) A. Salazar, P. Ferrón, R. Eccleston, J. Villa, P. Waring, R. Sheridan, D. Cooper, L. Bononi, and T. Schramer; (second row) Brother L.M. Luberts (coach), P. Carey (manager), X. Padilla, S. Reza, R. Rodríguez, E. Rodríguez, J. Van Gorder, R. Gutiérrez, W. Bilotti (manager), and J. Fleming (manager). (Courtesy of Lauro Montes.)

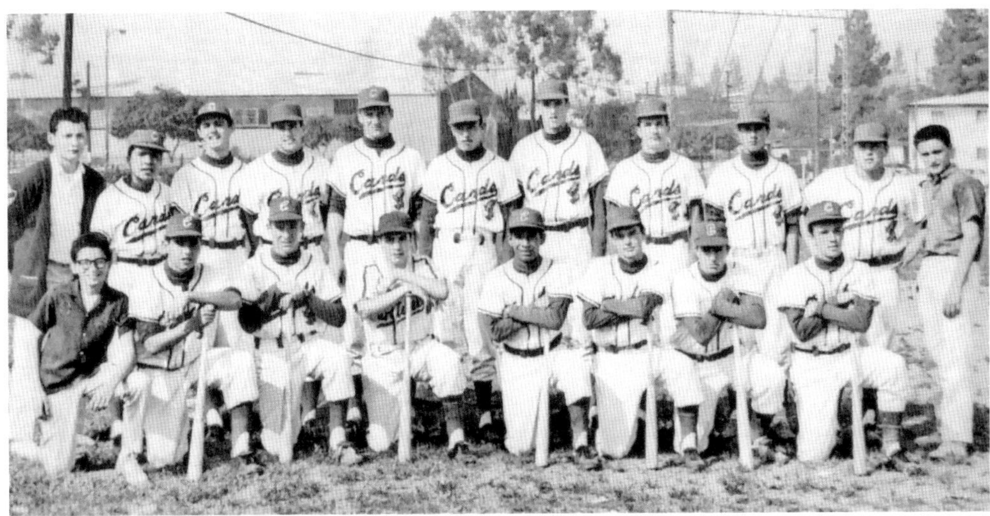

The 1962 Cantwell High School team was very good. From left to right are (first row) manager George Uranga, Bob Godinez, Jim Sweeny, Al López, Dan Ramírez, Bob Krup, Jim Hauser, and Bill Toby; (second row) John Schwable, Raúl Cardoza, Bob DeMoss, Ralph Sacco, Don Mette, Dave De La Torre, John Strange, Frank Klinger, Mike Cadilli, Charlie Anaya, and manager John Rogers. (Courtesy of Raúl Cardoza.)

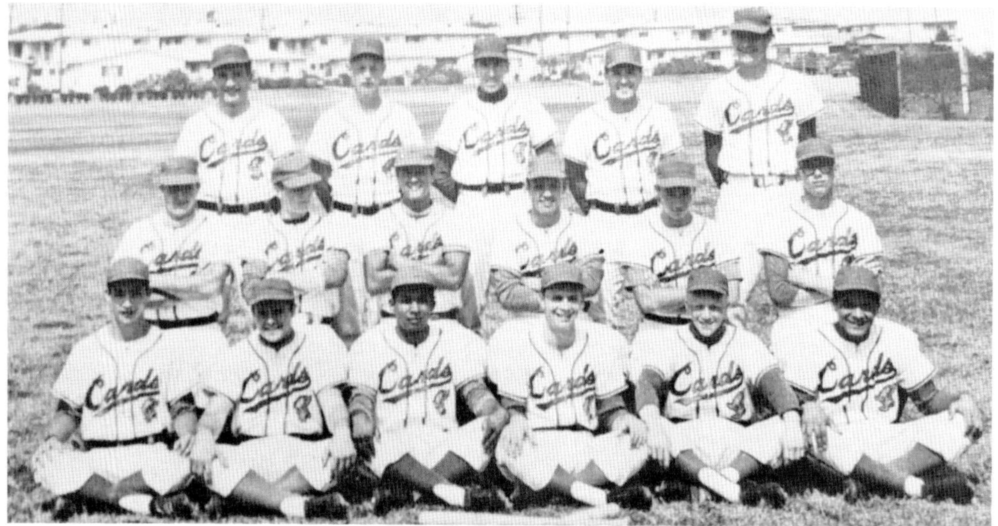


The 1964 Cantwell varsity team is the one by which all other Cantwell teams are measured. They advanced to the semifinal playoffs and set a school record with six first-team all-league selections. One player signed with the Boston Red Sox, and six played in college. Pitcher Frank Klinger earned All-League, league MVP, and All-CIF honors. He still holds Stanford University's lowest ERA season record. This squad also advanced to the playoff semifinals in 1963. (Courtesy of Lauro Montes.)

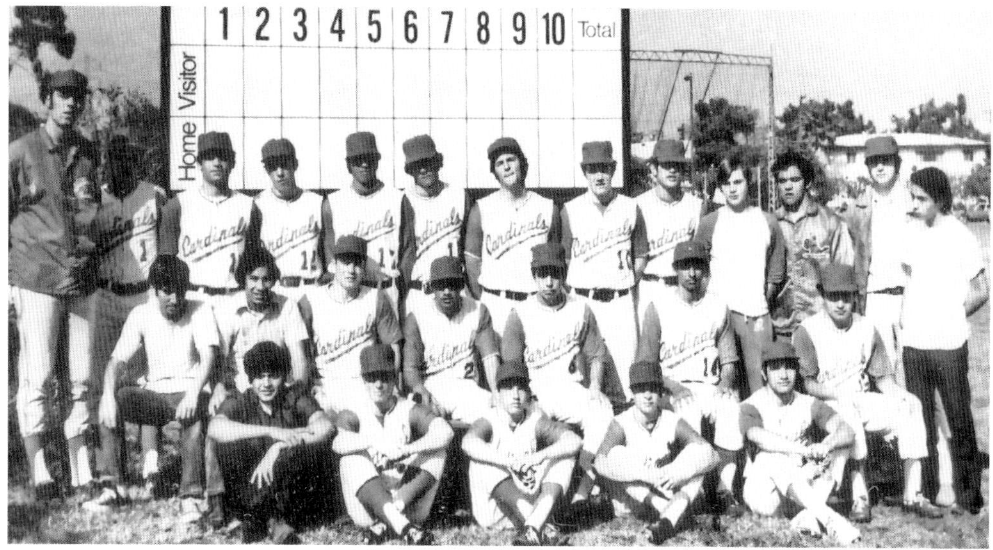


The 1972 Cantwell varsity team placed second in the Santa Fe League, finishing with a 14-5 record. Every Saturday before league play, they scrimmaged against Roosevelt, because Cantwell coach Rod Poteete had been an assistant coach under Ernie Rodríguez at Roosevelt. Cantwell was led by All-League pitcher Ray Gaitan, All-League second baseman George Villa (Cerritos College), pitcher Jimmy Carrillo (Pepperdine Malibu), and catcher Joe Villa. Joe Villa had a scholarship offer to Stanford but opted to sign with the Baltimore Orioles. His father, Joe, and brother, John, were also Cantwell players. (Courtesy of Lauro Montes.)

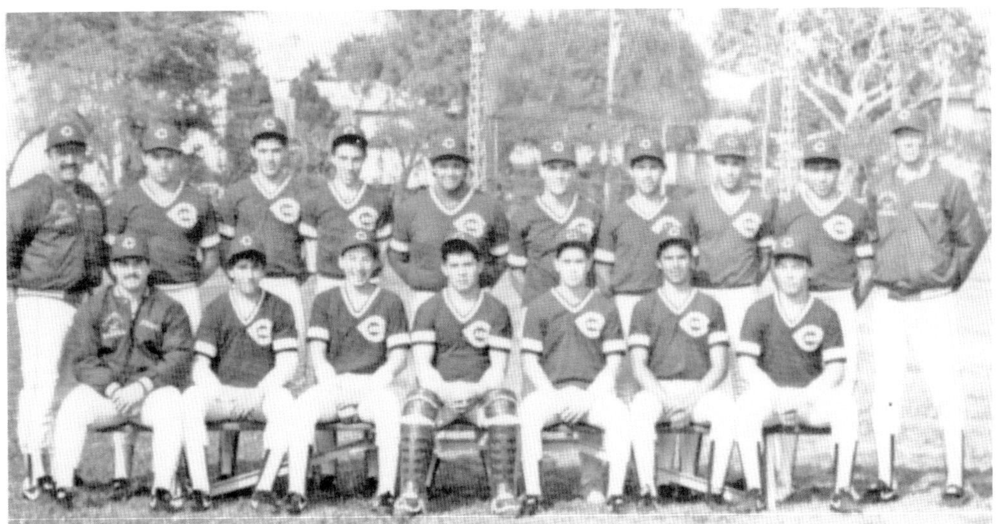

The 1986 and 1987 Cantwell varsity squads were coached by Richard Straight (second row, far right). The Cantwell baseball field was named in his honor in 2014. Ray "Flores" Walker, pitcher and outfielder, earned All-CIF honors twice. He later played at the University of California at Irvine. Joe Gonzáles, pitcher and shortstop, earned All-CIF honors and played at Lewis and Clark College in Idaho. He was coached by his father, Montebello alum Pete González Sr., and Joey's brother, Pete González, who played at Whittier College. (Courtesy of Lauro Montes.)

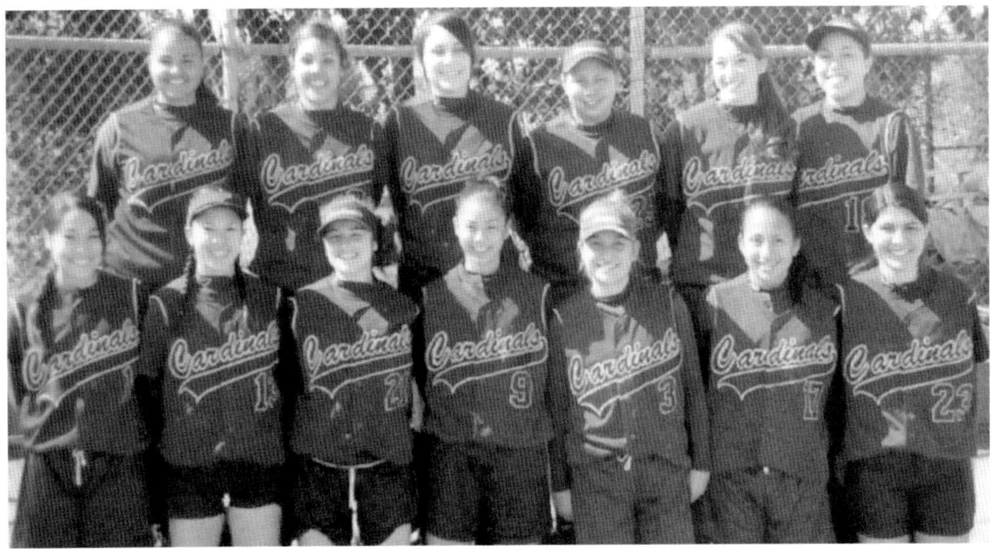

The 2006 Cantwell Sacred Heart of Mary varsity softball team captured its second consecutive CIF championship. From left to right are (first row) Roberta García, Roxy Gonzáles, Jackie Hernández, Lauren Yao, Lauren Alvarado, Michelle Sierra, and Veronica Méndez; (second row) Vanessa Carrasco, Jackie Reyes, Aileen Villareal, Armanda Ybarra, Bernadette Andrade, and Cynthia Duarte. Not shown is Lupe García. Villareal was head football manager at the University of Notre Dame and, after graduation, worked for the Houston Astros and Detroit Tigers in media relations. (Courtesy of Lauro Montes.)

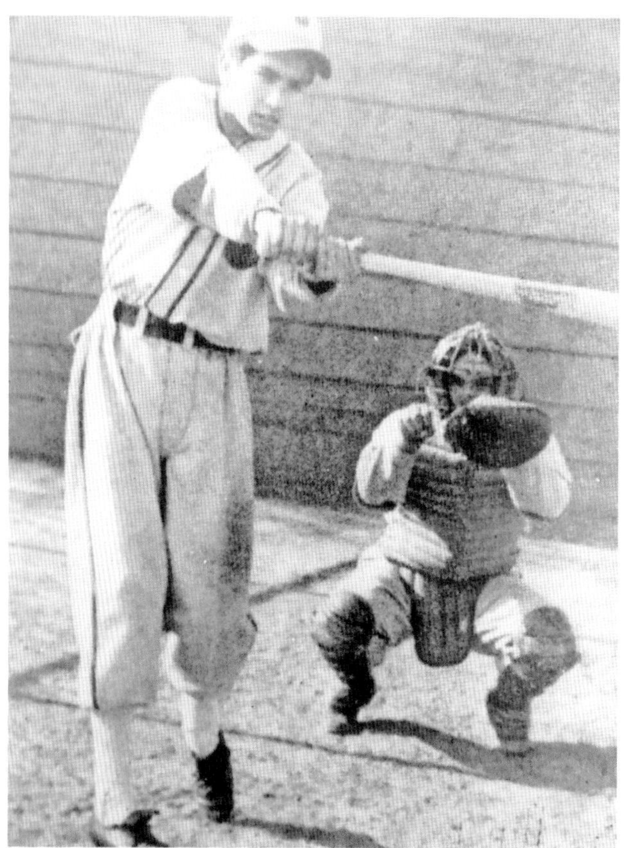

In 1945, the Cathedral Phantoms won the Catholic championship for the fourth consecutive time and were undefeated in league play. The team had outstanding pitching and hitting. Co-captain Lalo Portillo, shortstop and leading batter for the squad, played his third and final year for the team. Johnny Reyes was a sensational sophomore second baseman. (Courtesy of Cathedral High School.)

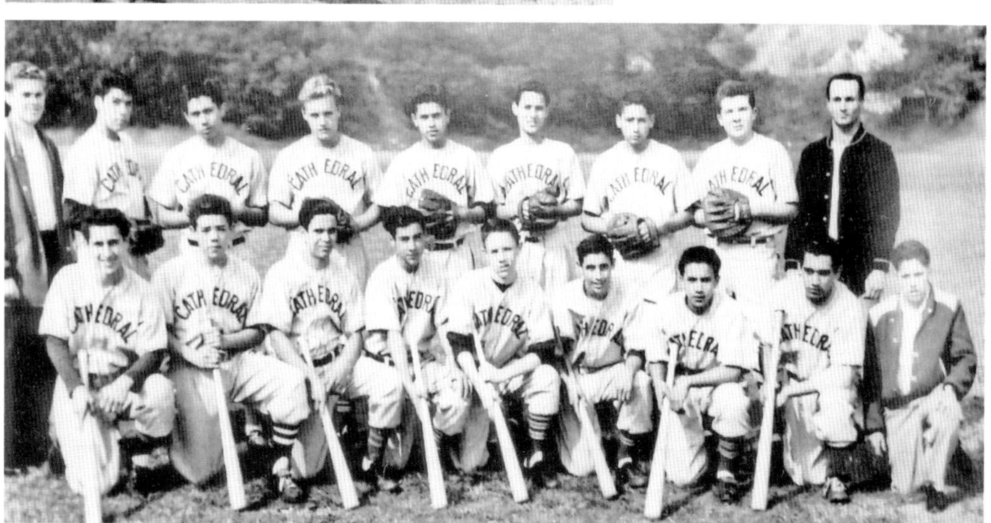

The 1958 Cathedral team continued the school's reputation as a solid team with strong pitching and hitting. From left to right are (first row) M. Cannis, R. Houser, J. Rocha, R. Meléndres, D. Hendrickson, H. Moreno, R. Villanueva, J. Juárez, and manager C. Stanton; (second row) manager R. McWilliams. R. Pedroza, R. Recendez, T. Davidson, A. Barrios, L. Varela, J. Férralez, T. Mullen, and Coach Marvin Sampson. (Courtesy of Cathedral High School.)

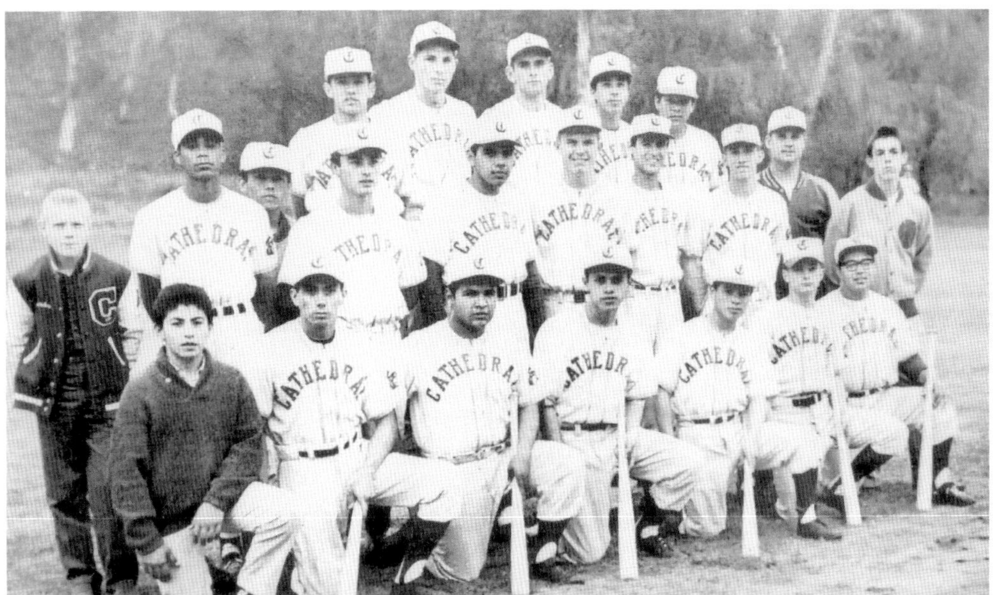

There were several outstanding players on the 1961 Cathedral baseball team. From left to right are (first row) manager A. Torres, R. Recendez, R. Nava, A. Barrios, N. Trinidad, L. Mestyanek, and W. Rodríguez; (second row) manager C. Saale, R. Galwey, G. Palacio, J. Soldó, J. Recendez, D. Sigaty, L. Varela, T. Bibbs, coach Dick Salter, and manager E. Espinoza; (third row) R. Ruedas, F. Bilderback, W. Terry, V. Escobedo, and D. García. Not pictured is E. Bertrand. (Courtesy of Cathedral High School.)

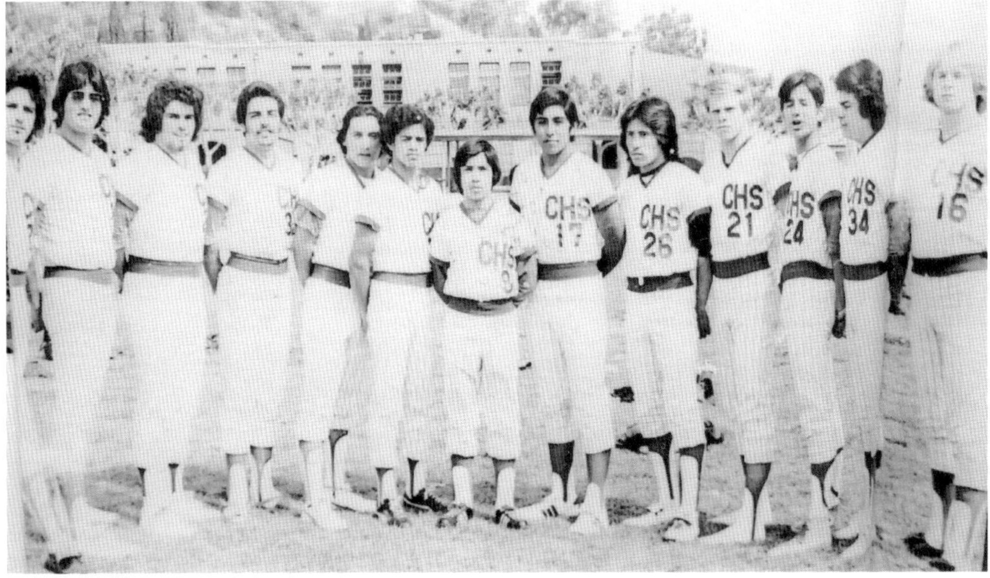


The 1976 Cathedral baseball team included, from left to right, Mike Contreras, Ed Domínguez, Joe García, Domingo Herrera, Albert Betancourt, Francisco Torrez, Larry Godinez, Lorenzo Tovar, Saúl Felamino, Phillip Ruiz, Nick Griego, Paul Provénció, and Sean Conway. (Courtesy of Cathedral High School.)

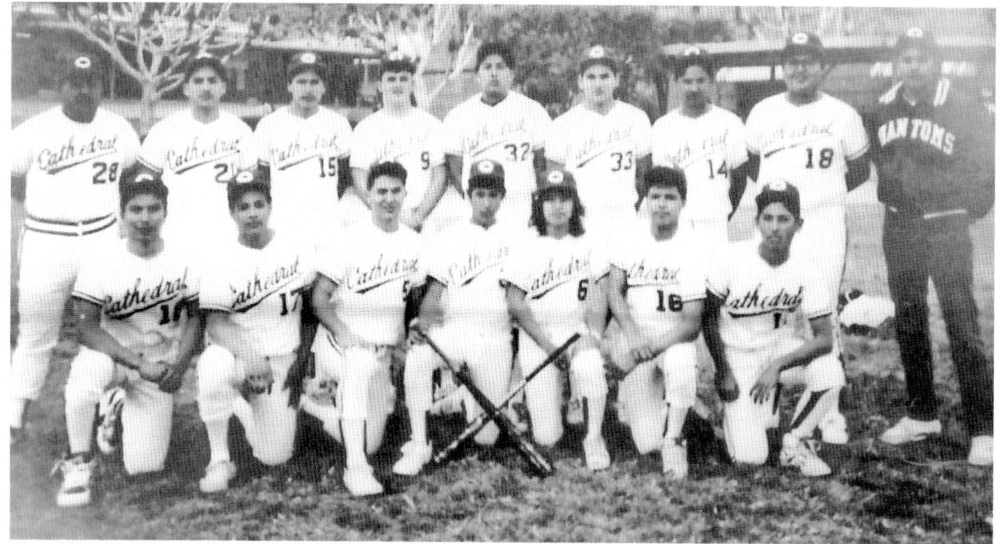

The 1989 Cathedral baseball team included, from left to right, (first row) Richard Murga, Joby Gutiérrez, Joe Kollsar, Michael Cox, Frank Espinosa, Davian Corona, and Rene Sánchez; (second row) coach Louie Moreno, Jesús Cisneros, Ray Soto, A.T. García, Tony Rodríguez, David Marín, Omar Villanueva, Gabriel Puga, and coach Roger Argomaniz. Not pictured is Marcos Sánchez. (Courtesy of Cathedral High School.)

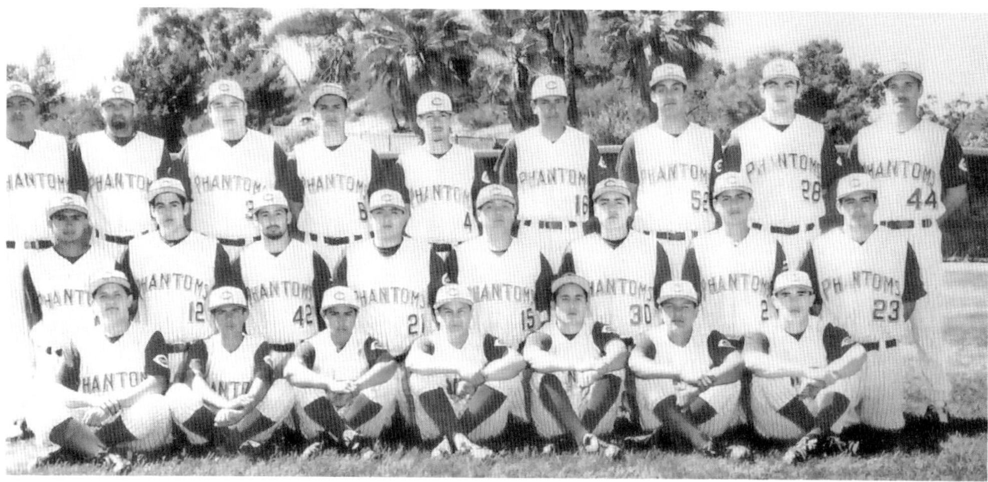

Over the years, Cathedral has had several great teams. The 2010 team was one of its finest, with outstanding hitting, amazing speed on the bases and in the field, and a first-rate pitching staff. From left to right are (first row) Alex Mayagoitia, Cal Moreno, Johnathan González, Jonathan Martínez, Jaime Figueroa, Joseph Díaz, and Kyle Merrill; (second row) Joe Gonzáles, Anthony Vásquez, Armando Bermúdez, Josh Ibarra, Tim Shiba, Brian Orozco, David Sánchez, and Sergio Luna; (third row) coaches Marcos Sánchez and Mickey Moreno, Christopher Centeno, Chris Flores, coach Juan Sánchez, Oscar Leong, Jimmy Lara, Phil Pérez, and coach Scott Pearson. (Courtesy of Cathedral High School.)

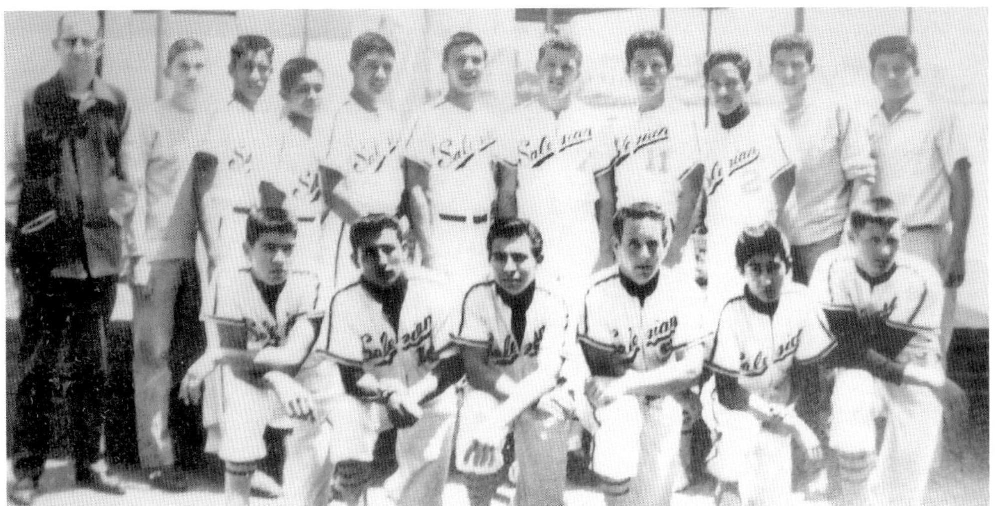

The 1960 Salesian Mustangs were the school's second varsity team. There is no photograph of the 1959 team. From left to right are (first row) Charles García, Xavier Avila, Jesse Baeza, Greg Cunningham, Frank Urias, and unidentified; (second row) Fr. Mike Ribotta, Alfred Gutierrez, Frank Pacheco, Mario Valdez, Ed Acosta, Jesse Romero, Thomas Benigni, Leonard Benavidez, Angel Rodríguez, Larry Frank Gaxiola, and Ed Chávez. The football stadium at St. John Bosco in Bellflower, California, is named after Father's Ribotta's brother Frank. Frank was a long time faculty member and coach. Acosta was the first student body president. (Courtesy of Salesian High School.)

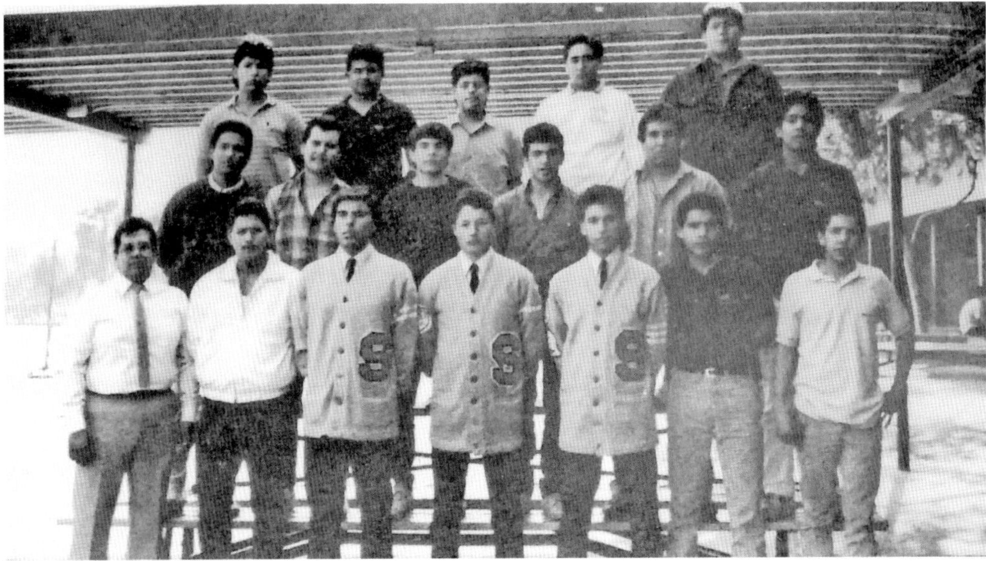

The 1985–1986 Salesian Mustangs were a solid team. From left to right are (first row) coach J. Rodríguez Sr., Adolfo Gutiérrez, Mark Rodríguez, Carlos González, José Huizar, Danny Díaz, and Jerry Meléndrez; (second row) Oscar Chávez, David Aguayo, Rick Vásquez, Henry Esqueda, Jimmy Pérez, and Nick Hernández; (third row) Al Valenzuela, John Martínez, Danny Mata, Victor Magallón, and Ramón Ortega. Not shown is Eddie García. Huizar currently serves on the Los Angeles City Council. (Courtesy of Salesian High School.)

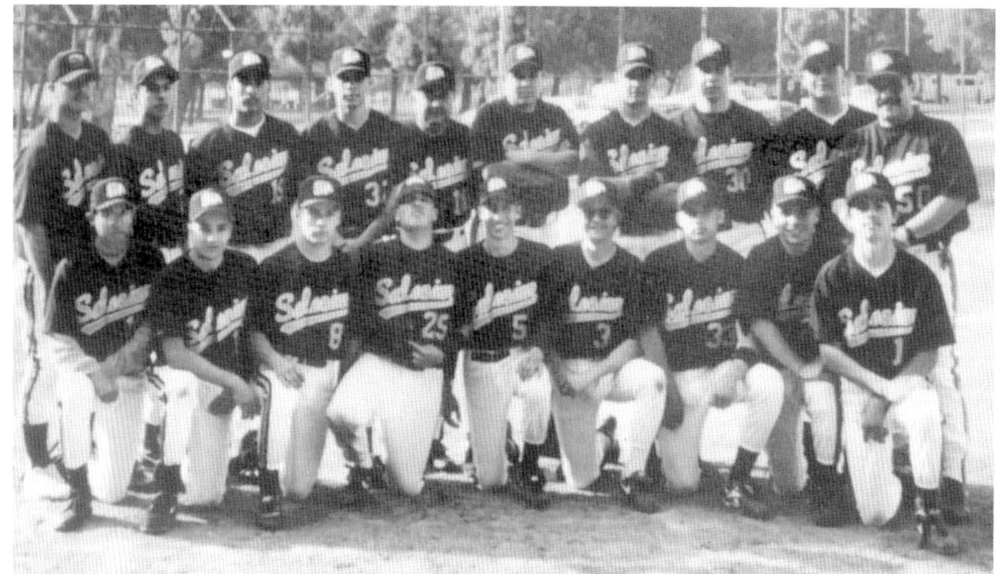

The 1994 Salesian team had outstanding hitting, a strong pitching staff, amazing speed on the bases, and a solid defense. One of the players, Alex Chacón (first row, center), is currently the principal of Bishop Mora Salesian High School. Besides Salesian, Chacón graduated from Santa Teresita School. Other players include Erasmo Aderete, Eddie Fernández, Mike Valdez, Luís Márquez, and Rafael Lomeli. The Catalonian Bishop Francis Mora was consecrated a bishop with right of succession by Bishop Thaddeus Amat in 1873. He is entombed in the Bishops' Crypt at the Cathedral of Our Lady of the Angels in Los Angeles. (Courtesy of Salesian High School.)

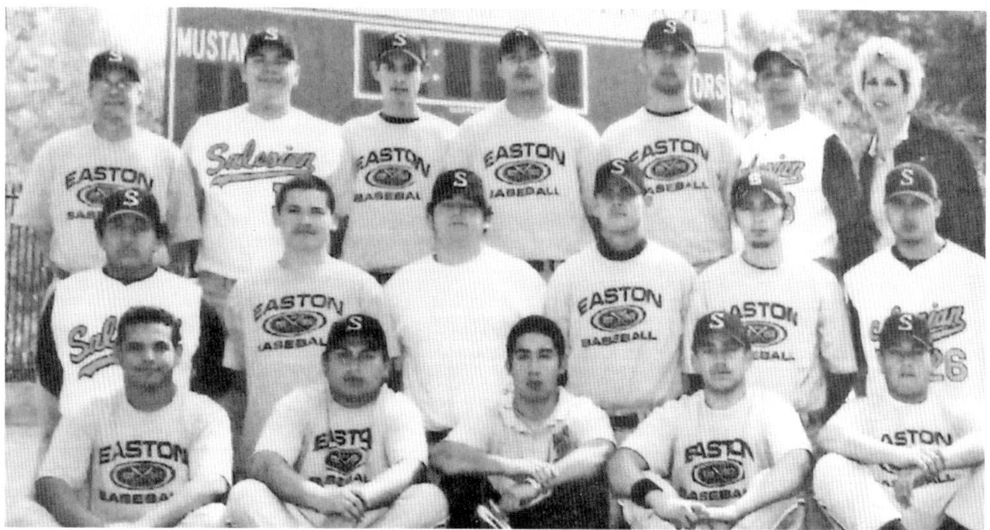

The 2003 Mustangs had a solid team and a female coach. From left to right are (first row) D. Canales, B. Conde, M. De León, J. Rodríguez, and A López; (second row) J. Grijalva, L. Hidalgo, J. López, L.A. López, L. Beltrán, and M. Ramírez; (third row) coach Richard Sacino, J. García, E. De la Cruz, J. Villafuerte, G. Bucio, G. Silva, and assistant coach Pearl Parker. (Courtesy of Salesian High School.)

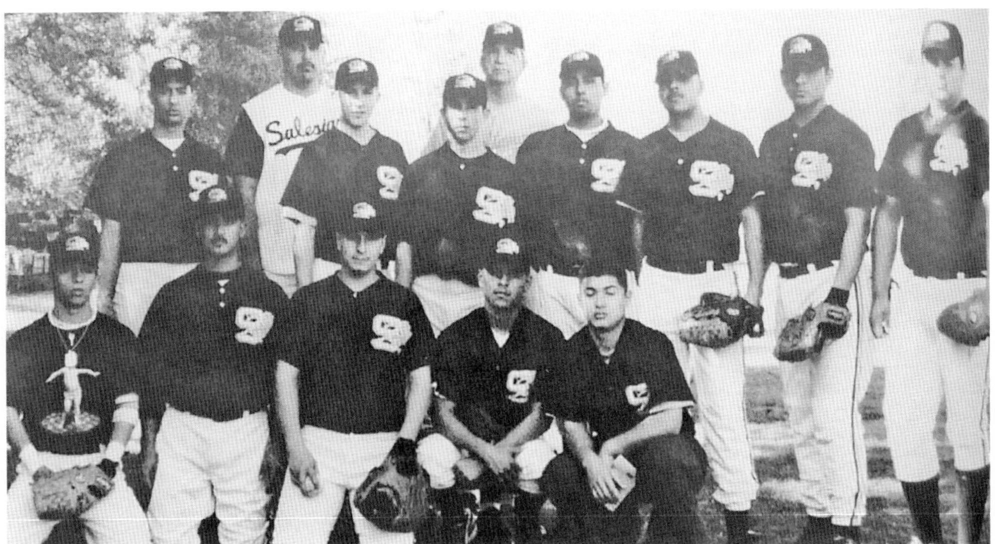

The 2000 Salesian Mustangs had an excellent group of players. From left to right are (first row) Eddie Ruiz, Jaime Pulido, Ernie Ortega, José Rodríguez, and coach Ronald Díaz; (second row) Jason Farabaugh, Victor Ruiz, Gerry Ruiz, Abel Eligio, Adrián Gamboa, Alex Navarro, and Héctor Sandoval; (third row) two unidentified. Not pictured are Joey Ibarra and David Vidaurri. (Courtesy of Salesian High School.)

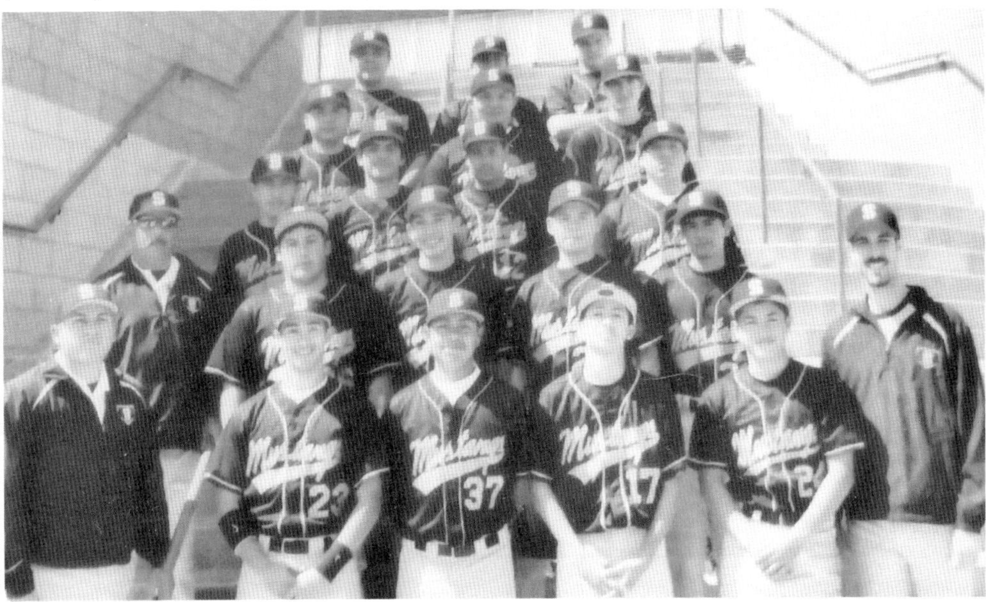


The 2015 Mustangs had outstanding hitting, amazing speed, and a tough pitching staff. From left to right are (first row) coach Andrew Jiménez, Jerry Barragán, Jonathan Cortéz, Steve Rostran, C.J. Rodríguez, and coach Chris Lanus; (second row) coach Joe López, Anthony Ceniceroz, Danny Fernández, Oscar Quintana, and Félix Romero; (third row) Julián Castro, Saúl García, Nick Gutiérrez, and Armando Favela; (fourth row) Peter Pérez, Augie Zepeda, and Ronald García; (fifth row) Arnie Robles, Jorge Esparza, and Garrett Malcor. (Courtesy of Salesian High School.)

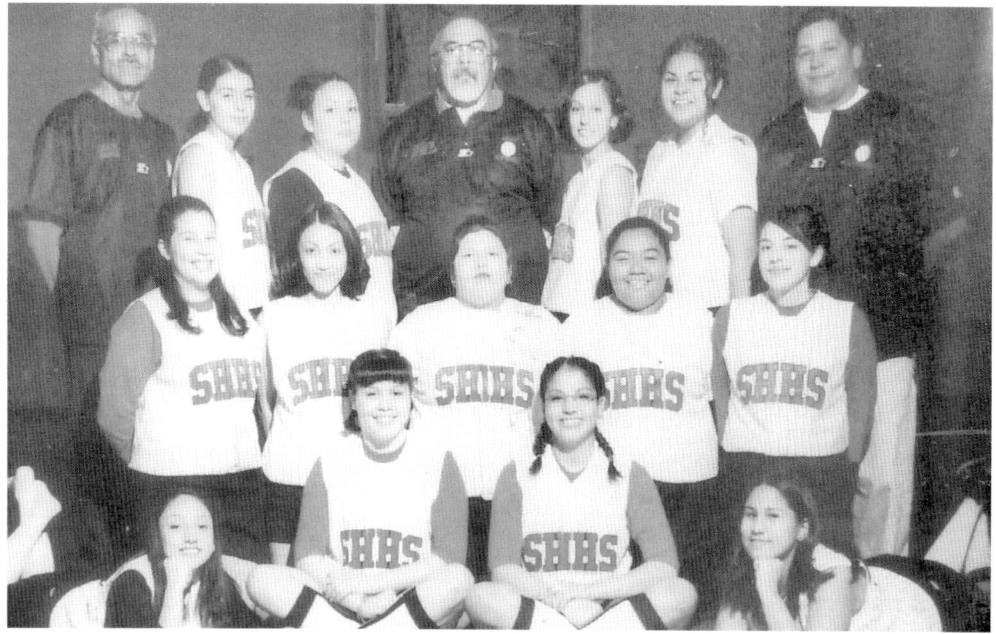

The 2001 Sacred Heart of Jesus softball team had excellent fielding, great pitching, speed on the bases, and outstanding coaches. In no particular order are coaches Amaya, López, and Padilla and players Carolyn G., Jessica F., Desiree F., Xochitl A., Raquel M., Amy M., Kathy R., Amalia Q., Michelle R., Jennifer A., Andrea F., Lisa T., and Jennifer M. (Courtesy of Sacred Heart High School.)

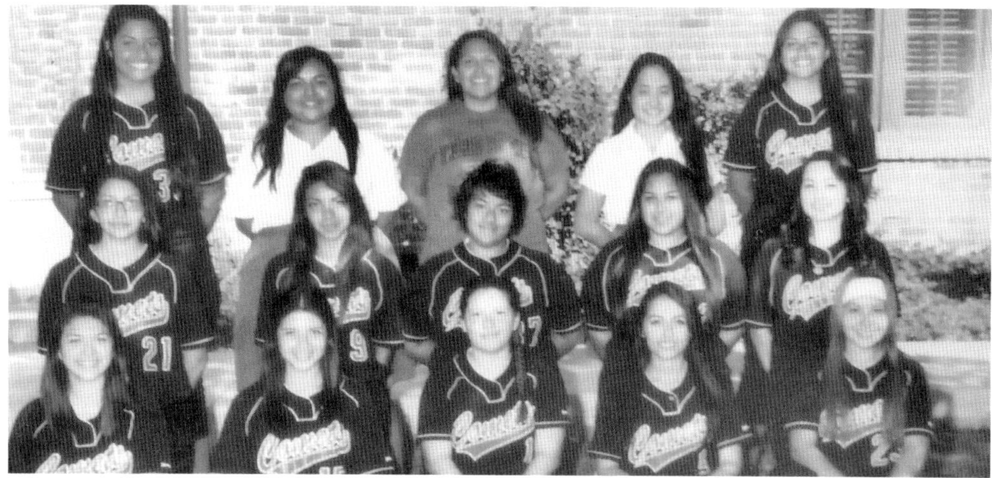

The 2015 Sacred Heart team included, from left to right, (first row) Jocelyn Carreon, Leslie Nuñez, Sara Rocha, Yessania, and Zsa-Zsa Ramos; (second row) Jezabel Carreon, Arianna Obligacion, Jasmine Khan, Rhiannon Mejia, and Samantha Anderson; (third row) Edith Estrada, Brittany Morales, Coach Christina López, Elen Devoux, and Judith Estrada. Rhiannon Mejia started playing T-ball at the age of four and played for Alhambra Little League for several years, making all-star teams. She pitched and played first and third bases. She also played six years in American Youth Soccer Organization (AYSO) Alhambra-Monterey Park District 60. She later played basketball at St. Thomas More and softball and volleyball at Assumption School. (Courtesy of Sacred Heart High School.)

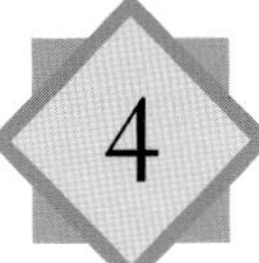

# COMMUNITY

Community baseball has been a major presence in the lives of Mexican Americans since at least the 1860s. The period between the 1920s and 1950s holds particular significance and is often referred to as baseball's golden age. On any given Sunday, there was daybreak-to-sunset buzz in the air as hundreds, even thousands of Mexican American fans cheered and gave allegiance to their storied teams and idolized hometown heroes. Truth be told, baseball was a serious business, a dogfight of pitching duels, and community pride was always at stake. By Sunday night, the gracious and dignified opponents were on their way home, having strengthened social and cultural ties with their Spanish-speaking brethren.

Nowhere was baseball more popular than East Los Angeles, home to the largest concentration of Mexican Americans in the United States and second only to Mexico City in population. Over the decades, hundreds of industrial, semiprofessional, neighborhood athletic club, municipal park, amateur, 40–60 club, and pickup teams have enriched the diamonds of "East Los." The euphoria of the games provided the jumping-for-joy multitudes with a special place for reaffirming their ethnic identity, language legitimacy, gender equality, and unbending unity; strengthening their unstoppable demands for social justice; and showcasing their unrelenting patriotism while at the same time displaying unrivaled athletic skill and jaw-dropping talent. These were the salad days for baseball in East Los Angeles.

With baseball and softball, Mexican American women and men had heroes to congratulate, teams to rally around, positive activities for their children, and the shared experiences that were the driving force that led the way for a common destiny of first-class citizenship. At the ballparks, which also served as political arenas, voter registration and citizenship drives took place, as did the recruiting of new union members, collecting donations to file discrimination suits, pressing the flesh by elected officials, and informing fans of boycotts against businesses that did not hire or serve Mexican Americans. Over the long haul, baseball and the civil and political rights movements coincided because playing on the fields and protesting in the streets were only a sidewalk apart.

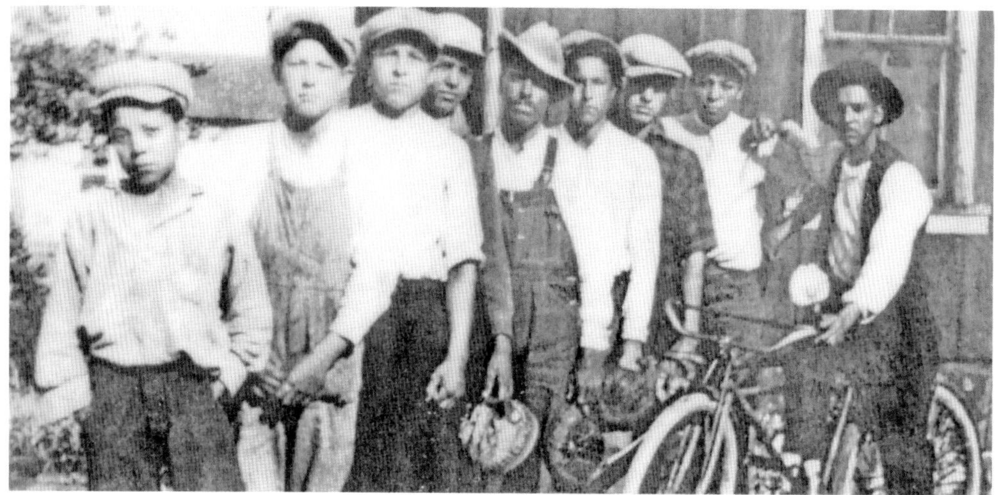

This 1917 photograph depicts an early Los Angeles Mexican American baseball team. Many teams during this era were comprised of brothers and cousins. This team had five brothers. Ventura Saiza is on his bike, while his brothers Manuel, Fidencio, Martín, and Pepe are directly to his right. Many of these brothers had children and grandchildren who played in East Los Angeles for decades. Mexican Americans were playing baseball in Los Angeles as early as 1870, and Mexican American women were playing as early as 1915 in the greater East Los Angeles area. (Courtesy of David Olmos.)

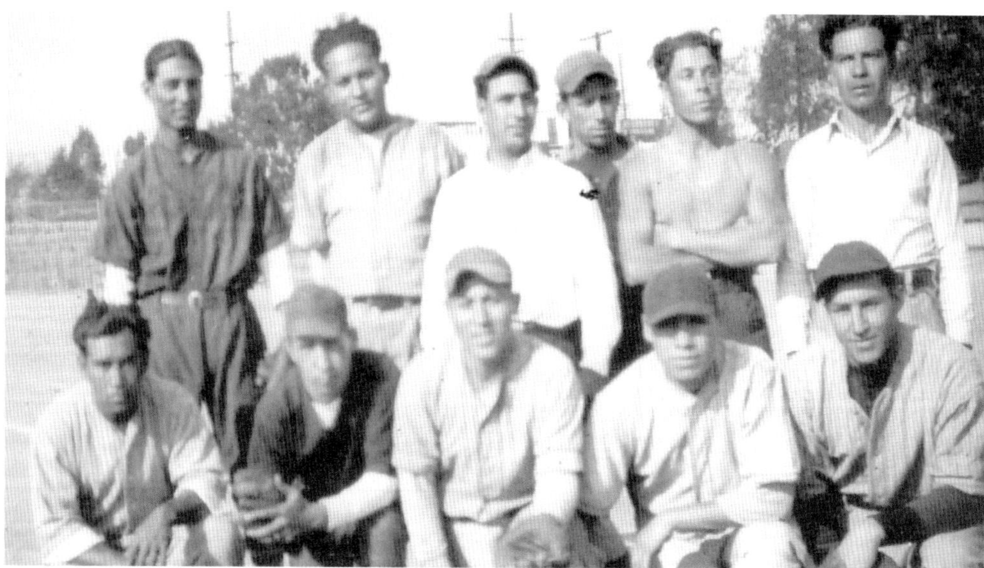

The San Jose baseball team from East Los Angeles organized around 1927. Due to lack of funds, they did not have uniforms, and their equipment was secondhand. Guadalupe E. López (second row, third from left) was the team manager, and three of his family members played on the team: cousin Steve Díaz (first row, second from left), brother Jesús (second row, far left), and cousin Vincent Macias (first row, center). (Courtesy of Carmen R. Reyes.)

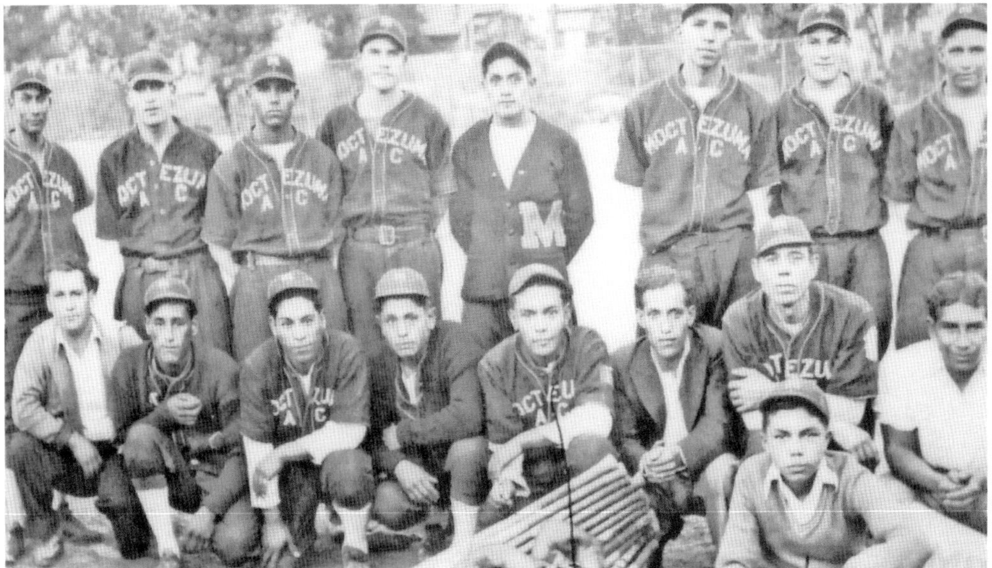

The Moctezuma baseball team is seen here at Downey Park in East Los Angeles in 1931. Players included two sets of brothers: Lalo and Adolfo Regalado, and Manuel and Pedro Barrios. Lalo (standing, far left) and Adolfo (standing, second from right) were the brothers of prominent baseball manager and promoter Manuel Regalado. Pedro (kneeling, fifth from left) and Manuel (sitting in front) also come from a distinguished family of players. Pete Encinas, wearing the sweater with the letter M, was Pedro's best friend. (Courtesy of Pete Barrios Jr.)

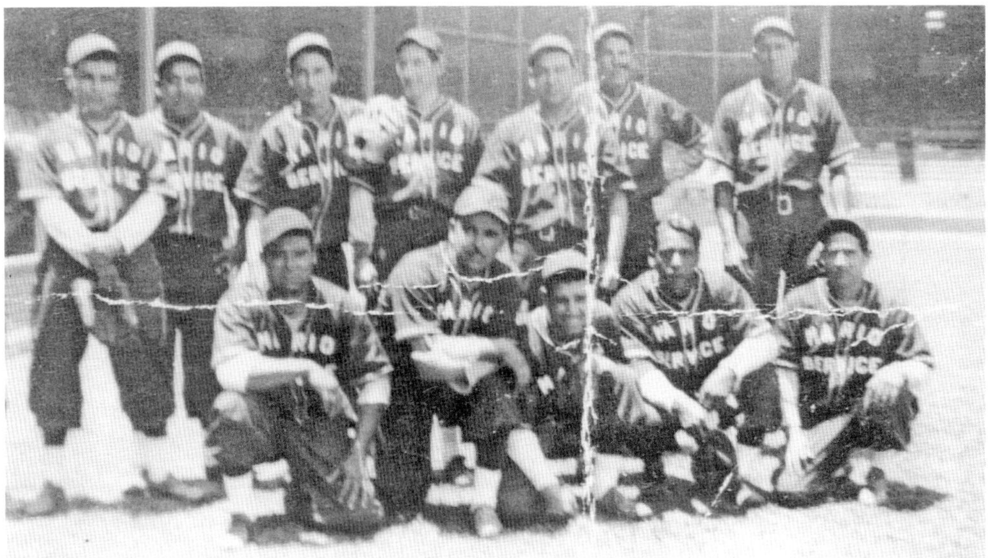

In 1942, Mario López (first row, center) decided to sponsor a team under the name of his business, Mario's Service Station. The team had excellent players, in part because López gave them free gas when they played well. Tommy Pérez (second row, far right), López's longtime friend, first managed this team. This photograph shows the team playing against the Pacific Coast League Angels at Wrigley Field in Los Angeles. (Courtesy of the López family.)

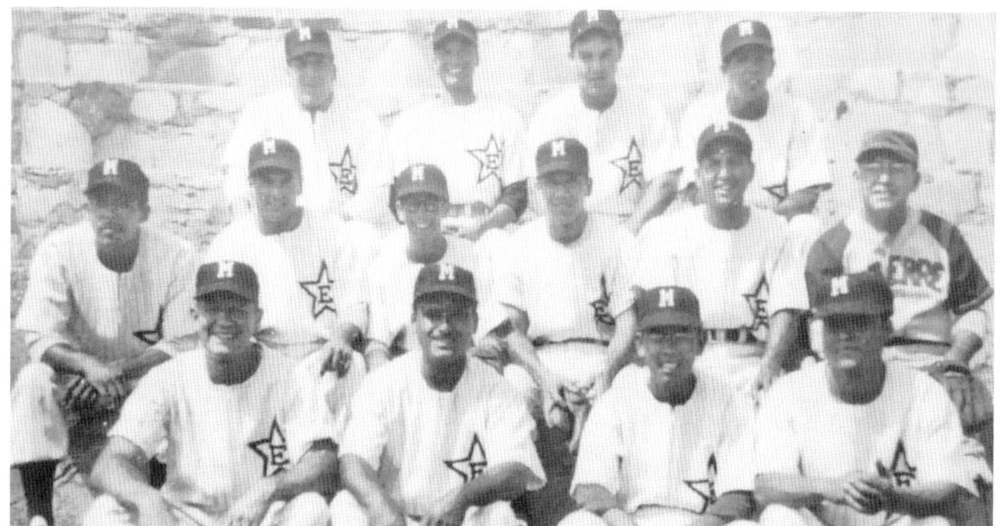

Baseball teams mushroomed in East Los Angeles immediately after World War II. The Eastside Merchants represented a group of businesses that pooled their meager resources to support a single team. Generally, the merchants were responsible for purchasing uniforms, equipment, gas for travel, food and beverages, trophies, and team photographs. From left to right are (first row) unidentified, Bobby Granillo, Wallie Poon, and unidentified; (second row) Duke Aloy, Rudy Farisi, and four unidentified; (third row) Vince Galindo, Gabe Peña, Rich García, and Babe Órnelas. (Courtesy of Bobby Recendez.)

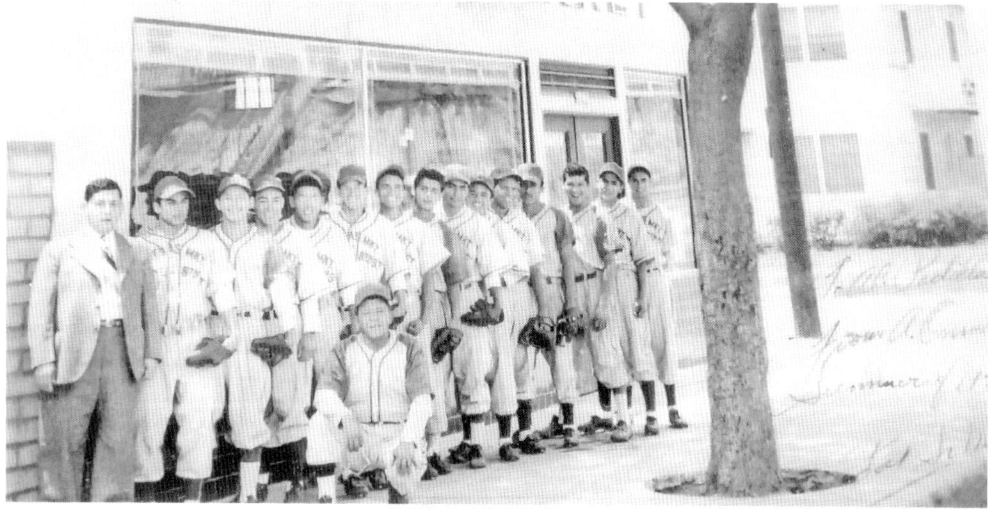

Most merchant teams lasted only a few years. There were, however, a handful of teams that lasted several years. This 1949 team was sponsored by Órnelas Market. Youth teams sponsored by businesses were regarded as a way to keep boys out of trouble with local gangs. A number of managers had multiple sons on teams in order to occupy them with positive activity. From left to right are Angelo Órnelas, Luís Gómez, Benny García, Eddie Peña, Wallie Poon, Chimino Magaña, Gabe Peña, unidentified, Lugo ?, Jesús Reza, Al Padilla, Pat Molina, Johnny Ruelas, and two unidentified. Kneeling is manager Pat Molina Jr. (Courtesy of Richard Peña.)

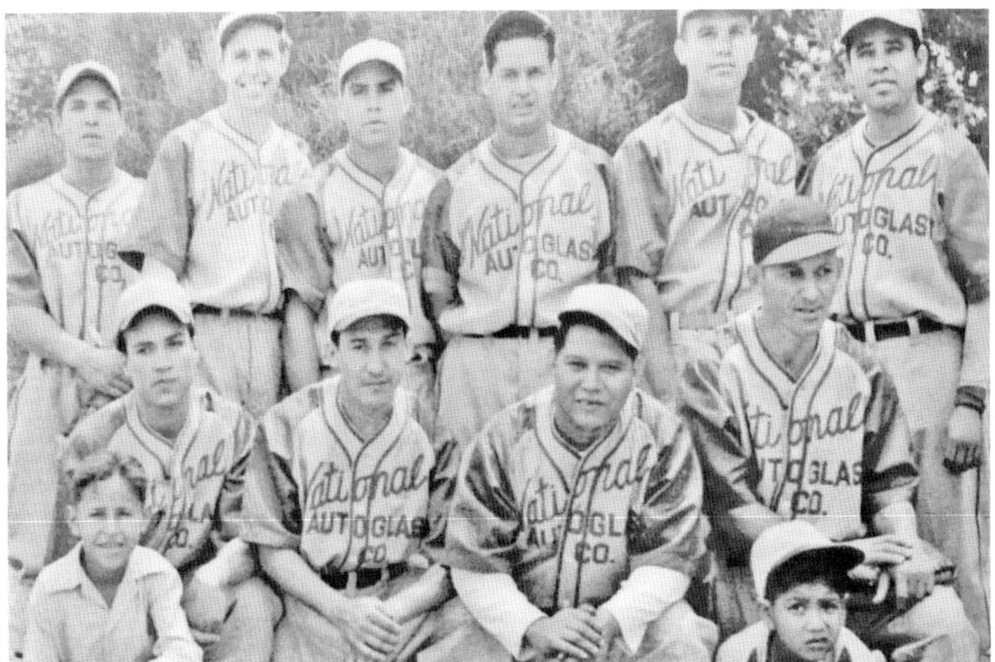

The National Auto Glass Company team dominated for years during the 1940s. From left to right are (first row) George Peña, unidentified, manager Manuel "Shorty" Pérez, and unidentified; (second row) Ed Castro, unidentified, Richard Álvarez, Joe Corea, unidentified, and Ray Armenta. The batboy to the right is Eddie Pérez. The best players wanted to play for "Shorty" because of his knowledge of the game and his record. Players often left other teams to be on his squad. (Courtesy of Richard Peña.)

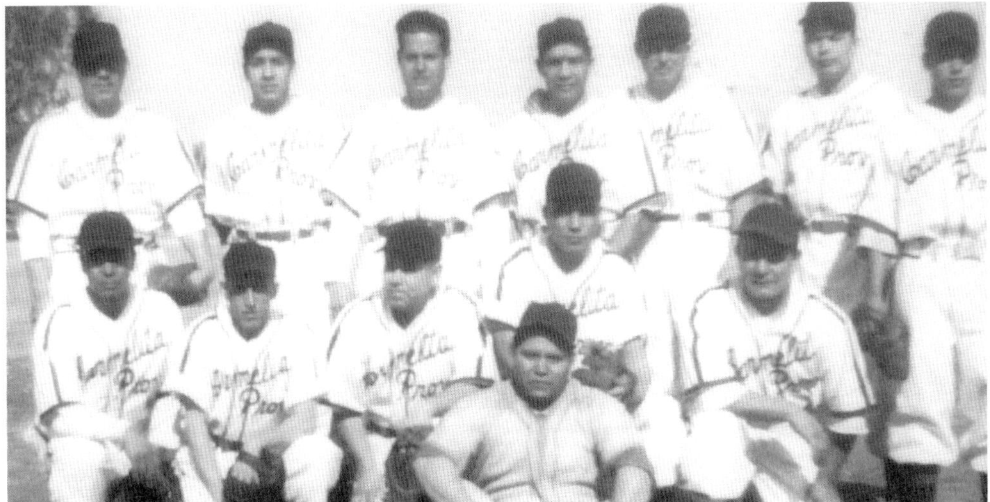

The Carmelita Provision Company was one of the few local markets that sold popular Mexican food. The team was nicknamed "Los Chorizeros" (the sausage makers). The 1947 team is seen at Evergreen Park. Manuel "Shorty" Pérez (sitting) managed them for decades. Players include, in no particular order, Ray Armenta, Joe Corea, Al Castañeda, "Chavalo" Zumbía, Ernie Sierra, Sandy Sandoval, Freddy and Yam Yánez, "Lefty" Ocampo, and Richard Peña. (Courtesy of Richard Peña.)

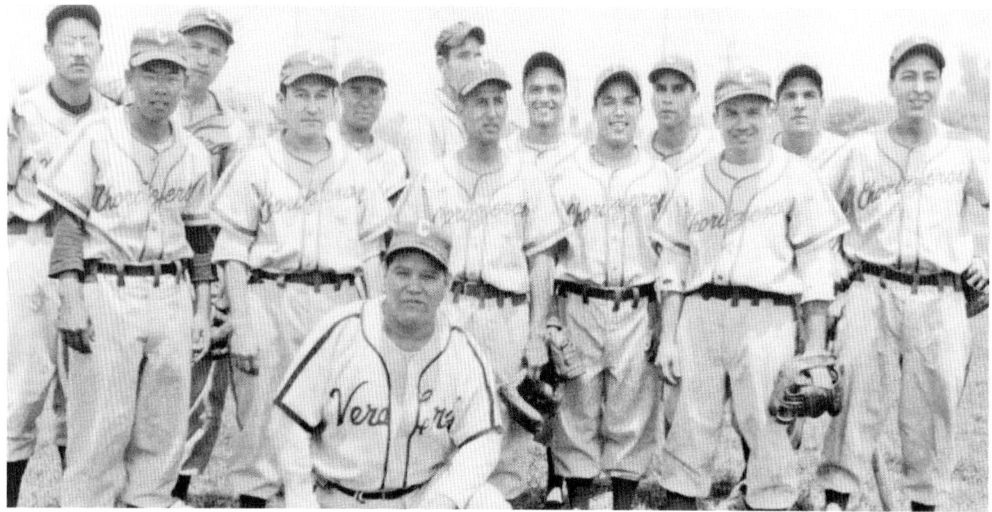

In 1948, Mario López closed his gas station and opened the Carmelita Provision Company, one of the few East Los Angeles markets that carried popular Mexican food such as pigs' feet, pork rind (*chicharrones*), and pork sausage (*chorizo*). After winning its first community championship in 1948, Saul Toledo nicknamed the team "Los Chorizeros," and the moniker stuck. Kneeling is "Shorty" Pérez; standing from left to right are unidentified, Wallie Poon, two unidentified, "Lefty" Rodríguez, unidentified, Ray Alderete, Gabe Peña, Richard Peña, Richard Álvarez, Saúl Toledo, Eddie Castro, and Dan Salazar. (Courtesy of Richard Peña.)

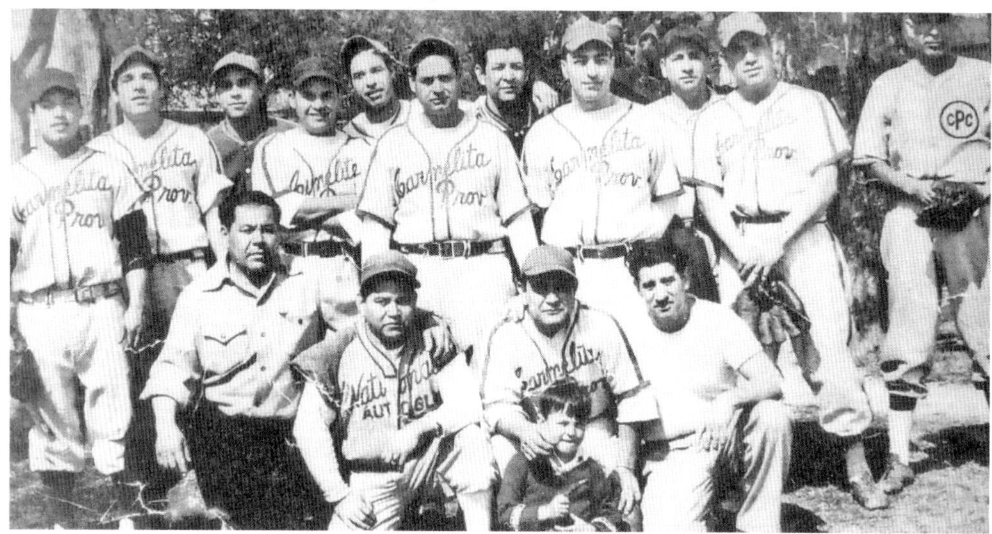

The Carmelita Provision Company teams were known as the "New York Yankees of East Los Angeles," because they won several championships and produced extraordinary players. From the 1940s through the 1970s, it is believed they won 19 Los Angeles city championships. The 1949 team included, from left to right (first row) Frank Sornoso, Manuel "Shorty" Pérez, "Lefty" Gómez, and Mario López; (second row) Richard Peña, Eddie Castro, Richard Álvarez, Larry Ochoa, unidentified, Joe Corea, Sam Gallindo, Dan Salazar, Gene Conda, Luís ?, and ? Morales. López and Sornoso were the co-owners of Carmelita. The little boy is unidentified. (Courtesy of Richard Peña.)

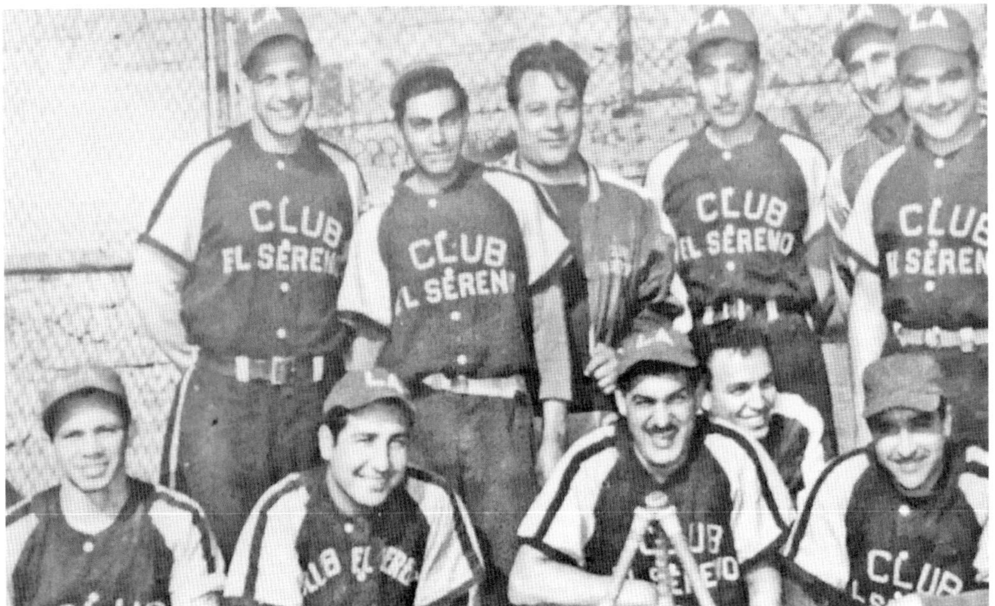

The 1948 El Sereno team played in the Los Angeles Winter League. Players included Manuel López, "Lefty" Ortega, Alex Velásquez, Bobby Peña, Manuel Salcido, George Acuña, ? Herrera, Tom Echevarria, Trino Cervantes, Norbert Castel De Oro, and John Apodaca. Norbert (first row, far left) was the second of five children born to Sylvian and Louise Castel De Oro, who migrated from Mexico. Norbert married Gloria Palanco in 1950. They had five children and five grandchildren. (Courtesy of Jaime Castel De Oro.)

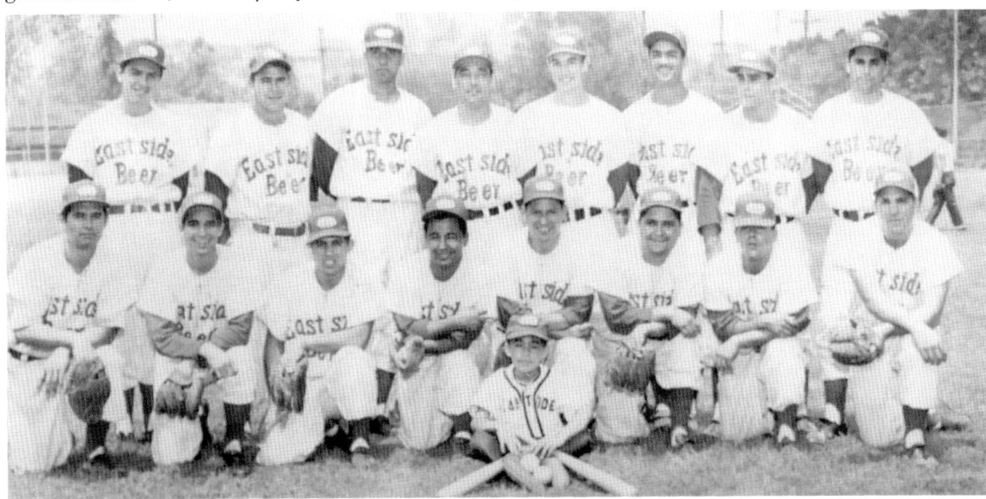

The Eastside Beer team, pictured in 1951, played for about four years before the club was disbanded due to the brewery going out of business. From left to right are (first row) Gil Blanco, unidentified, Ernie Blanco, Pepe ?, unidentified, Rudy Gonzáles, unidentified, and Eddie Castro; (second row) two unidentified, Gil Gamez, manager Rudy Morinas, two unidentified, Richard Álvarez, and unidentified. The batboy is unidentified. Ernie and Gil Blanco are brothers. Ernie was only 17 years old when he played for the team. (Courtesy of the Latino Baseball History Project.)

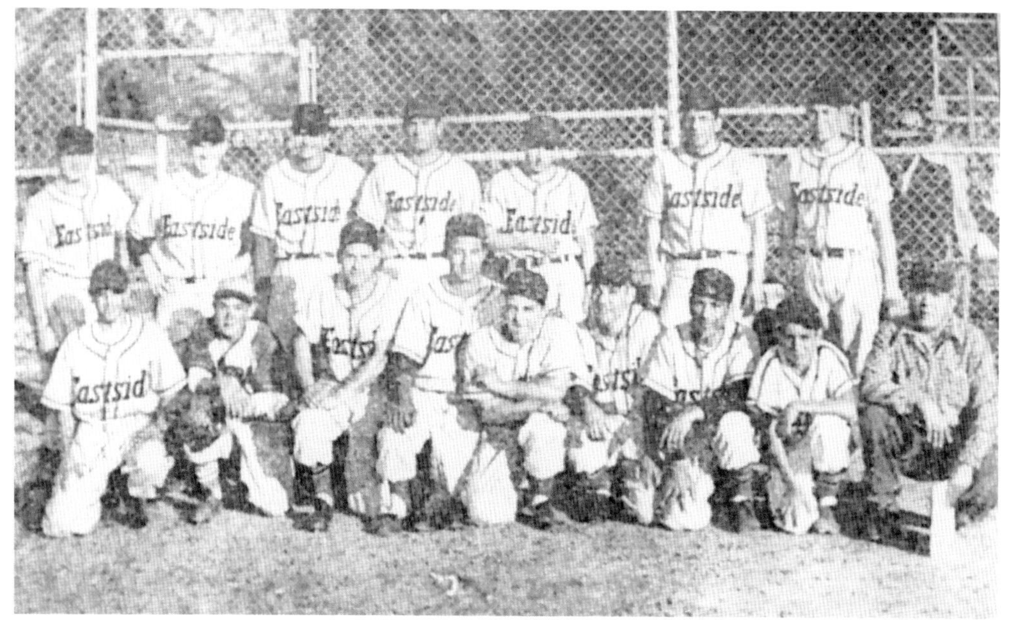


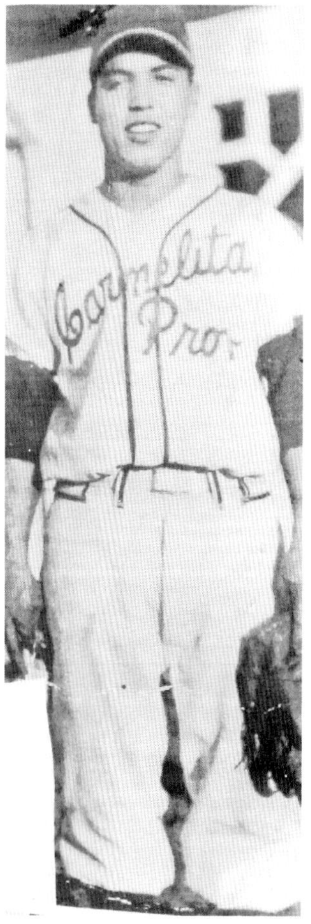

This Eastside Beer team was a heavy favorite to win the Los Angeles playoffs tournament. From left to right are (first row) Bobby Resendez, Rudy Figueroa, Eppie González, Pepe Figueroa, Cheche Hernández, Rudy Martínez, Ray Puente, batboy Charley Nava, and manager Pat Molina; (second row) Don Watson, Frank Clantanoff, Joe Miranda, Larry Silva, Ernie Mesa, Sal García, and Randy Olea. Not pictured are "Lefty" Ortega and Arnold Figueroa. (Courtesy of Bobby Resendez.)

Richard Peña is seen here in 1950, when he pitched for the Carmelita Provision Company. He was the most sought-after player because he was an outstanding left-handed pitcher and speedy centerfielder. The Peña family settled in East Los Angeles in 1918. By 1968, Richard's parents, William and Victoria, had 11 children, 25 grandchildren, and 11 great-grandchildren. William, who himself was an outstanding player in New Mexico, spent most of his days attending Little League, community, and high school games watching his sons. All nine of his sons played football and baseball at Roosevelt High School. Richard was an excellent quarterback and gymnast in high school, but his true love was baseball. The nine Peña brothers formed their own teams while their sons were the batboys, including Greg, Bill, David, Richie, Steve, Marc, Michael, Bobby, Gabriel, John, and Ted. (Courtesy of Richard Peña.)

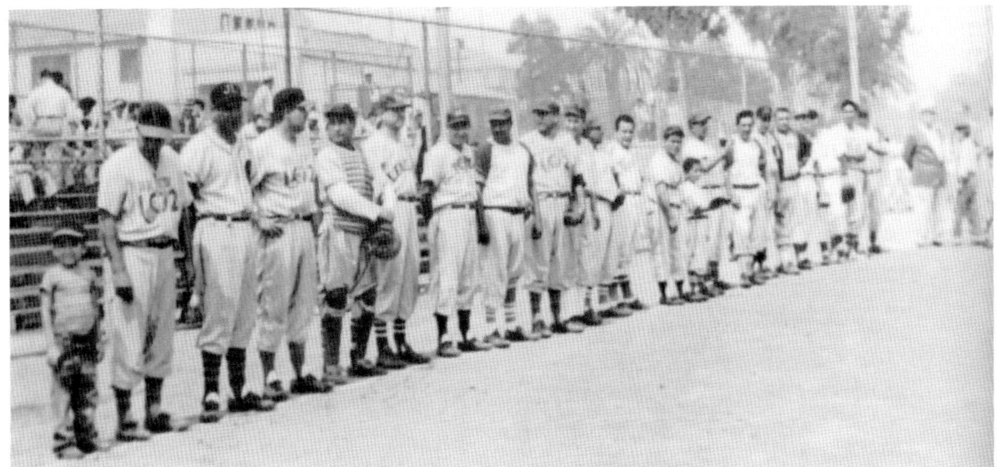

Many community and ex-professional players refused to quit as they became older and instead joined the Los Angeles 40–60 Club. This club and a similar club in El Paso scheduled goodwill games twice a year in each other's venue, often on a holiday weekend such as Memorial Day or Labor Day. The games in El Paso often attracted family and friends, who would cross the international border from Ciudad Juárez to attend the games and the dances that followed. During the 1950s, the Los Angeles team played Mexican teams from Hermosillo, San Luís, Chihuahua, Juárez, Delicias, and San Luís Rió Colorado. (Courtesy of the Regalado family.)

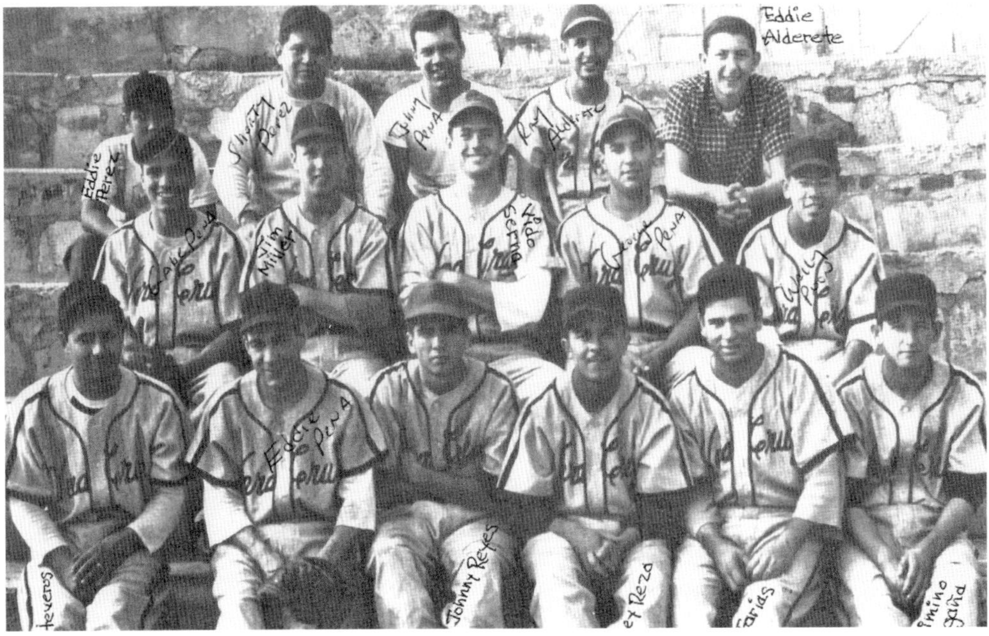


The Vera Cruz team played at Fresno Playground in East Los Angeles. The players on this 1950s team are, from left to right, (first row) Vic Onterveros, Eddie Peña, Johnny Reyes, Chuey Reza, Rudy Farias, and Chimino Magaña; (second row) Gabe Peña, Jim Miller, Vido Serra, George Peña, and Wally Poon; (third row) Eddie Pérez, "Shorty" Pérez, Johnny Peña, and brothers Ray and Eddie Aderete. (Courtesy of Richard Peña.)

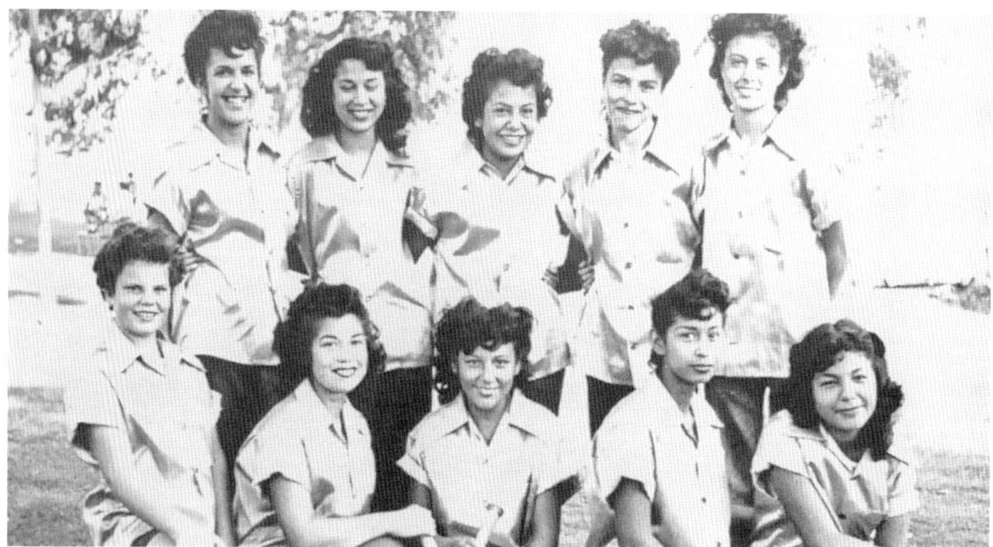

The 1950–1951 East Los Angeles Columbianas played at Belvedere Park and were sponsored by the Columbia Utility Company. The team was comprised of girls around 15 years of age, most of whom knew each other from Kern Avenue Junior High School and Garfield High School. Like many girls' teams, there were several sets of sisters and cousins who played together. Jo Galindo O'Dell (second row, far left) played catcher and outfield. Jo's father, Sammy Galindo, played baseball in East Los Angeles for years. (Courtesy of Jo Galindo O'Dell.)

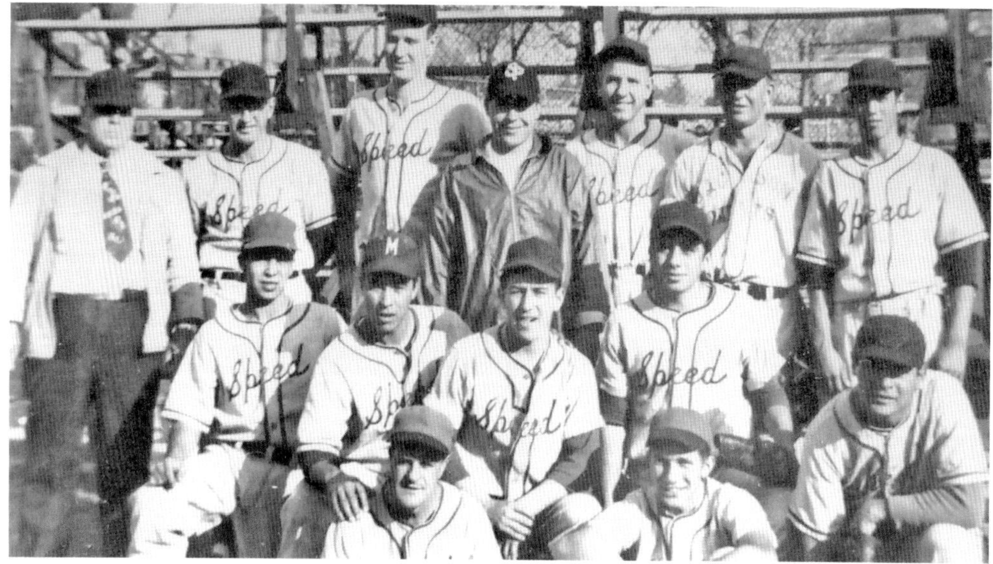


Speed Liquor store sponsored this team, seen in 1953 at Griffith Park in Los Angeles. Speed Liquor was a farm team for the Carmelita Chorizeros. Several Chorizeros saw action in Korea, which gave Speed players an opportunity to play for the Chorizeros. From left to right are (first row) manager Gordy Leach and ? Morton; (second row) Joe and Chano Gaitan, Ernie Rodríguez and Mando Pérez, and Greg Regalado; (third row) scorekeeper ? Leach, three unidentified, Sy Vernal, Chuck Sarni, and Bobby Recendez. (Courtesy of Bobby Recendez.)

In 1953, sixteen-year-old Conrad Muñatones played for the East Los Angeles Lucky Lager Beer team. In 1954, he was named player of the year for Los Angeles Southern District as a pitcher. He was senior class president at Roosevelt and later played college ball at UCLA, where he was captain and was selected as a college all-star. Conrad was named to the California Intercollegiate Baseball All-Star team as an outfielder. In 1954, he was named Player of the Year for the Los Angeles Southern District as a pitcher. He signed a contract with the Los Angeles Dodgers, and played in Canada. He coached many years in East Los Angeles, including at Roosevelt. He retired from a long career in education. Conrad was one of the founders of the Latino Baseball History Project and continues to lend his expertise to promoting the long and rich history of Mexican American baseball. (Courtesy of Conrad Muñatones.)

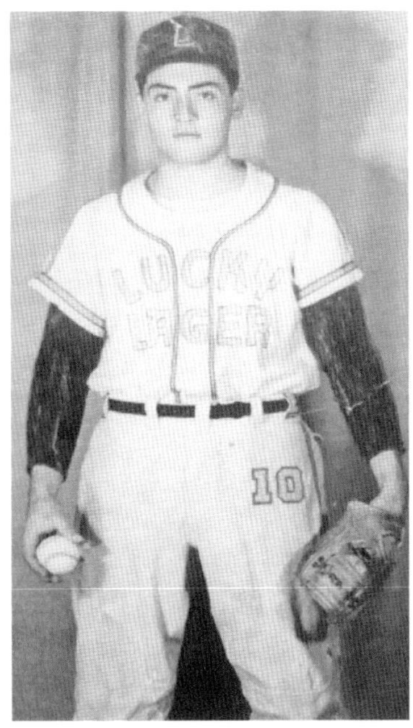


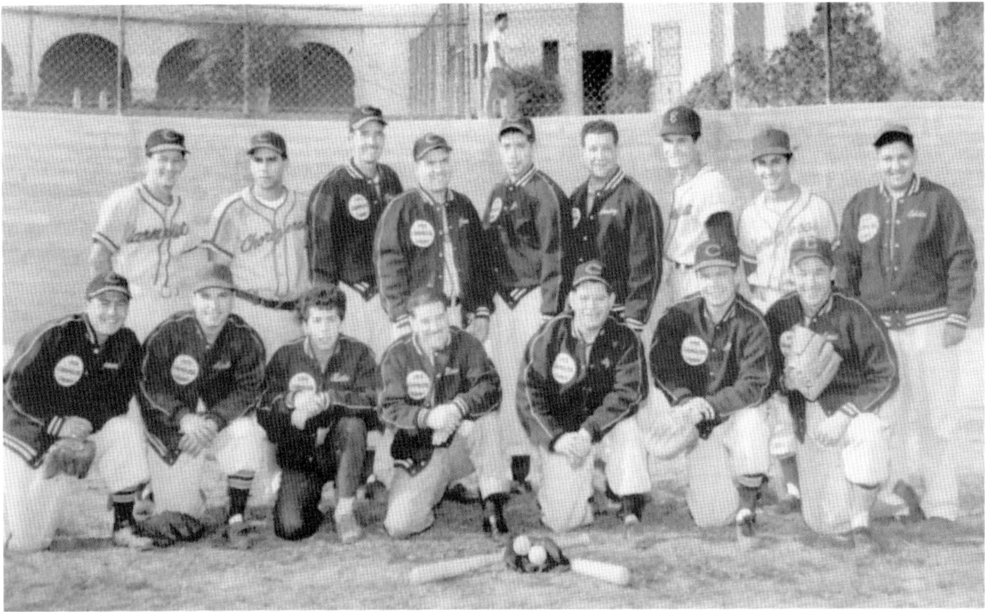

The 1953 Chorizeros won the city championship. From left to right are (first row) unidentified, Richard Peña, Babe Órnelas, Mario López, "Shorty" Pérez, Yam Yánez, and unidentified; (second row) Chimino Magaña, Richard Álvarez, unidentified, Johnny Peña, Joe Valasuella, Sammy Galindo, unidentified, Fernando Farfán, and Eddie Pérez. Mario López liked to invite the players to an East Los Angeles restaurant-bar named the Joker's Den, located on the famous Cinco Puntos (Five Points) on Lorena Street and Brooklyn Avenue, or to the Silver Dollar on Whittier Boulevard. He picked up the tab for beer and tacos. The young man in the background is Pete Barrios Jr. Pete's father, Pedro, played baseball in East Los Angeles in the 1920s and 1930s. (Courtesy of the López family.)

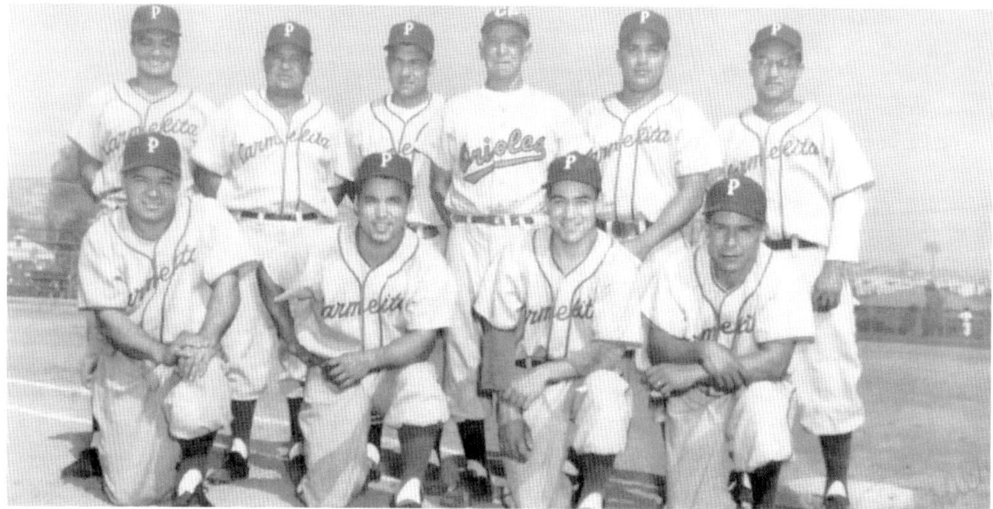

At one time, nearly the entire Chorizeros team was comprised of nine Peña brothers managed by their father. This 1950s photograph was taken at Belvedere Park. This family includes, from left to right, (first row) Pete, Richard, Eddie, and Albert; (second row) Gabe, Ray, Johnny, father William (manager), George, and Victor. The letter *P* on their caps stands for Peña. William, also known as Bill, played catcher for the Barelas, New Mexico, team in 1907. Five of his sons were catchers too. This photograph appeared in *Ripley's Believe It or Not*. (Courtesy of Richard Peña.)

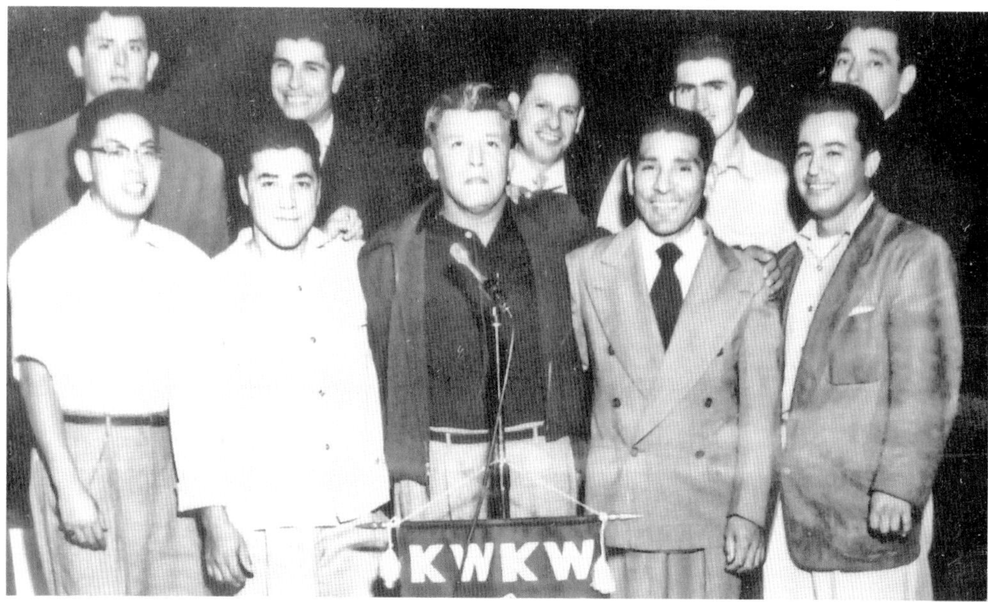


Members of the Eastside Beer team were interviewed in 1956 by radio host Milt Nava (not pictured). KWKW was one of the largest Spanish-language radio stations in the United States and broadcast Dodgers games in Spanish when they first moved to Los Angeles from Brooklyn. From left to right are (first row) Wally Poon, "Cheche" Hernández, manager Pat Molina, Ray Puente, and Pepe Figueroa; (second row) Larry Silva, Joe Miranda, Eppie González, unidentified, and Rudy Martínez. (Courtesy of Bob Recendez.)

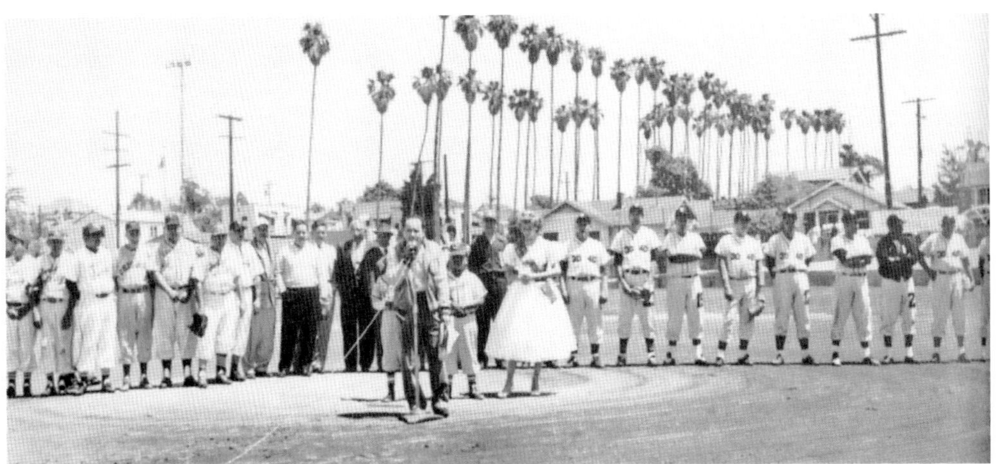

This c. 1959 game was between the Los Angeles 40–60 Club and the Hermosillo 30–40 Club from Mexico at Evergreen Park. At the microphone is Saúl Toledo. The 40–60 Club queen is Margie Sepúlveda, and veteran manager Manuel Regalado is behind her in the black outfit. The club's name indicated the age range of the players. Other leagues consisted of players from 20 to 39 and from 61 to 80. These types of age-bracket teams are still found throughout the United States in Mexican American communities. (Courtesy of Ron Regalado.)

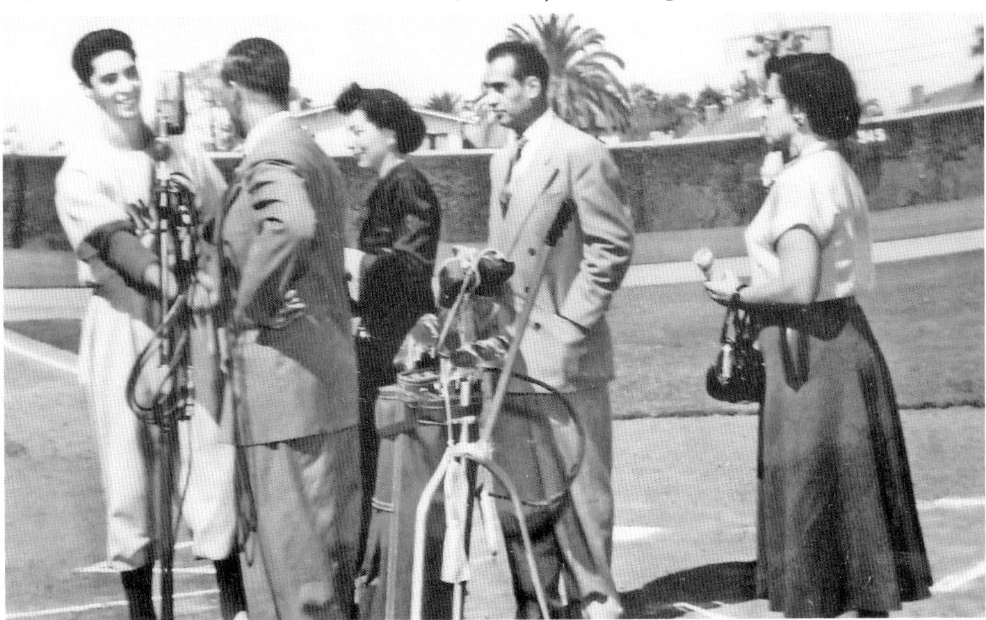

Edward Roybal (fourth from left) is seen at Wrigley Field, the home of the Pacific Coast League Angels, honoring Memo Luna (left) from the San Diego Padres in the 1950s. Roybal was a graduate of Roosevelt High School, a World War II veteran, and in 1949, the first Mexican American elected to the Los Angeles City Council since 1881. In 1962, he became the first Mexican American from California to serve in Congress. Congressman Roybal was a great baseball fan, often seen at the parks in East Los Angeles watching his favorite sport. He passed away in 2005. (Courtesy of the Latino Baseball History Project.)

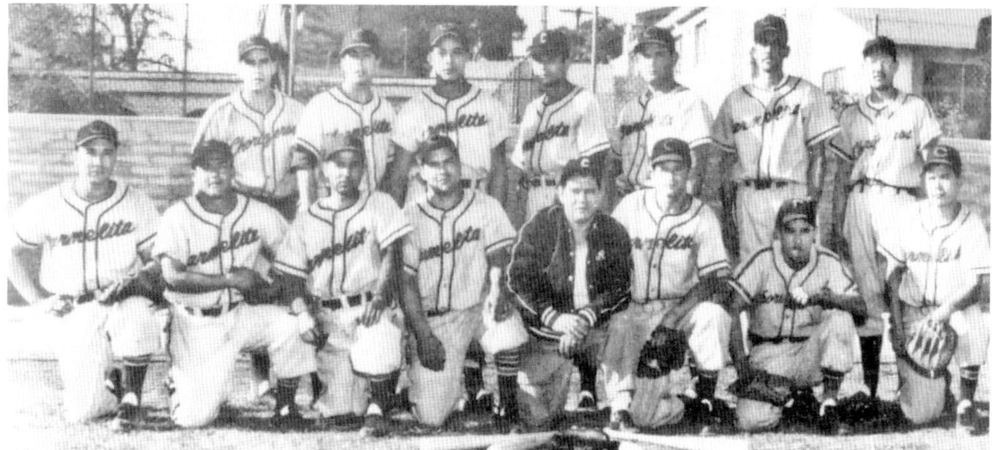

This 1950s Carmelita Chorizeros team includes, from left to right, (first row) Freddie Yánez, unidentified, Ray Aldrete, Johnny Peña, manager "Shorty" Pérez, Chimino Magaña, unidentified, and Yam Yánez; (second row) Richard Álvarez, Babe Órnales, Joe Valenzuela, Joe Miranda, Larry Silva, and two unidentified. Mexican Americans played on Sunday, but during the week, some were active in political and labor organizations. The baseball field became an instrument for organizing for civil and human rights. (Courtesy of Richard Peña.)

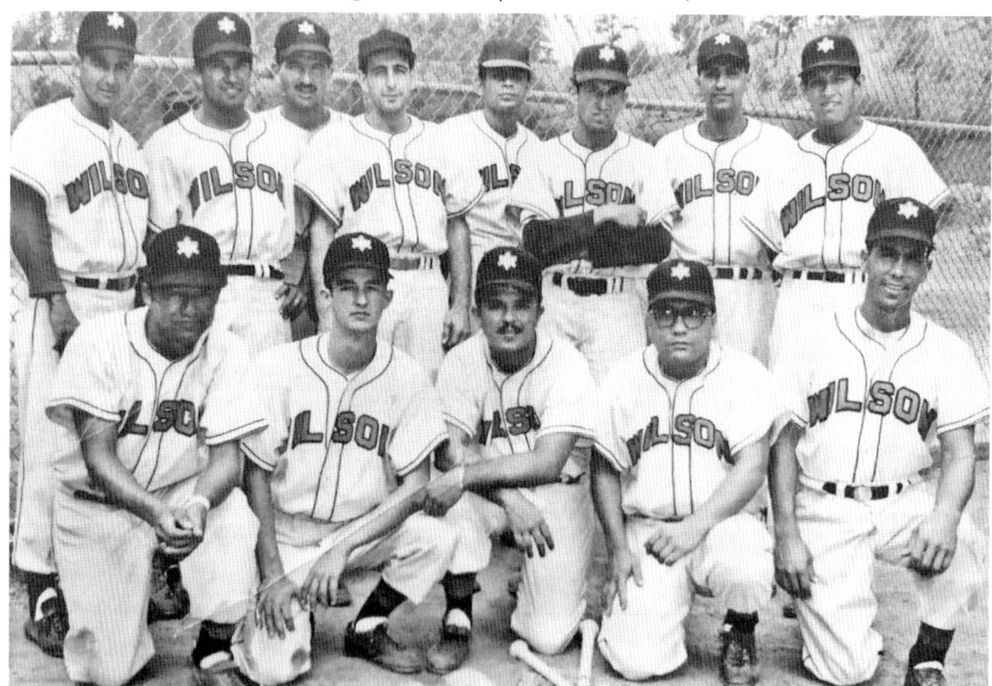

The 1970 Wilson baseball team played at Hazard Park, located behind the General Hospital in East Los Angeles. The club was sponsored by the Wilson Packers, the same Wilson Sporting Goods company that made uniforms for the San Diego Padres. Their uniforms were pro quality. Some of the players are Paul Falcón, Ralph Núñez, Mario Chávez, Lolo Chávez, and Jesse Reza. The manager is Cave William. (Courtesy of the Ralph Núñez family.)

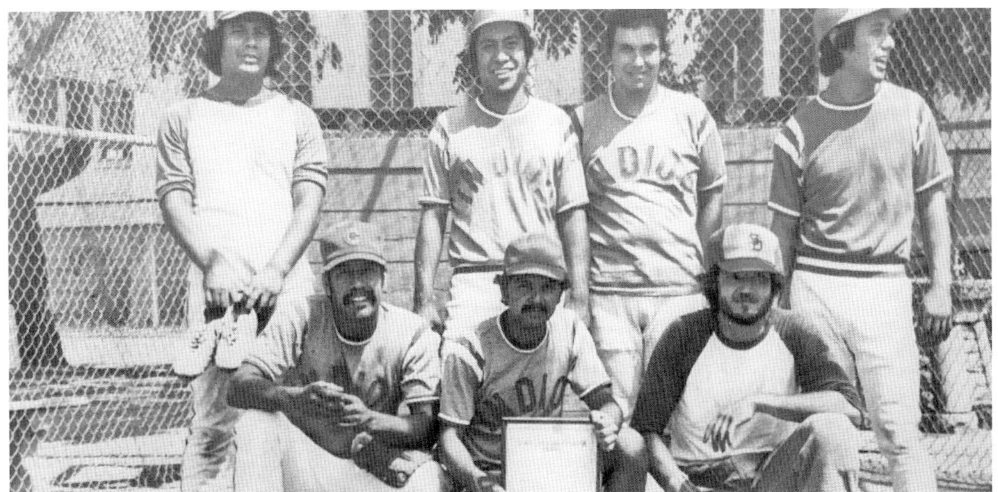

Elías and Jacinta De La Rosa moved from Fabens, Texas, to Los Angeles in 1956, raising nine children. Softball was a deeply rooted family affair, as they enjoyed picnics and games on Sundays. The De La Rosa brothers formed a family fast-pitch softball team, Los Indios, in Boyle Heights. They called themselves Los Indios because they were dark skinned. Most of the brothers played baseball at Roosevelt. The team included De La Rosa brothers Refugio, Al, Frank, Rubén, and Elías Jr., brothers-in-law Frank López and Raúl López, and close friends Gerardo López, Mando Subía, Peter Ramírez, and Danny López. Elías (first row, left) earned a Bronze Star in Vietnam. Los Indios played from 1973 through 1989. They played their home games at Castello, Hazard, and Evergreen Parks. They won two Parks and Recreation championships. (Courtesy of Frank De La Rosa.)

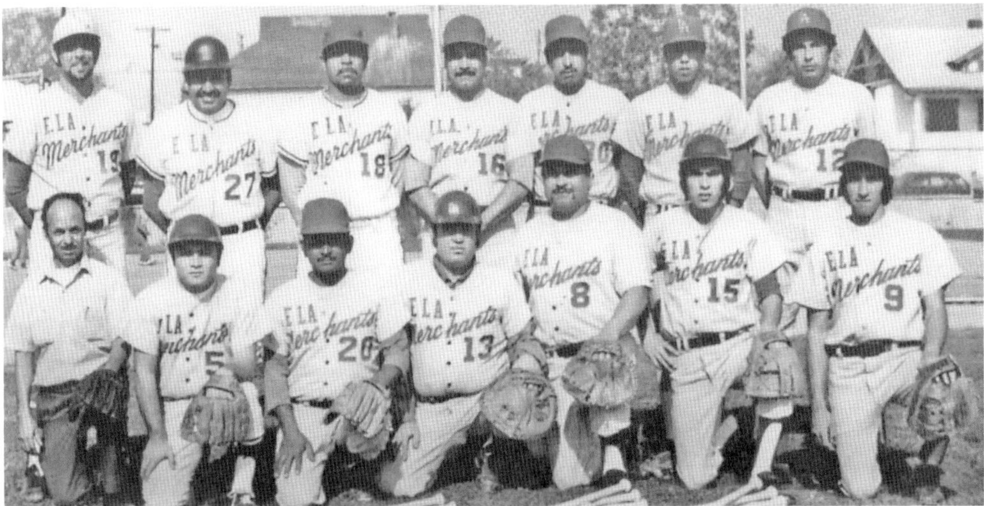

The East Los Angeles Merchants were a powerful team in the 1960s and 1970s. They are seen in 1971 at Evergreen Park. From left to right are (first row) Carlitos Morales, Jack Arenas, Ramiro ?, Cylindro Santillán, Alfonso Villaseñor, Ray Lara, and Joel Palomares; (second row) Ray Loya, Tacho Morales, Carlos Nix, Alberto Villaseñor, Lencho Vásquez, Paul Franco, and Rudy Martínez. The Merchants later changed their name to the California Stars. The team was known for physicality and high-octane passion on the field. (Courtesy of Jack Arenas.)

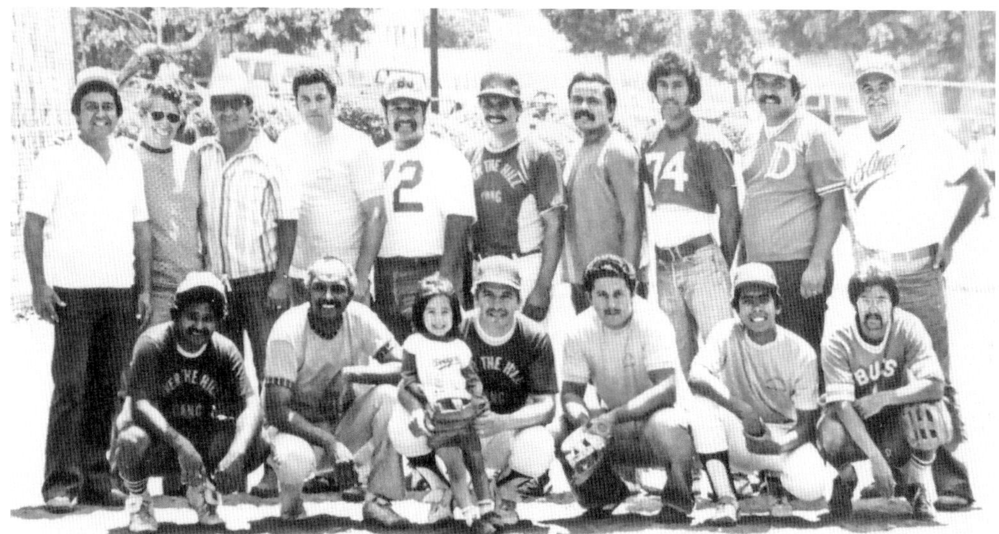

The 1971 Hazard Park All-Stars represented the Los Angeles men's fast-pitch league. Most of these players were originally from El Paso, Texas. The players included Mike Ríos, Rudy Orosco, Jaime Farfán, Lance Rubio, and Gilbert Gamboa Jr. Gilbert Jr. played for an international program in which the El Sereno Angels traveled to Sinaloa, Mexico. This collaboration remained for years. Gilbert was an exchange student in high school to Helsinki, Finland, where he was on the baseball and track teams. After graduating from high school, Gilbert played softball in East Los Angeles and El Paso. (Courtesy of Victor Gamboa.)

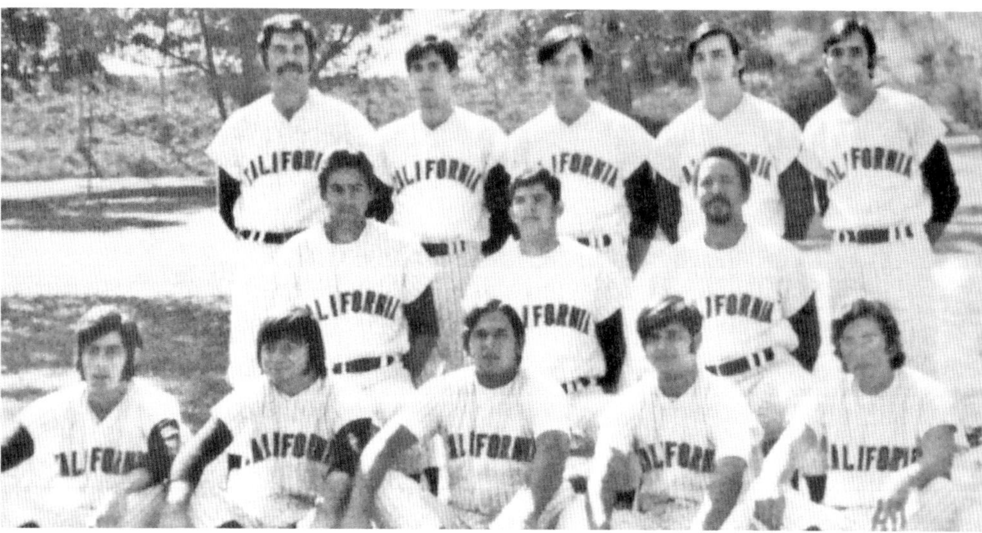

The 1974 California Stars are, from left to right, (first row) Ray Lara, Jack Arenas, Robert Murietta, David Vidaurazaga, and Nacho Muñoz; (second row) Lencho Vásquez, David Armenta, and Carlos Nix; (third row) Ray Loya, Paul Franco, Frank Seañez, Félix García, and David Ferrell. Lara was the stolen-base champion four consecutive years in the Mike Brito League. Ray Loya has mentored several major league pitchers including Fernando Salas and Trevor Hoffman. (Courtesy of Chris Kolotzis.)

Chuey Reza was one of the finest first basemen to come out of Roosevelt High School in 1948. He reminded the Boyle Heights community of another great first baseman to come out of Roosevelt, Charlie Sierra. Reza played for several community teams, including Órnelas Market, Club Vera Cruz, Carmelita, and Lucky Lager. In the 1950s, Reza played for one of the best teams ever in the Los Angeles Municipal League, the Órnelas Market "Wonder Boys." The team manager was Pat Molina. Other teammates included Chimino Magaña, Chano Gaitan, Al Padilla, and Richard Peña. Reza is seen here at Fresno Playground. (Courtesy of Bobby Recendez.)

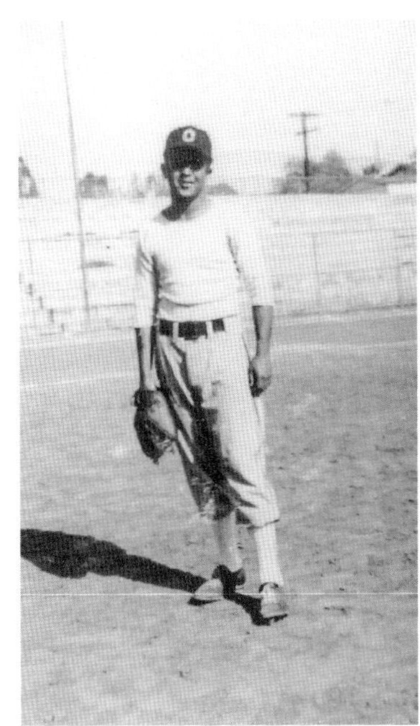

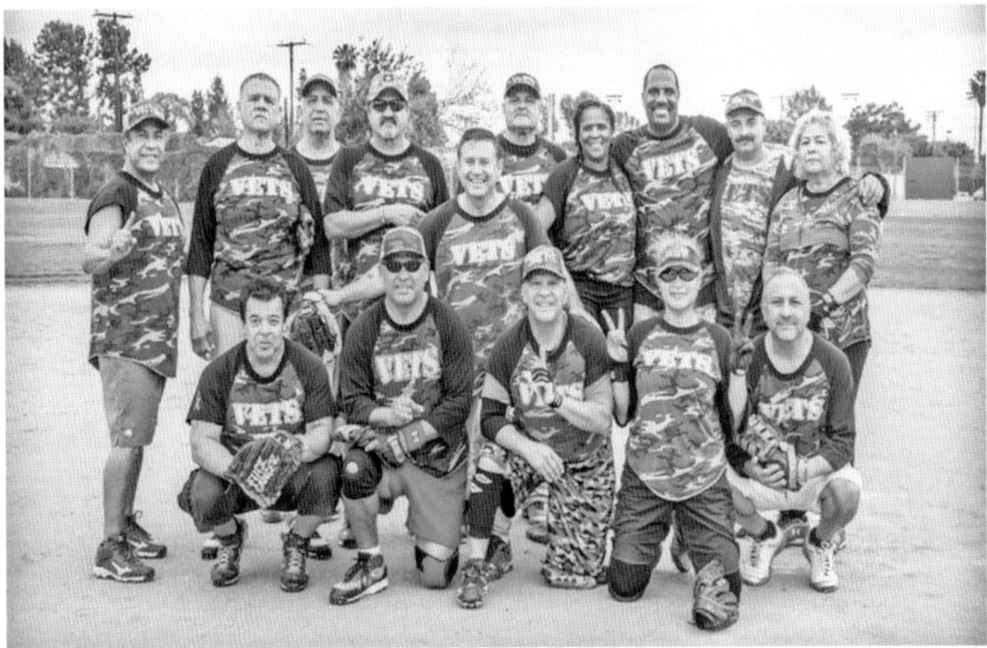

The Vets were born and raised in East Los Angeles but now live throughout Los Angeles County. They play in Pico Rivera at Smith Park and Rio Hondo Park. The Vets started around 2010. About eight of the players served in Vietnam. The Vets are, in no particular order, Manny Saldivar, Art Montano, David Perales, Bob Chávez, Eddie Jiménez, Nicky Escamilla (standing, with sunglasses), Sylvia Page, Reggie Mason, Rick Iglesias, Kala Carbajal, Randy Pico, Art Estrada, Adam Sandoval, Anna Sánchez, and George Cuellar. Escamilla played for East Los Angeles College in 1970 and 1971 under coach Rob Hertel. (Courtesy of Nicky Escamilla.)

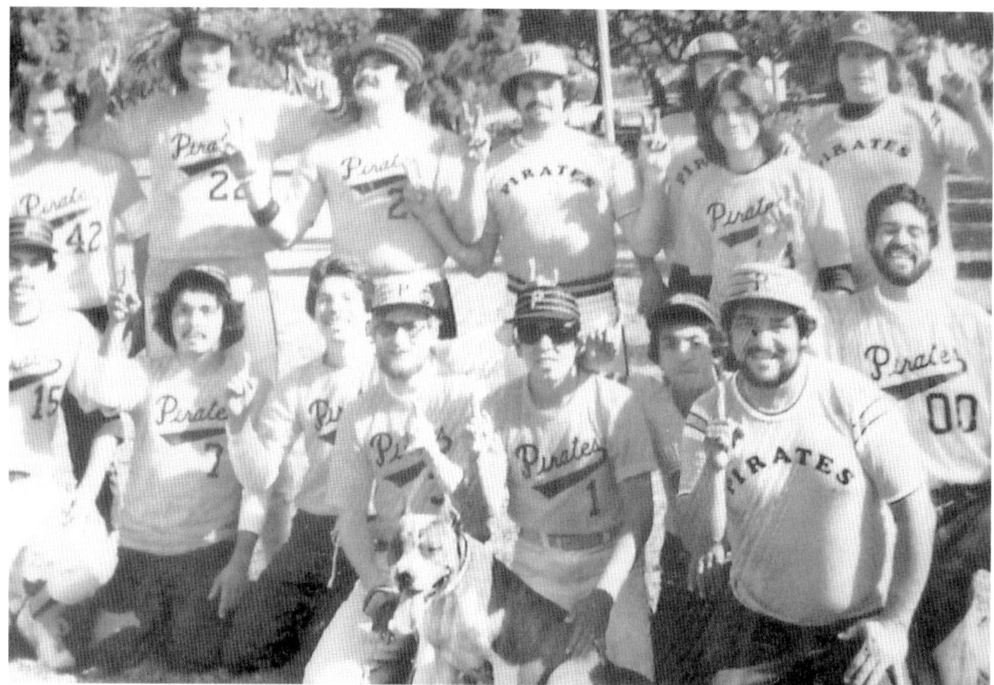

The 1977 El Sereno Pirates played at El Sereno Park. Six of them are now deceased. Nearly all had played at Wilson High School. They played against other El Sereno teams, including the Aces and Spoilers. Prior to the Pirates, the team was called the Dusters. Nicky Escamilla was the coach when they beat the Raiders for the championship. From left to right are (first row) Terry López, Bobby Acala, Richie Ruiz, Tim Saxeby, Rudolph (mascot), Mando De La Loza, Tudy Tovar, Ernie Acala, and Richard Meléndez; (second row) Danny Lujan, Manny Domínguez, Nicky and Ricky Escamilla, John Greenlee, Ralph López, and Ernie Terrazas. (Courtesy of Nicky Escamilla.)

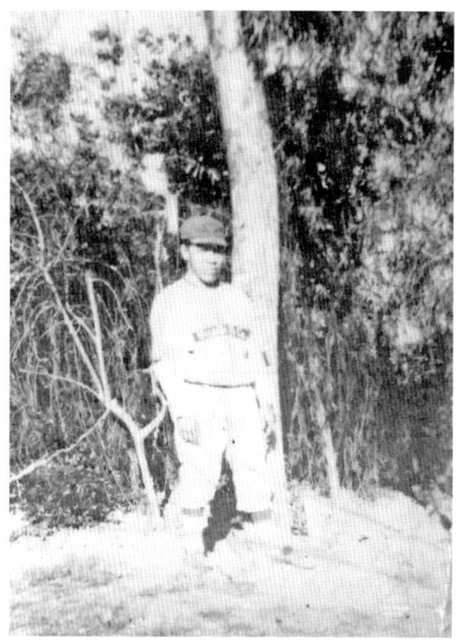

Antonio "Tony" Gaitan was born in Chihuahua, Mexico, in 1908. He is seen in 1931 at Hazard Park. As a young boy, his family settled in Fillmore, California, where he picked fruit with other newly arrived Mexicans. In 1928, he met his future wife, Aurora Cortes, and settled in East Los Angeles. There were few jobs during the Depression, so Tony boxed professionally to support his family. They moved to Indiana Street near Olympic Boulevard, where the 5 freeway later displaced residents. He later purchased three homes on a lot and built a pitching mound for his boys. He also had a daughter, Vera. His three boys, Chano, Tony, and Joe, played baseball at Garfield and ELAC. Joe played for Fresno State. He and Chano played in the military. Chano also played in the Pittsburgh Pirates farm system. (Courtesy of Ray Gaitan.)

Manuel "Shorty" Pérez (left), pictured here around 1959 with Saúl Toledo (center) and Mario Lopez, is considered the greatest manager in East Los Angeles history. As a youth, he played for a 1930s team called Elysian Park from the old neighborhoods of Chavez Ravine, where Dodger Stadium was later built. His baseball knowledge was extraordinary. Shorty coached for over 40 years with several teams, including the Chorizeros, the Auto Glass Company, and Club Vera Cruz. During his reign, the Chorizeros won nearly 20 championships in 30 years. Players loved playing for Shorty. He passed away in 1981. In March 2011, a ceremony at Belvedere Park honored him with a plaque commemorating his achievements. (Courtesy of Gil Pérez.)

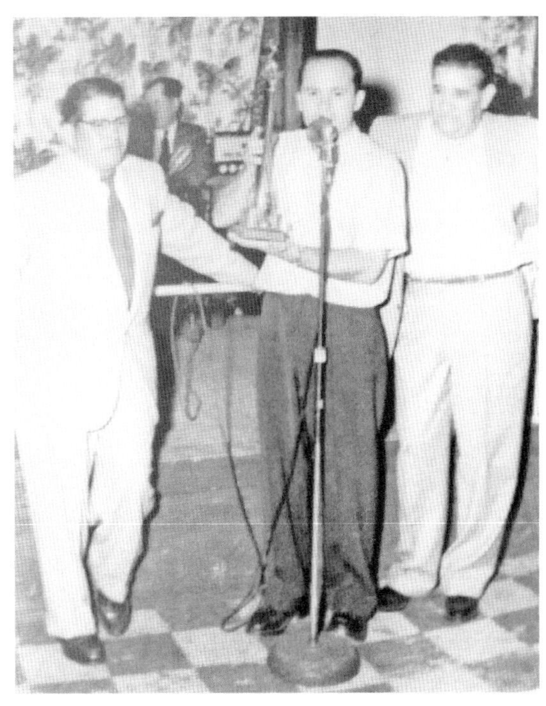

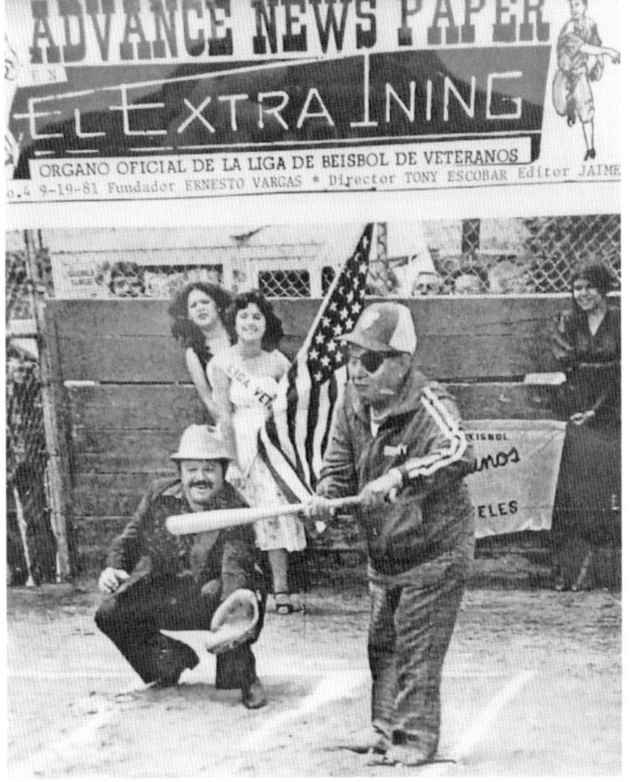


This 1981 photograph shows two close friends and giants of East Los Angeles baseball, Manuel "Shorty" Perez (batting) and Mike Brito (catching). Nearly every outstanding player from East Los Angeles played for Shorty and in the Mike Brito League. Willie Davis, a former Dodger from Roosevelt, played for Shorty. In fact, Davis was signed by Dodgers scout Kenny Meyers at Evergreen Park around 1960. Brito managed the Evergreen Baseball League and his own league, which continues after 50 years. Both men loved Cuban cigars. Brito is also famous for signing Fernando Valenzuela and Robert "Babo" Castillo to the Dodgers. (Courtesy of Gil Pérez.)

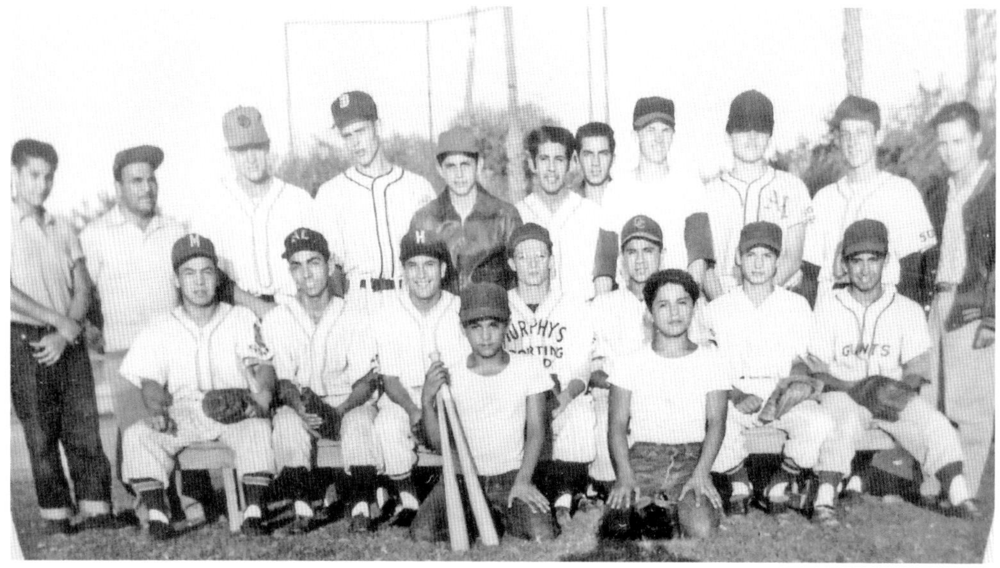

Feliziano "Chano" Gaitan (not pictured) was born in 1930, the first son and second child of Antonio and Aurora Gaitan. He started his baseball career in East Los Angeles at several playgrounds, including Evergreen, Fresno, Hazard, and Belvedere. Feliziano played at Garfield High School, in the military, professionally, and with several community teams. With community teams, he was a sought-after player because of his amazing skills. He married Felicitas (Phyllis) Soto in 1952 and used his signing bonus to purchase a home in Pico Rivera. His brother Joe is seen here in the first row at far left. (Courtesy of Raymond Gaitan.)

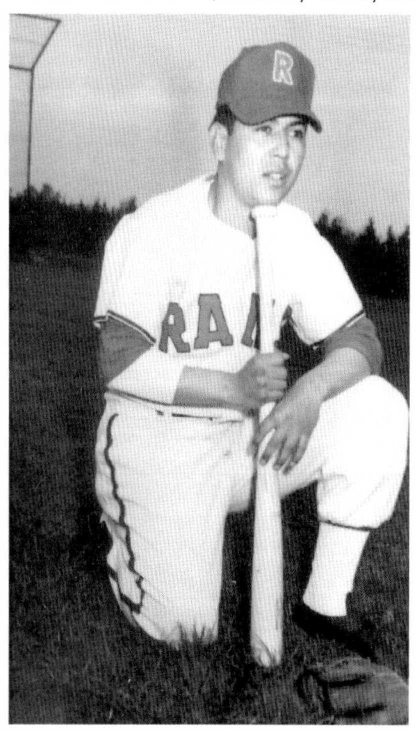

Adolfo García grew up in the "Happy Valley" section of El Sereno. He played little league baseball for a travel team that was part of the Golden State Baseball League in Pico Rivera. At Lincoln High School, he was the All-City quarterback while playing baseball. He was coached by the legendary Hall of Fame referee Jim Tunney. After graduating from high school in 1955, Adolfo was drafted by the Army, and joined an Army team that played ball throughout Germany. He married his high school sweetheart, Carmen, and they had three sons, Mark, Steven, and Greg. Adolfo coached youth ball in El Sereno. Many of his players excelled in local high schools and colleges. One of his players, Victor Bernal, played at Wilson High School, Cal Poly Pomona, and with the San Diego Padres. (Courtesy of Mark García.)

# PROFESSIONAL

Like all young boys, Mexican Americans dreamed about playing in the big leagues a century ago. The Cubs, the Pirates, the New York Giants, the Red Sox, and the Brooklyn Dodgers were the first teams scouting and signing players from the Southwest and Midwest. These teams have been evaluating Mexican American talent since at least the early 1920s.

It should be noted that these teams, from the ownership down to the managers, did not proactively encourage the recruitment of Mexican Americans. Instead, this recruitment was covertly carried out by enlightened baseball scouts who witnessed first-hand that Mexican American players had the athletic skills and emotional makeup to help their clubs. Despite their racial tolerance, these scouts understood that only light-skinned Mexican Americans could be signed. The first Mexican Americans signed to professional contracts passed as white. A few of them made it to the big show. Only light-skinned Cubans were allowed to play ball as well. This was baseball's unwritten rule regarding Latino players.

After World War II and Mexican Americans' fight for racial equality, more major-league teams began to scout darker-skinned Mexican Americans. For these players, the excitement of signing a major-league contract was offset by racism and bigotry. Most major-league teams had spring training and minor-league affiliates in the Deep South. Dark-skinned Mexican Americans were subject to the same Jim Crow laws as African Americans. In countless interviews, Mexican American players described the racial tension even among their own teammates, who saw them as unwanted competitors for the few scarce spots on rosters when major-league baseball had only 16 teams.

At spring training and on minor-league teams, Mexican Americans remembered that the all-white coaching staff spent considerably more time with white players than with them and African Americans. Even when Mexican American prospects were clearly better hitters and pitchers and had better defensive skills and speed, they were ignored. Often, less talented white players were called up to play at the big club while the more talented players of color stayed put. Their baseball fate rested in the hands of unconcealed racism. This was a recurring pattern for years and negatively affected countless players of color.

After a short time, some Mexican American players naturally decided to return home, fatigued by overt bigotry, while many were simply homesick. Their dream of playing major-league ball was shattered forever. Nevertheless, they played locally and in Mexico, coached Little League, high school, and college, and managed semiprofessional teams, and some became umpires. Ironically, a few later became major-league scouts specifically recruiting Mexican American and Mexican players.

Mexican Americans began seriously joining major-league teams in the 1960s and 1970s. This chapter highlights a few lucky ones from East Los Angeles who signed major-league contracts. It also salutes the trailblazers who helped set in motion the social forces that ended institutional racial animosity towards future generations of Mexican American players, who continue to have the same dreams as their great-great-grandfathers.

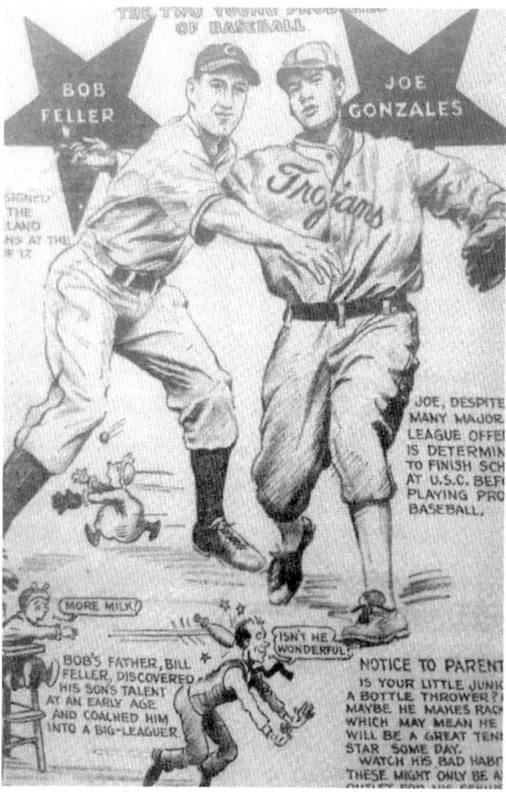


Joe Gonzáles was born and raised in San Francisco. His family eventually moved to Boyle Heights. Joe and his brother Candido played at Roosevelt under coach Charles "Coney" Galindo. Galindo, from San Diego, had played in the 1920s for USC. After he graduated, Joe went to USC too. He led the Trojans to several championships. Joe was signed by the Red Sox, one of the first Mexican Americans to play professionally. When World War II broke out, Joe and his four brothers enlisted. Joe lost a brother in the war. After coming home, Joe coached baseball at Roosevelt. In 1951, he became the baseball coach at Loyola University in Los Angeles and also coached at Westminster High School, winning six championships. He was a field judge for the NFL for 21 years, the first Mexican American referee. He died in 1996. (Courtesy of Al Padilla.)

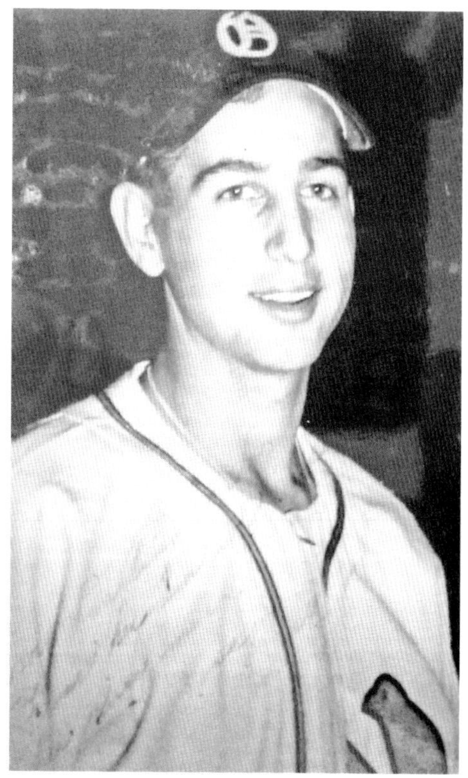

Ray Alderete was signed by the Ontario Orioles in 1947 as a second baseman and shortstop. The Orioles played in the Sunset League, comprised of teams from El Centro, Riverside, Las Vegas, San Bernardino, Reno, Calexico, Tijuana, and Mexicali. During the summer, the temperature soared over 100 degrees in the desert, and players had to keep their mouths closed throughout the game or risk swallowing the bugs that filled the air. Ray was signed by Babe Dahlgren. Dahlgren is better known for replacing Lou Gehrig in the lineup on May 2, 1939, ending Gehrig's 14-year, 2,130-game streak. Dahlgren had a homer and double in that game. Ray and his wife, Anna, had five children: Robert, Ray Jr., Linda, Lorraine, and Loretta. Both boys played ball. Later, the two boys and Loretta became outstanding golfers, with Loretta joining the LPGA. (Courtesy of Ray Alderete.)

Ray Alderete played for the Riverside Rubes in 1948 and the Riverside Dons in 1949. Both teams played in the Sunset League Class C. Ray started playing at a young age in East Los Angeles. Joe G. Macias promoted bringing Mexican teams to play against teams in Los Angeles. Macias managed the Los Angeles Cardinals and all-star teams during the late 1920s, and offered seven-year old Ray the position of batboy. Ray later married Macias's daughter Anna. She attended all of his games at home and on the road. Anna was born in Los Angeles in 1926. She was a singer and as a young girl would often sing for the players before and after her father's games. She attended Euclid Elementary School, and played softball at Hollenbeck Junior High School and Roosevelt High School. She remembered playing a game against the Ramona School for Girls team. She attended Los Angeles City College to be an airline stewardess but married to raise her family. (Courtesy of Ray Alderete.)

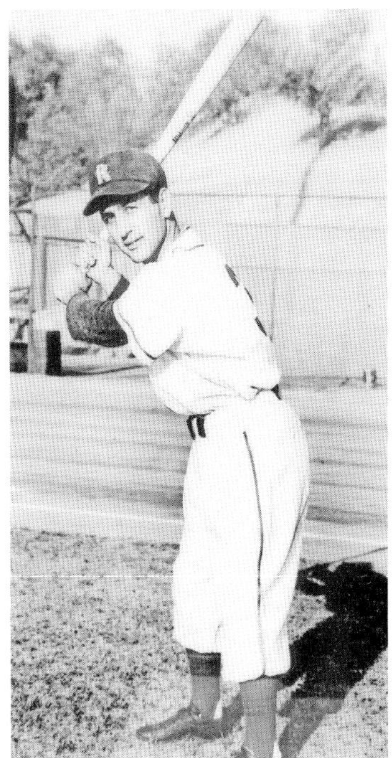

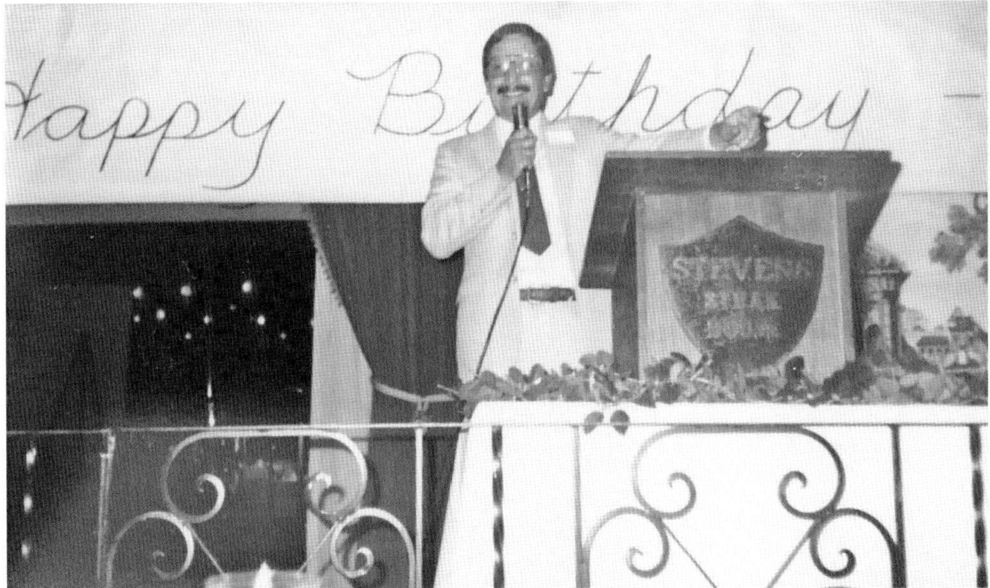


Pete Ortega (pictured) was a teammate of Tom Robles throughout their youth in East Los Angeles. They played together in American Legion ball and at Garfield. Pete was born in Ajo, Arizona. Like Tom, he signed a contract with the Chicago Cubs, and was later traded to the Pittsburgh Pirates, starting his minor-league career with the Gainsville, Florida, Owls in 1954. That same season, he played for the Magic Valley Cowboys in the Pioneer League. Pete later played in the Arizona-Mexico League for both the Globe-Miami Miners and the Mexicali Eagles. In 1955, he and Tom Robles were briefly united in Billings, Montana. (Courtesy of Joe Gaitan.)

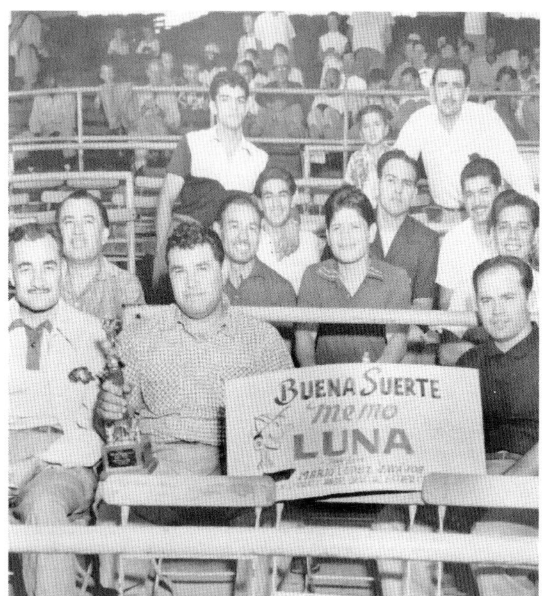


Several prominent residents attended a game honoring Memo Luna from the Pacific Coast League San Diego Padres. From left to right are (first row) Pete Despart, Rubén Aldapa, and Saúl Toledo; (second row) Raúl Morín, Ramón Fuentes, Lauro Salas, and Lalo Ríos. Standing at far left is boxer Ramón Tiscareno. Despart was the first Los Angeles resident drafted in World War II. Morín wrote the book *Among the Valiant*, about Mexican American Medal of Honor winners during World War II and Korea. Salas and Fuentes were boxers. Ríos appeared in 10 Hollywood films. (Courtesy of the Latino Baseball History Project.)

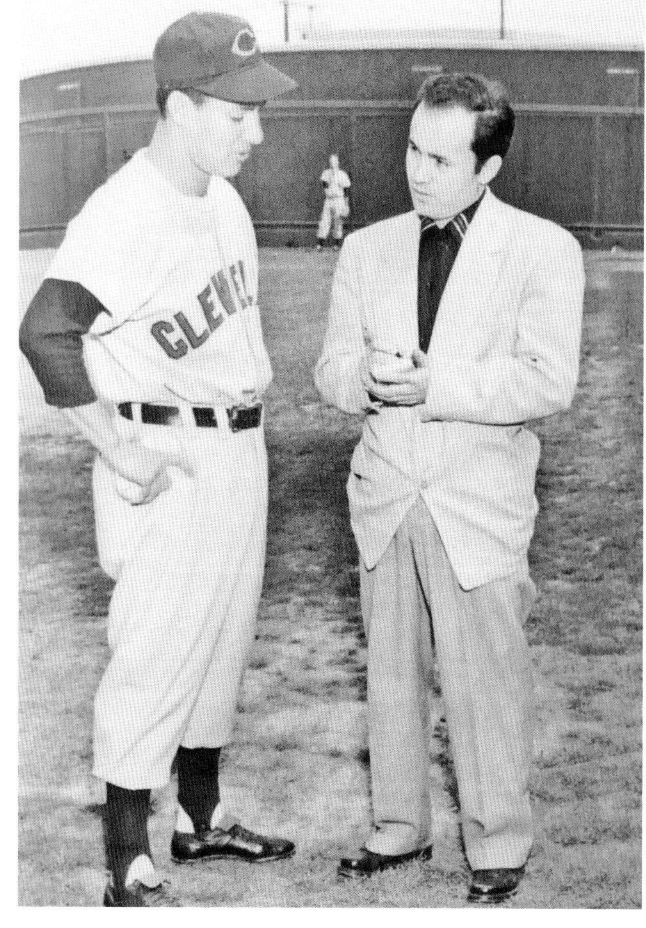

Saúl Toledo (right) interviews Roberto "Bobby" Gonzáles Ávila of the Cleveland Indians. Toledo was an amazing sports enthusiast as a player, coach, sportswriter, radio broadcaster, public address announcer, promoter, and administrator. Until his death in 2010 at the age of 90, he was known as "Mr. Baseball of East Los Angeles." He interviewed countless professional baseball players as well as players of other sports, especially boxing. He was one of the founders of the Latino Baseball History Project. Ávila was the first Latino player to win the batting title, hitting .341 in 1954. (Courtesy of Saúl Toledo.)

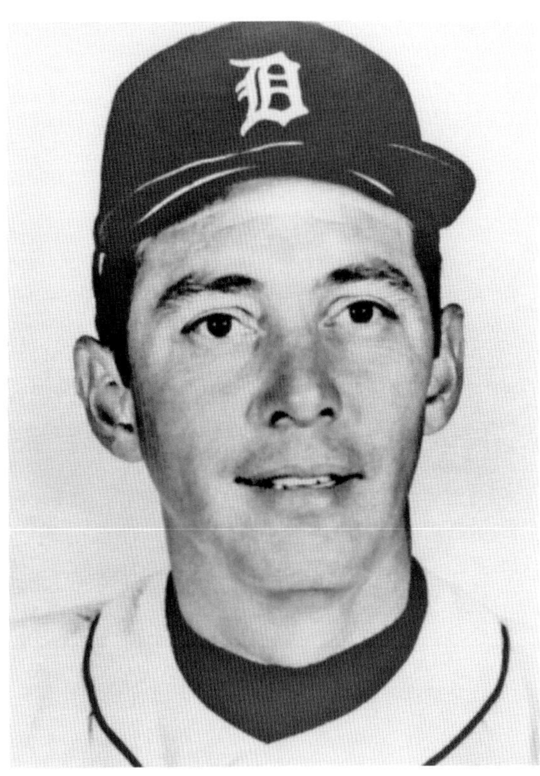

Henry John "Hank" Aguirre was nicknamed the "Tall Mexican" by sportswriters because of his six-foot, four-inch height. Born and raised in Azusa, California, he delivered tortillas for the family business before playing sandlot and American Legion ball. He was also an outstanding basketball player. While playing baseball at East Los Angeles Junior College, Aguirre was signed by the Cleveland Indians and played for the top club in 1955. He had a highly successful 16-year career as a starter and relief pitcher. His best year was 1962, when he won 16 games and led the American League with an ERA of 2.21 for Detroit. Aguirre played for the Dodgers in 1968. His five brothers and sisters still reside in Southern California. (Courtesy of the Latino Baseball History Project.)

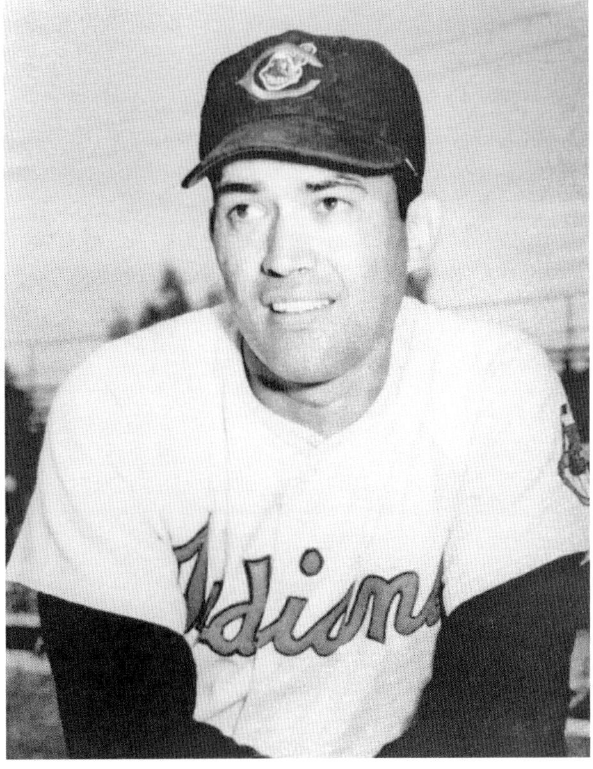

Rudolph Valentino "Rudy" Regalado, son of longtime East Los Angeles baseball manager and organizer Manuel Regalado, starred at Hoover High School in Glendale and at USC in 1949 and 1950. Regalado was signed by the Cleveland Indians and played for the big club between 1954 and 1956. He played in the 1954 World Series at the age of 23. He also played three seasons in the Venezuelan League, winning the batting title with Pampero in 1958–1959. Rudy was born in Los Angeles in 1930 and still lives there. (Courtesy of the Regalado family.)

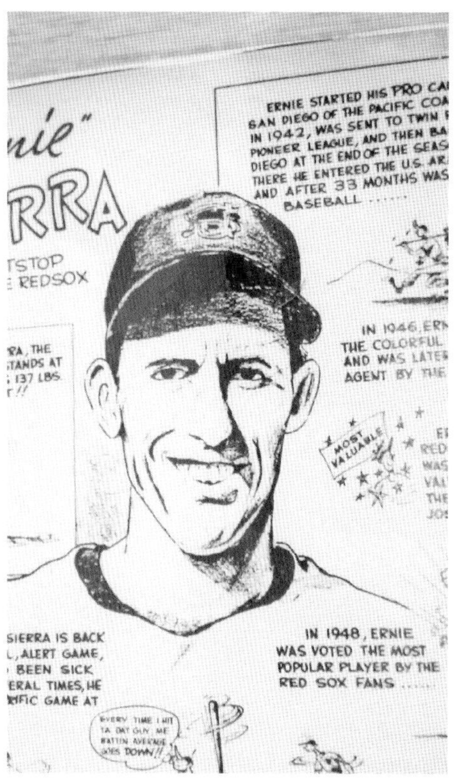


Ernie Sierra was an outstanding athlete. He was an infielder for the San Jose Red Sox in the California League from 1947 to 1951. Ernie was the team's MVP and an all-star for three years. He excelled at second base, shortstop, and third base. Ernie's professional career spanned 11 seasons, beginning in the early 1940s with the Twin Falls Cowboys in the Idaho Pioneer League. When World War II broke out, he served in the US Army Air Corps, flying dozens of bombing missions over Europe and Asia. After the war, he returned home and then traveled to Mexico to play for the Tampico Alijadores in 1946. He also played ball in Mexico in 1951 with the Nuevo Laredo Tecolotes. He later played for the Tri-City Braves (1953), Idaho Falls Russets (1953), and the Boise Pilots (1954). Ernie's father, Ernesto, was an outstanding player in Arizona in the 1920s. (Courtesy of Charlie Sierra.)

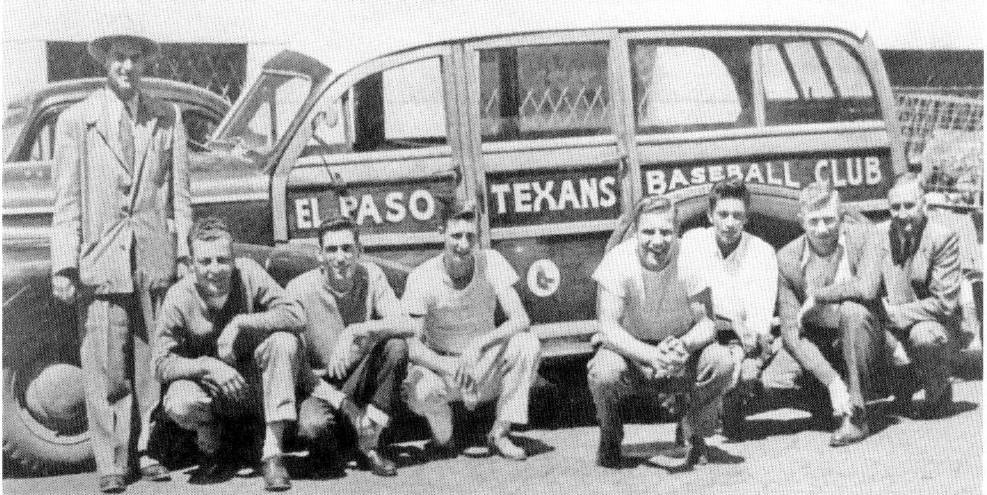


Charlie Sierra (third from right) played with the Boston Red Sox farm team in El Paso in 1947 and 1948 in the Class C Arizona-Texas League. Sierra recollected that in 1947, the team had departed from Bisbee, Arizona, when their station wagon flipped over in the desert. He was asleep in the back seat and fortunately was not injured. Sierra also recalled the harsh racial discrimination he confronted in Texas. Many fans from Juarez crossed the border to see the three Mexican Americans on the Red Sox minor-league team. Charlie and Ernie are brothers. Charlie played at Roosevelt High School and in the military. (Courtesy of Charlie Sierra.)

Tom Robles was signed by the Pittsburgh Pirates when he was 18. He was sent to their farm team in Merida, Mexico, bordering Guatemala. The Pirates sent him to play in Davenport, Iowa, and Great Falls and Billings, Montana, in 1955. He later played for the Mexico City Tigers, the Kinston Eagles in the Carolina League, and the Lewiston Broncos in the Northwest League. Tom tried one last time to play professionally with the Hollywood Stars. In the minors, he played against Don Drysdale and befriended Dick Stuart of the Pirates. Tom was an outstanding catcher at Garfield, making first-team All-City. His professional career started in 1954 with the Salinas Packers in the California League. (Courtesy of Mary Robles.)

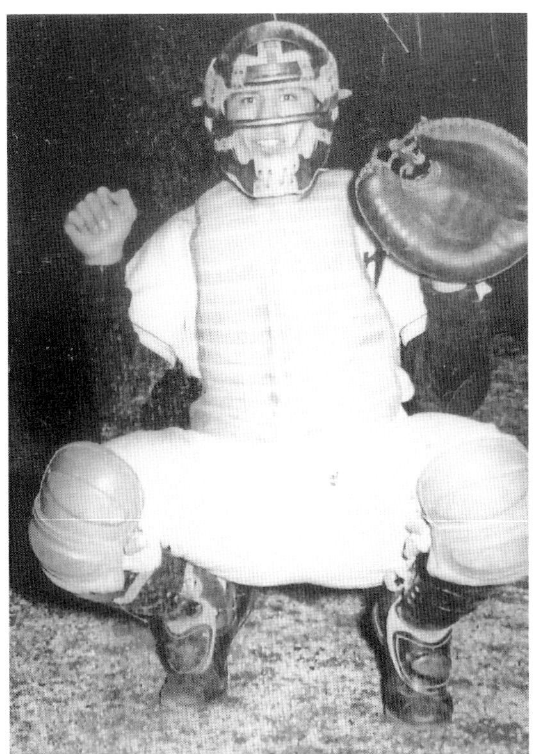

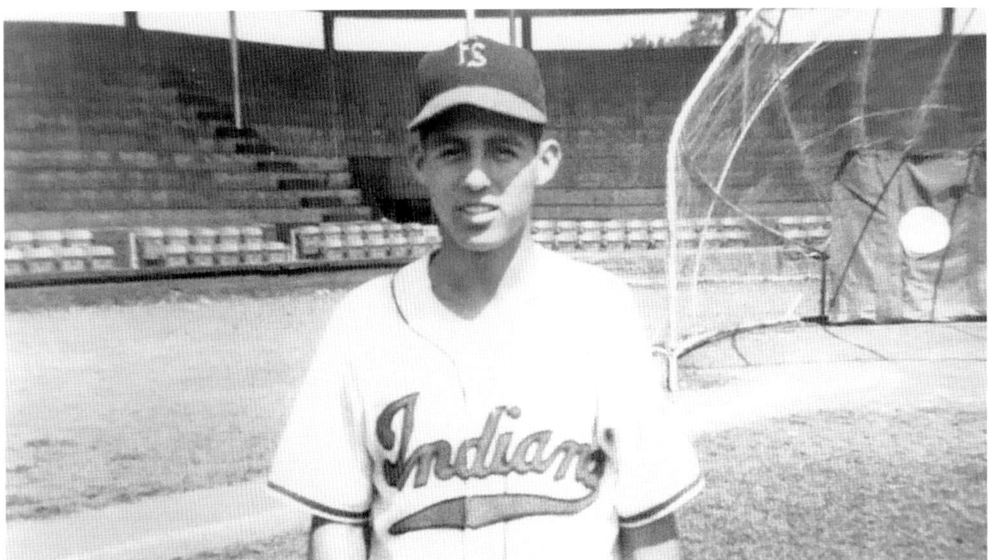


After playing at Roosevelt and with Eastside Beer, Ernie Blanco signed with the Cleveland Indians and reported to spring training in Daytona Beach. He was assigned to the Class C Spartanburg, South Carolina, Peaches and was named to the 1952 Minor League All-Star team, beating out several excellent players who later played in the major leagues. In 1952, Ernie was drafted, serving in the Korean War and playing service ball for a year. After the war, he played with Cleveland's minor-league team in Fargo, North Dakota. (Courtesy of Ernie Blanco.)

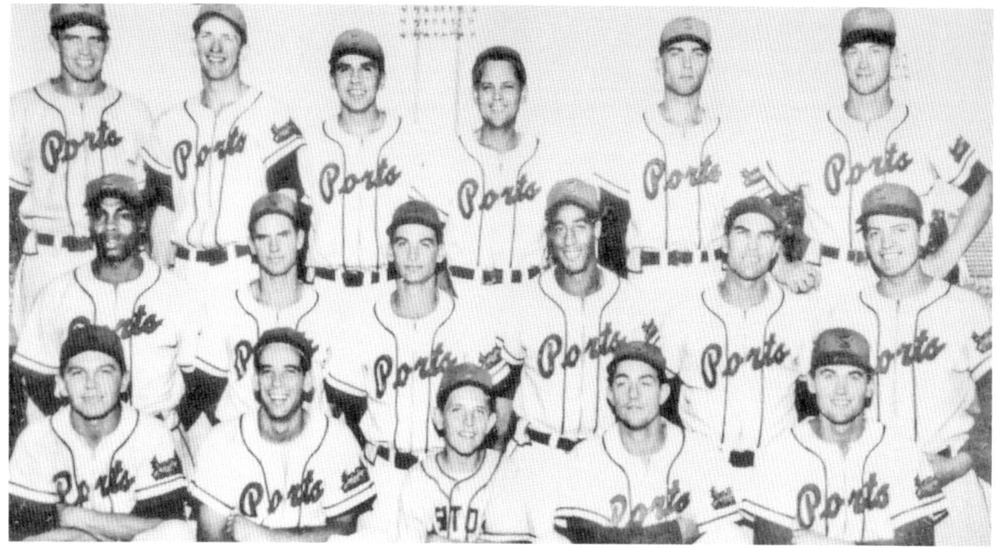

Armando Pérez (third row, third from left) was an outstanding player at Roosevelt and East Los Angeles Junior College. In 1956, he signed a contract with the Baltimore Orioles and played outfield for two of their minor-league affiliates, the Pacific Coast League Vancouver Mounties and the California League Stockton Ports. He later earned a master's degree in counseling and devoted his life to education. In 1970, he founded the Montebello Stars, providing scholarships and mentoring to outstanding student athletes. (Courtesy of Armando Pérez.)

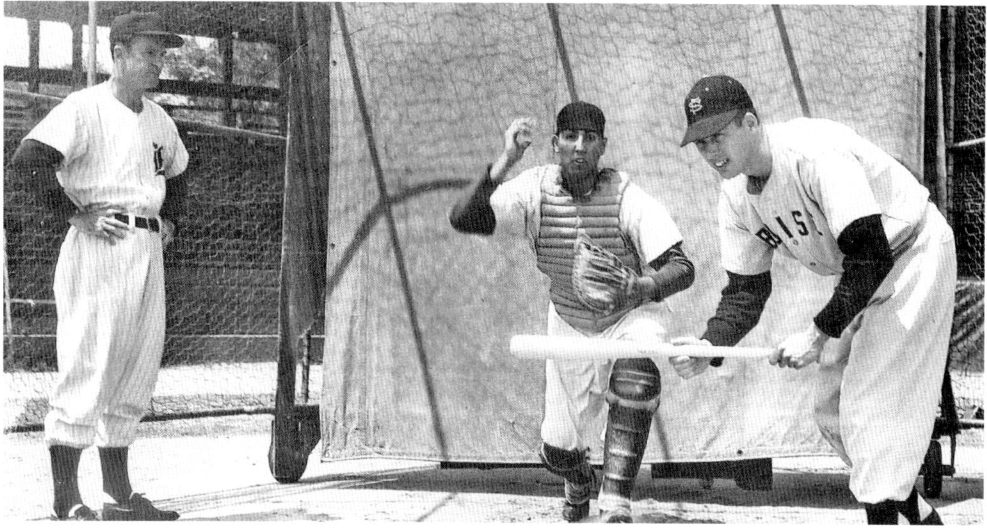

Gil Gamez Jr. (center) was a catcher and first baseman during the 1950s for the Boise Braves, Paris Orioles, Phoenix Stars, Portland Beavers, Salem Senators, Salt Lake Bees, and Stockton Ports. He always believed that racism prevented him and other Mexican Americans from making it to the major leagues. He was an outstanding player at Roosevelt and for the Carmelita Chorizeros. Gamez was an umpire for 22 years. He managed teams in Mexico and later became a scout for the Seattle Mariners, California Angels, Kansas City Royals, Milwaukee Brewers, and Montreal Expos. (Courtesy of Gil Jr. and Alma Gamez.)

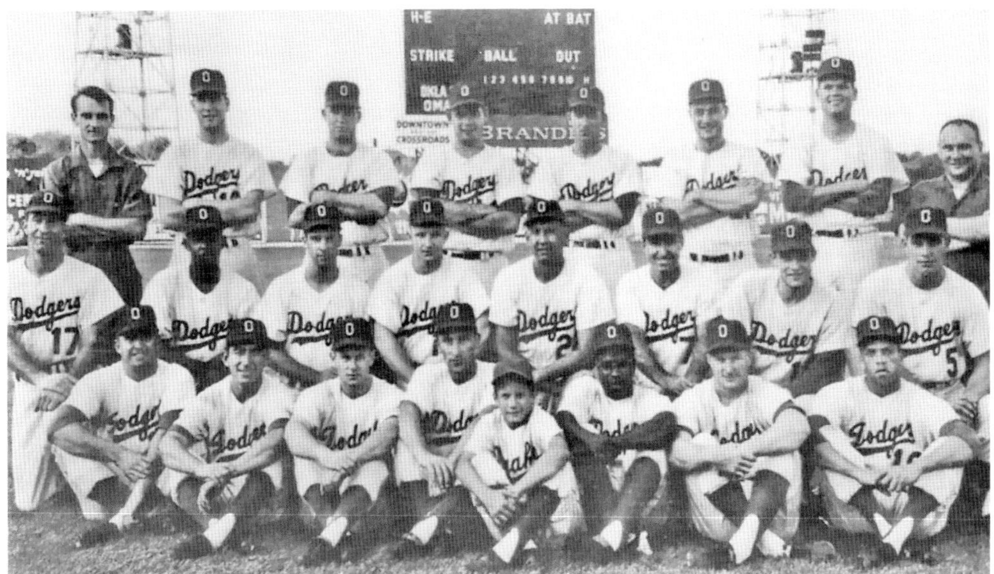


Ernie Rodríguez successfully transitioned from professional player to coach. He managed the Pocatello, Idaho, Posse in the Independent League, the Great Falls, Montana, Giants in the Rookie League, and other teams. He later returned to his alma mater, Roosevelt High School, to manage the baseball team and teach. Ernie has served as a critical link for high school, collegiate, and professional players. He is seen during his playing days with the 1962 Omaha Dodgers (first row, second from left). (Courtesy of Ernie Rodríguez.)

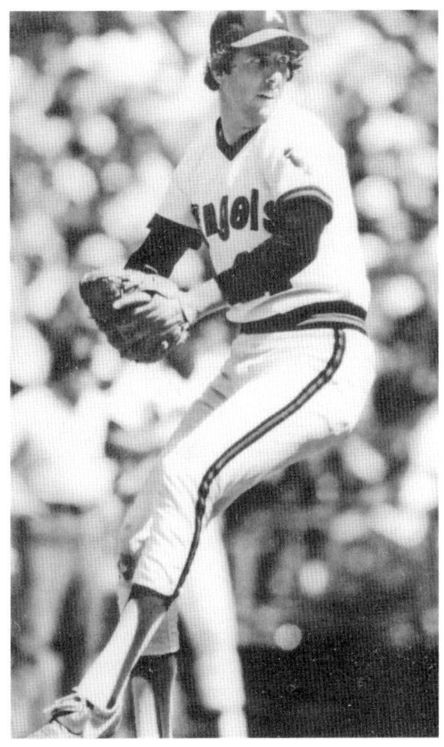

Fred Martínez grew up in Lincoln Heights and played ball at Downey Playground for Dan Alessi. He is proud to have been a Downey Playground Gremlin. He pitched and played first base at Lincoln High School in the 1970s. He played for Whittier College, ELAC, and Cal State Los Angeles. He was drafted by the New York Mets in 1977, playing in their minor-league system for three years. Fred's contract was purchased by the California Angels in 1979. In 1980, he started 23 games for the Halos and was named Angel Rookie of the Year. His manager was Jim Fergosi, and his pitching coach was Larry Sherry. He is currently a Los Angeles fireman. Fred's father, Rodolfo, played in Monterey, Mexico, in the 1940s and 1950s. He could not have known at the time that 35 years later, his son would play on the same field with the Monterey Sultanes in the Mexican League. (Courtesy of Fred Martínez.)

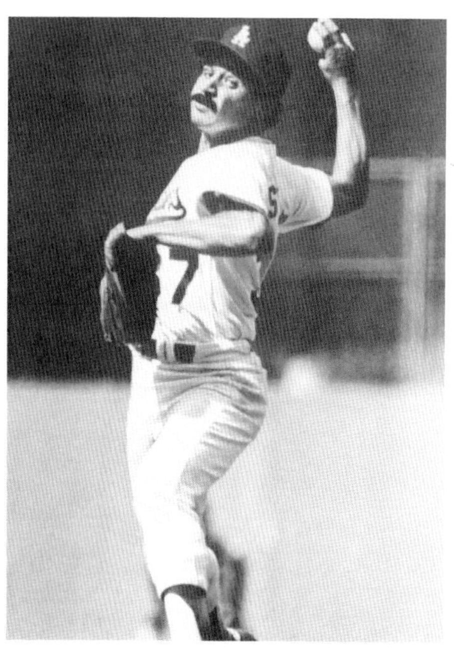

Bobby "Babo" Castillo was one of the great baseball stars from Lincoln Heights in East Los Angeles. Castillo was a three-time All-City player at Lincoln High School. He made his major league debut on September 19, 1977, retiring hall-of-famer Johnny Bench for his first major league out. He pitched in 250 professional games for the Los Angeles Dodgers and Minnesota Twins in a nine-year career from 1977 to 1985, winning the 1981 World Series with the Dodgers. He is often credited for teaching young Fernando Valenzuela how to throw the screwball, which became Valenzuela's signature pitch. Castillo pitched in Japan with the Chunichi Dragons in 1987. He died in 2014 at the age of 59. (Courtesy of Richard Santillán.)

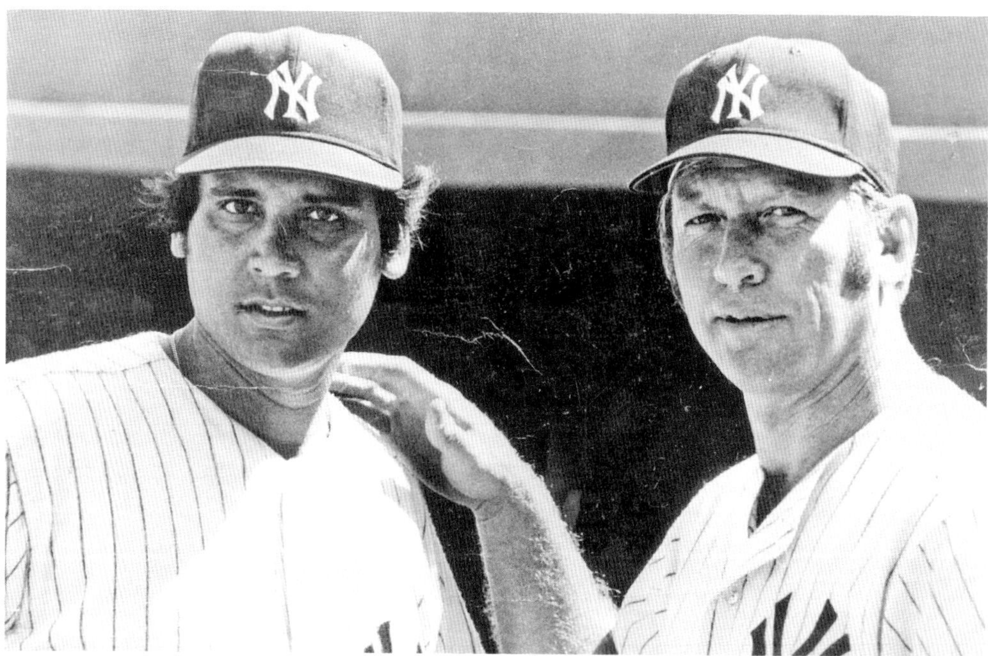

George Peña Jr. (left) is seen with Mickey Mantle. Peña was signed by the California Angeles out of Montebello High School and later played for the Chicago Cubs farm team in San Antonio, Texas. Between 1963 and 1975, George played for several minor league teams, including the Quad-Cities Angels, Reynosa, Mexico Broncs, San Jose Bees, El Paso Sun Kings, Tacoma Cubs, Dallas–Fort Worth Spurs, Syracuse Chiefs, Toledo Mud Hens, Tacoma Twins, and the Iowa Oaks. George's father, George Sr., was an all-league football player at Roosevelt High School and played one year of minor league baseball in Ventura County. (Courtesy of Richard Peña.)

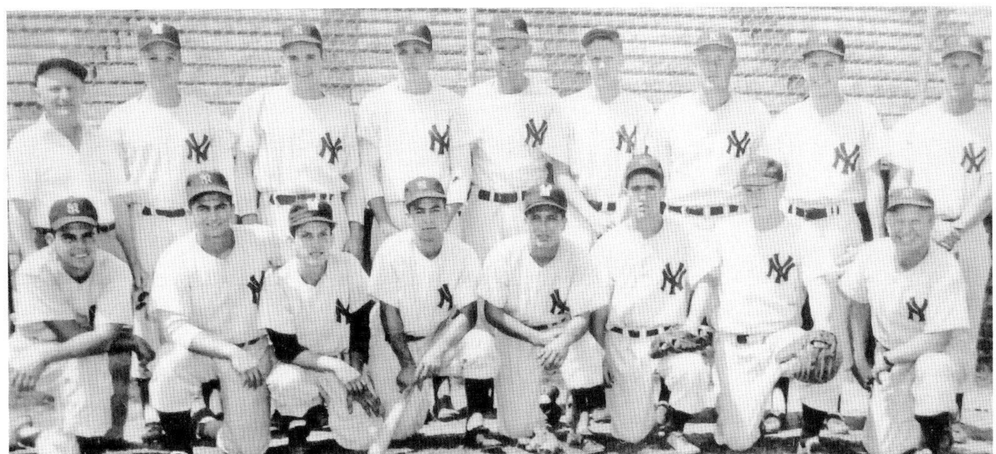

The 1953 Pasadena Yankees played at Brookside Park, not far from the famous Rose Bowl. The manager, Terry Bartron, was the Rosemead High School baseball coach and also a scout for the New York Yankees. Joe Gaitan (first row, fourth from left), Peter Ortega (first row, fifth from left), and Ángel Figueroa (first row, third from right) all played on the 1952 Garfield High School championship team. Ortega and Figueroa played in the minor leagues. Figueroa later scouted for the St. Louis Cardinals. Bob Lagunas (not pictured) from nearby Pico Rivera also played with the New York Yankees scout team. (Courtesy of Joe Gaitan.)

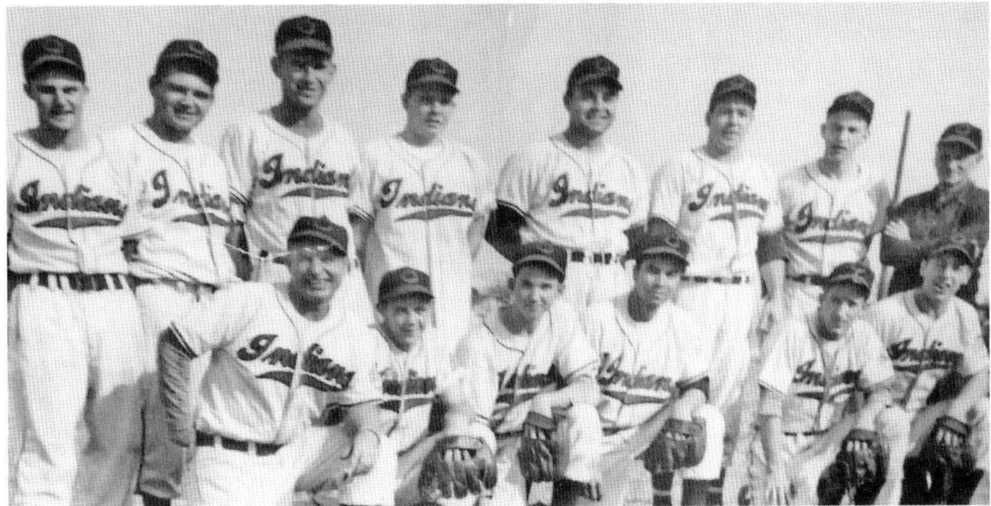

Around the time he was discharged from the military, Chano Gaitan spoke with scouts from the Chicago White Sox. He was invited for a tryout at Gilmore Field, where the Hollywood Stars played their home games. He had a very good session but was told that he was too small to make the White Sox roster. He is seen here in the first row, fourth from left, with the semi-pro Cleveland Indians scout team. Chano and his brothers, Frankie, Johnny, Willie, Tony, and Jimmy, had a softball team called the Over the Hill Gang at Evergreen Park. Johnny, who Chano said was the athlete in the family, put together several teams for years. Chano's son Damon and daughters Devon and Lanee played ball. The girls became excellent softball players at Wilson High School, making All-City teams. (Courtesy of Ray Gaitan.)

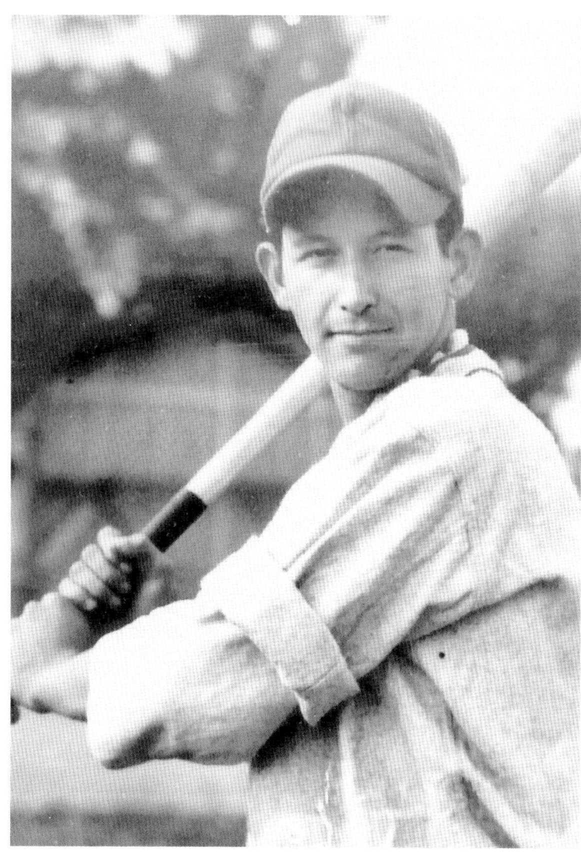

Fermín Magaña, also known as Chemino, was one of the greatest shortstops to come out of Roosevelt High School. After high school, he signed with the Philadelphia Phillies. Later, Magaña played for several East Los Angeles community teams, including Órnelas Market, Vera Cruz, Lucky Lager, and Carmelita. Magaña was an outstanding coach who mentored nephews Bobby Recendez and Fernando Farfán. His brother, Luís B. Magaña, was a well-known boxer and also a very good baseball player. Luis was an well-known boxing figure. He was the publicist and promoter for the famous Los Angeles Olympic Auditorium for 40 years. He was a sports writer for *La Opinión* newspaper. (Courtesy of Bobby Recendez.)

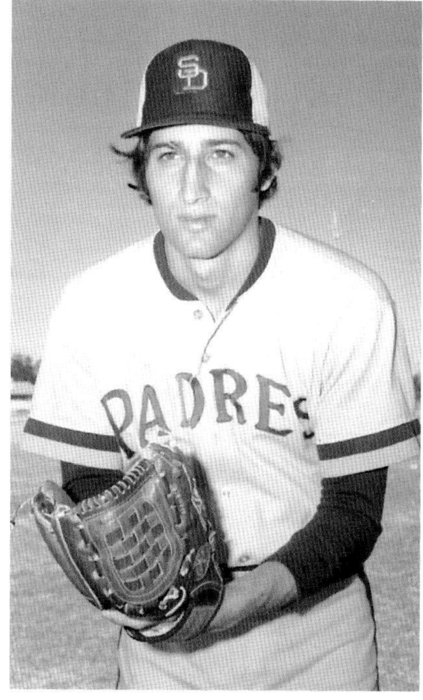

Victor Hugo Bernal's passion for baseball began when he was in elementary school. He grew up in Hillside Village, where his parents Marina and Jesus Bernal still reside, and started playing at Multnomah Elementary and Little League at El Sereno Recreation Center, where he played until high school. Bernal played third base and pitched for Woodrow Wilson High School, and after graduation, was recruited to play baseball for Cal Poly Pomona University. While at Cal Poly Pomona, he made the US all star team and played against Japan. He also caught the attention of professional baseball scouts, in particular the San Diego Padres. After playing for the minor and major leagues, his passion led him to coach baseball at the high schools where he taught and the Little League where his sons played. Bernal is survived by his wife, Kathy, and two sons Matthew and Andrew, and fondly remembered by family and friends. (Courtesy of the Bernal family.)

Fred Scott signed a AAA contract with the Baltimore Orioles in the fall of 1959 and started in Vancover, Canada. He was optioned to Stockton in the California C Class (now A ball) and was an all-star shortstop. The next year, he was playing A ball in Aberdine, South Dakota. But for two years, he did not move higher in the minor-league system, and asked for his release. He went back to play in Stockton, where his professional career ended in 1962. He was disappointed for not getting a shot to play in the major leagues. (Courtesy of Fred Scott.)

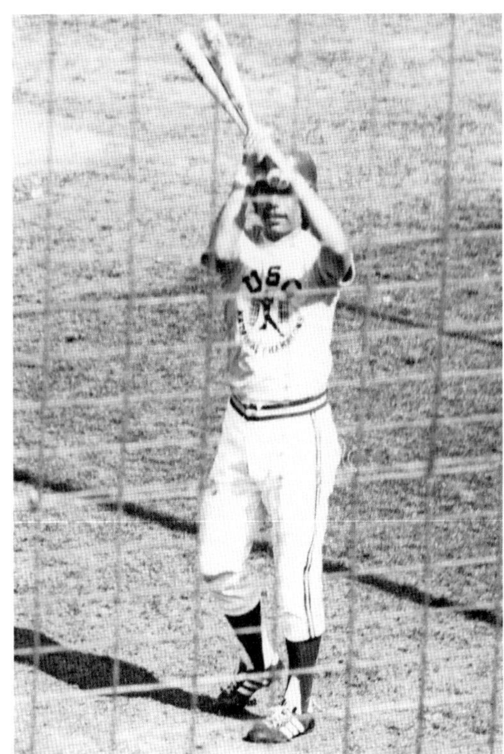

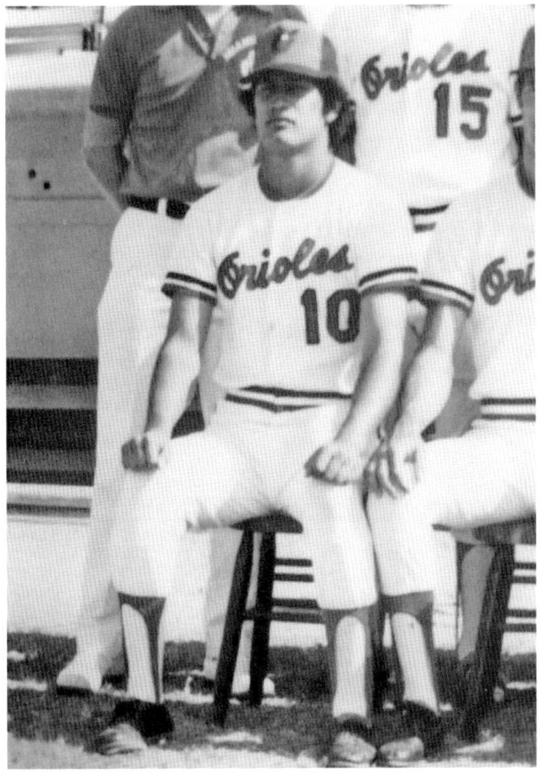


Joe Villa Jr. played at Cantwell High School in the early 1970s and had a powerful bat, a rifle arm, and the intelligence to be an All-CIF catcher and the league MVP his senior year. Joe was drafted by the Baltimore Orioles and played two years for the Miami Orioles. Joe's father, Joe Sr., also played at Cantwell as a catcher, while Joe Jr.'s uncle John played third base in 1951 at Cantwell. Joe Jr.'s brother, John, played at Cantwell in 1976 as a pitcher. (Courtesy of Lauro Montes.)

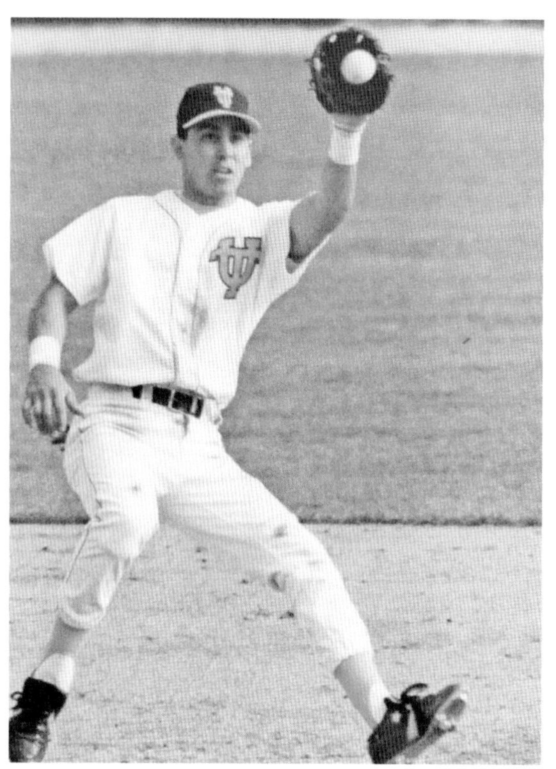

Danny Ramírez played at Cantwell High School in the mid-1980s, earning All-League honors. He played at Cerritos Community College and at the University of Tennessee. There, he earned the 1990 MVP award along with All-Conference second-team honors. Danny was drafted by the Baltimore Orioles and played for their minor-league affiliates before concluding his minor-league career with the Bowie Redsox double-A team in Maryland. Several Cantwell players later went on to play college ball including Rick Chval, Don Rizzi, Tom Quigley, Ron Arnold, Rick Arzula, Pete Levin, David Ávila, Marco Márquez, Willie Hernández Galbraith, Albert Chavarra, Chris Trujillo, and Andre García. (Courtesy of Lauro Montes.)

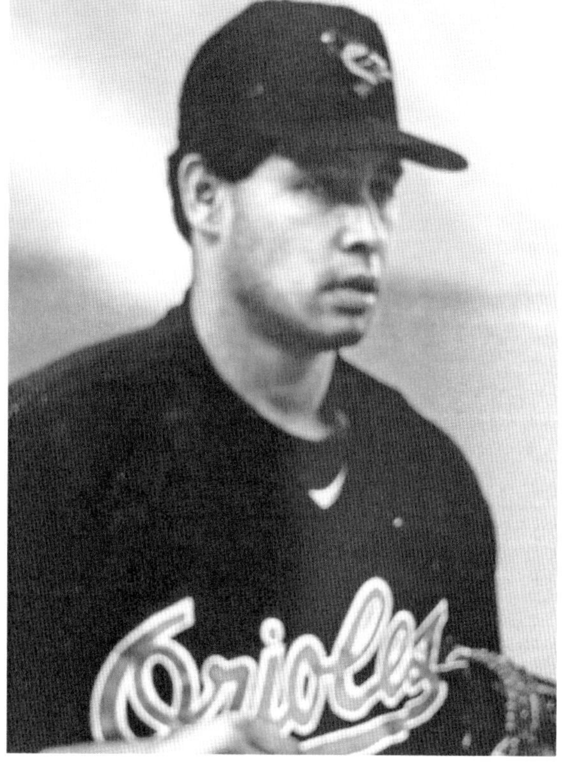


Craig Piedra Worthington played at Cantwell High School during the early 1980s. He was All-League and All-CIF before continuing his baseball career at Cerritos Community College in Norwalk. He was drafted by the Baltimore Orioles in 1985 and led the Carolina League in 1986 with 105 RBIs. Craig earned MVP honors with the International League when he played for Rochester, New York. In 1989, he made his major-league debut and hit 15 home runs. He played eight years in the major leagues with Baltimore, Texas, Cincinnati, and Cleveland. (Courtesy of Lauro Montes.)

# 6

# TRANSNATIONAL

The Latino Baseball History Project has uncovered an extraordinary history of Mexican Americans playing ball outside the United States. Hundreds have played in Mexico dating back to the late 19th century. They chose to play professionally in Mexico rather than the United States for several reasons, including better salaries, larger stadiums, a fanatical fan base, better coaching, extensive news coverage, familiarity with the language, food, and religion, less racial discrimination, and a higher caliber of competition.

Military service has also been a major contributor to Mexican Americans playing ball around the globe. This was especially true during World Wars I and II, Korea, and Vietnam. Even during times of peace, Mexican Americans have played military ball at home and abroad. During World War I, Mexican American doughboys played ball in France, often writing home to family and friends about their exploits on the diamond. Since World War II, Mexican Americans have played service ball in the Philippines, Germany, England, France, India, Morocco, Australia, Puerto Rico, New Zealand, Korea, Vietnam, Canada, Japan, Guam, Panama, Guadalcanal, China, Portugal, and near the Russian border.

These special globetrotters have had amazing experiences that few Mexican Americans have ever known. Their wide-ranging trips have provided them with a unique international perspective regarding different cultures and languages, a national perspective when meeting other Mexican Americans from different parts of the United States, a state perspective when meeting Mexican Americans from other parts of their states, and of course, a local experience already shaped by their upbringing. These extraordinary free spirits have multiple levels of geographical viewpoints to draw upon in all aspects of their lives.

With these various degrees of awareness, in addition to taking full advantage of the GI Bill to go to college and buy a home, these military wanderers launched civil, labor, and political movements demanding greater participation in American society and first-class citizenship. Mainstream baseball research has often ignored the rich history of Mexican Americans playing in Mexico and the personnel who played ball while risking their lives in the military.

After World War II, several Mexican American players wore their military belts and buckles with their baseball uniforms, symbolically shouting out loud that they had fought for this country and deserved respect, social justice, and equality. The immense contributions of these players, who played for the *patria* and for Uncle Sam, have left a lasting legacy. A memorial park on Lorena Street and Cesar Chavez Avenue in East Los Angeles honors Mexican Americans from World War I to the Gulf War. Directly across the street, a plaque pays tribute to Raul Morin, who wrote *Among the Valiant*, highlighting Mexican Americans who earned the Congressional Medal of Honor in World War II and Korea. This chapter pays homage to these deserving baseball idols who played for *la patria* and those who defended their nation while bringing baseball entertainment to the troops.

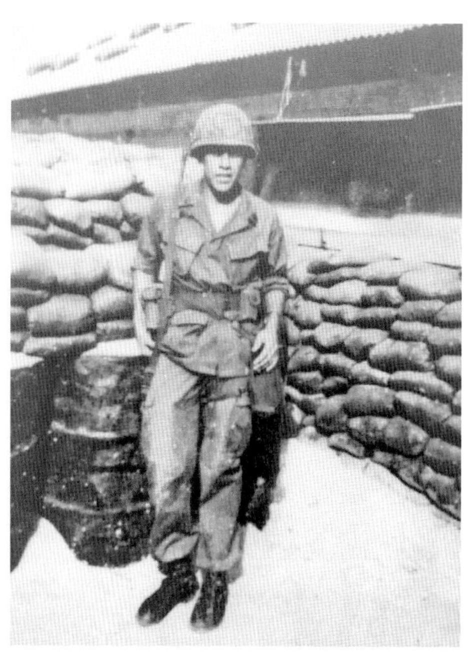

Elías De La Rosa Jr. was raised in East Los Angeles and drafted into the Army in 1968. He did his basic training at Fort Ord, California, and was assigned to Fort Bliss, Texas. He was the only Mexican American to make the military team and played outfield and third base. After only four games, he received orders for Vietnam, where he was stationed at Chu Lai with the 23rd Infantry near the North Vietnamese border. He was assigned to the antiaircraft unit. (Courtesy of Elías De La Rosa.)

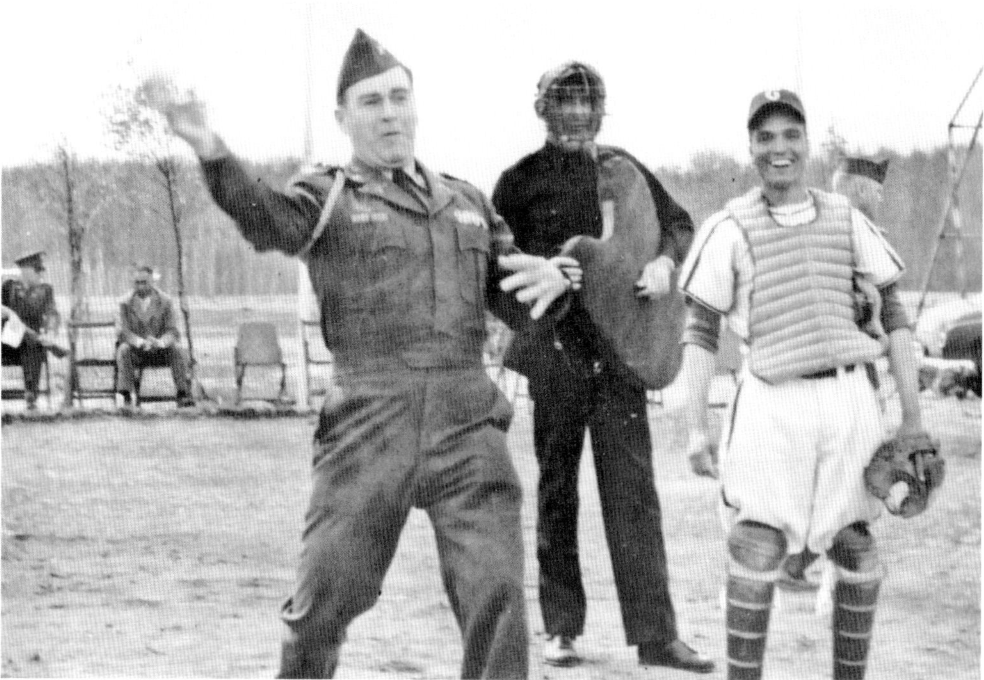

Gabe Peña was raised in East Los Angeles. He completed his basic training at Fort Ord and was stationed at Kirchgons Base, near Frankfurt, Germany, for 18 months in the 1950s. His unit, the 4th Division, 22nd Infantry, worked with mortars. Peña (right) was a catcher for the base team against teams from the 8th Infantry, 12th Infantry, division artillery, and special troops. He was also quarterback for the football team and helped with boxing matches and basketball games. (Courtesy of Gabe Peña.)

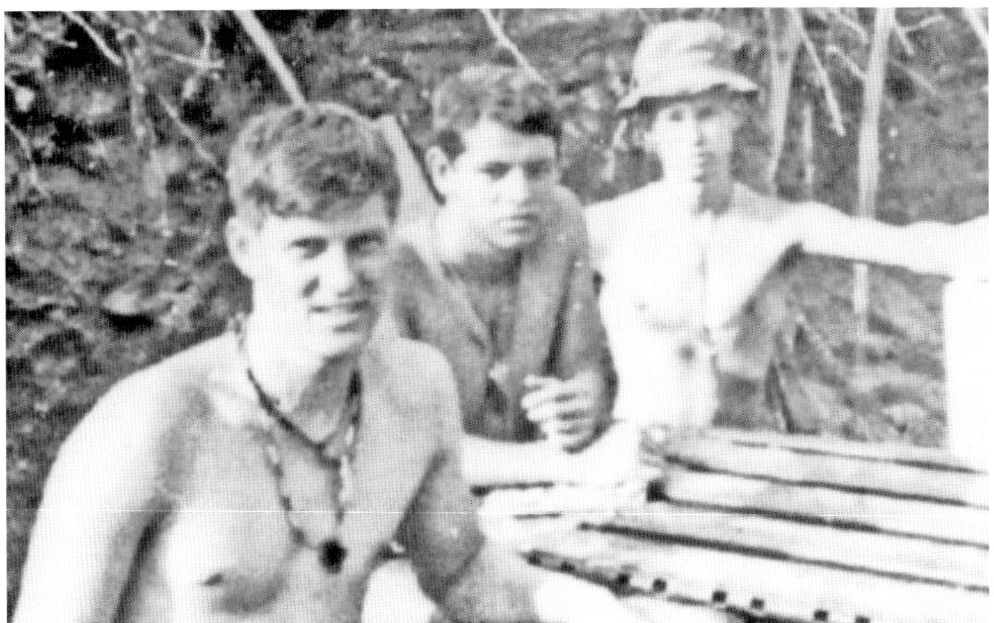

Alfonso Olmos (center) was drafted by the San Francisco Giants and the US Army. He did his basic training in 1968 at Fort Ord, where he played ball before being shipped to Vietnam with the 506th, 101st Airborne Division. He was an infantryman in the Ashua Valley in Thau Thien Province. Alfonso kept his Giants contract inside his helmet. He was killed in action on July 19, 1969. The movie *Hamburger Hill* depicts the battle where he lost his life. (Courtesy of David Olmos.)

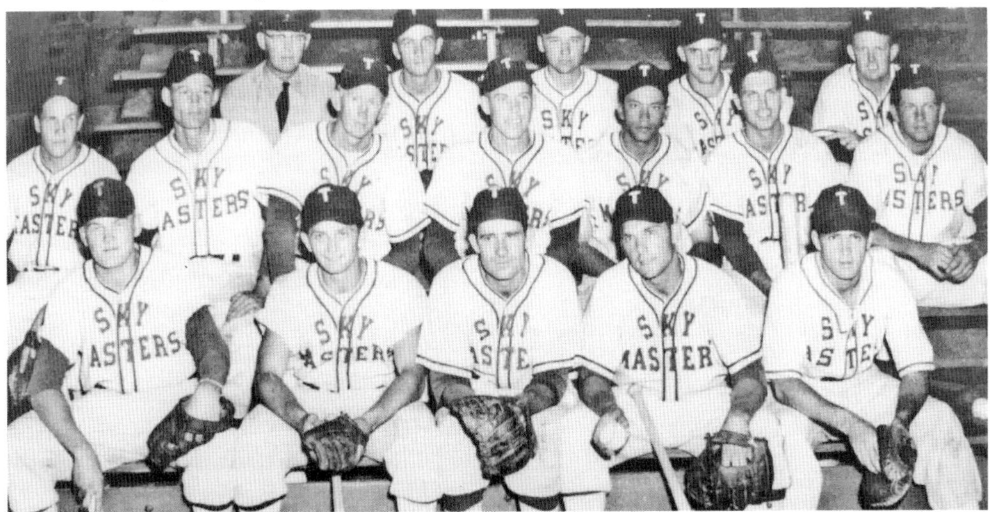

Charlie Sierra (second row, third from right) was an outstanding player at Roosevelt High School. He played at Travis Air Force Base, California, with the 14th Air Division. The Skymasters won the California and Pacific Championships in 1952 against the Hickam Flyers from Hawaii. The Skymasters played in the World Wide Air Force Championship at Eglin Field, Florida. In 1951, Charlie played for the Yokota Raiders, winning the Far East Air Force baseball championship at the Tokyo Coliseum. (Courtesy of Charlie Sierra.)

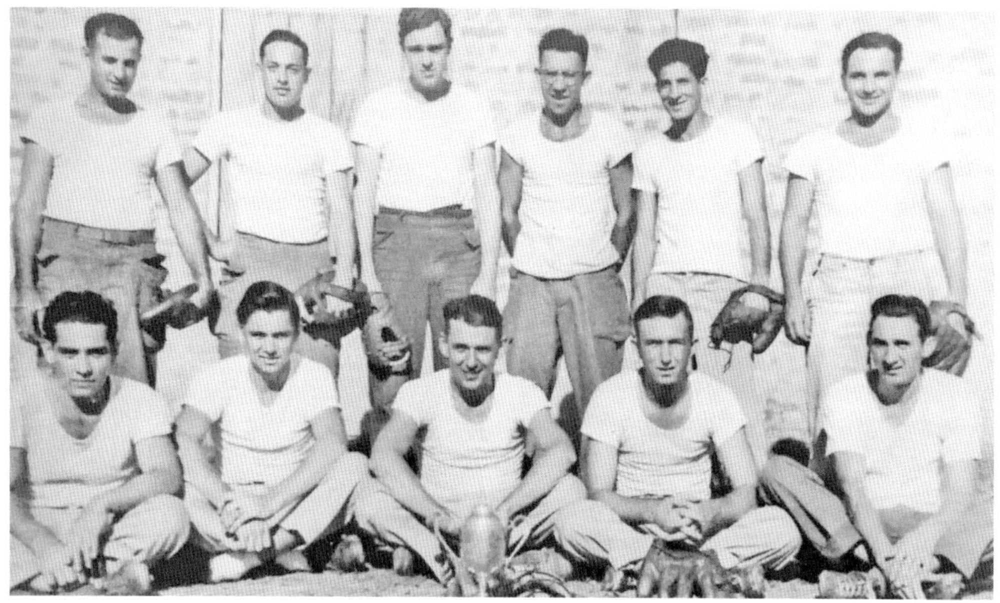

Jesús Paz (first row, left) served in World War II in the China-Burma-India theater. He is seen in 1945 with a softball team in Calcutta with the 142nd US Army Regiment. The team won the Calcutta softball championship. Paz was an outstanding youth player in East Los Angeles and coached for many years, earning the nickname "Mr. Boyle Heights" for his tireless dedication to coaching and maintaining the fields and parks for the youth. (Courtesy of Kelvin Paz.)

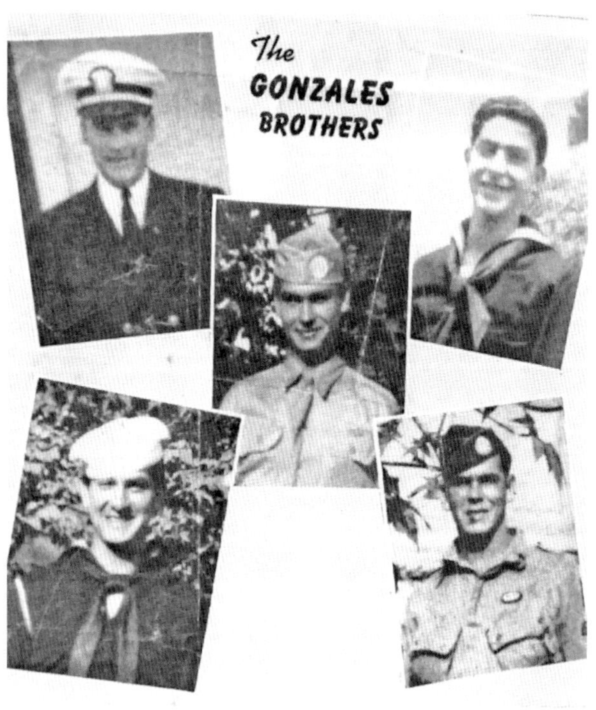


The Gonzáles brothers—Joe (far left), James (far right), Ernest (center), Freddy (lower left), and John (lower right)—were outstanding baseball players at Roosevelt High and East Los Angeles parks. Like thousands of Mexican Americans throughout the United States, they enlisted when World War II broke out. Another brother, Candido, worked in the war industry. Since Mexican American families were very large, it was not uncommon to see five or more brothers in the service. The Gonzáles family was no exception. Ernest was killed in action, and John was wounded in battle. Joe played and later coached baseball at Roosevelt and was on the same team as his brother Candido in 1932. (Courtesy of the Gonzáles family.)

Carlos V. Santillán was born in Tampico, Mexico, in 1923. His family migrated to East Los Angeles, where he sold newspapers in front of the Coliseum during the 1932 Olympics. He graduated from Stevenson Junior High School, then from Roosevelt in 1942. Although he did not play sports in high school, many of his friends were athletes, including George Peña. Almost 75 years later, Carlos's son Richard and George's younger brother Richard are coauthors of this book. Carlos took his two sons, Richard and Charles, to see the Pacific Coast League Angels play at Wrigley Field and to the Coliseum to watch the Dodgers and Rams. Carlos was wounded twice during World War II (in Anzio, Italy, and at the Battle of the Bulge) and received the Bronze Star. (Courtesy of Richard A. Santillán.)

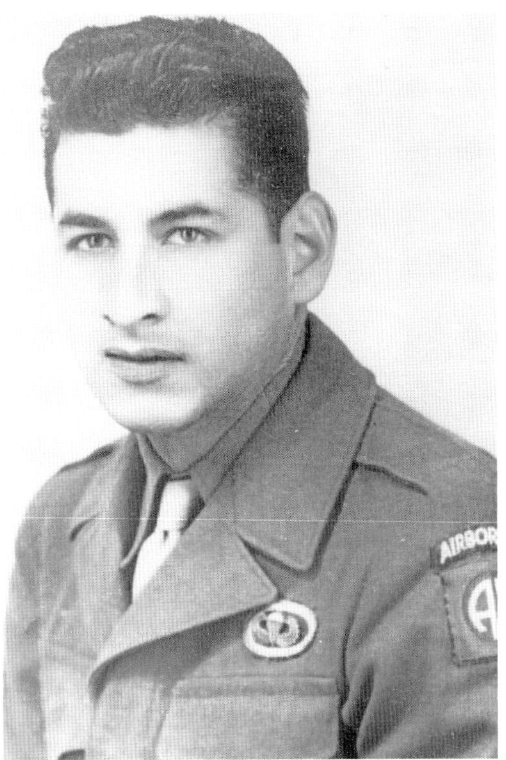

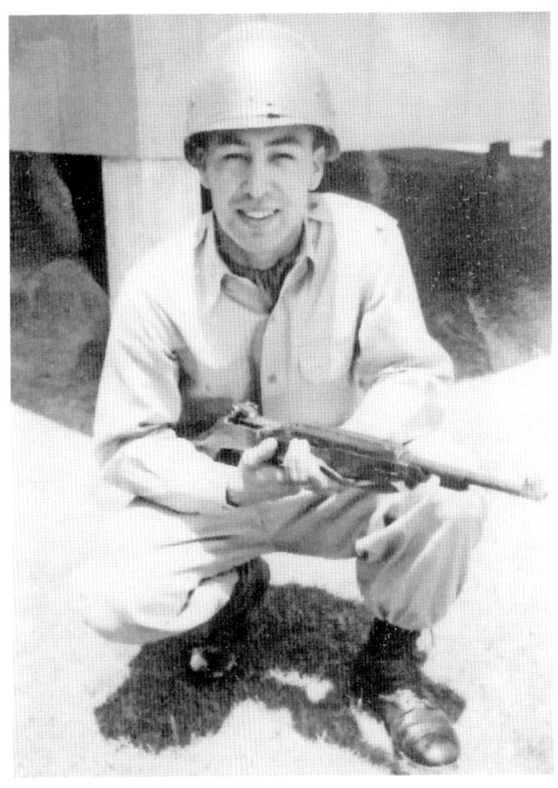

Joe Gaitan enlisted in the US Army in 1958 and is shown here at Fort Sill, Oklahoma, where he made the baseball team in the summer of 1958. His older brother Chano also played ball in the service. Joe currently resides in Montebello, California, with his wife of 58 years, Lillian. They have five children who graduated from college and 16 grandchildren (eight of whom are currently in college). Their professions include dentist, doctor, professor, pharmacist, and attorney. (Courtesy of Joe Gaitan.)

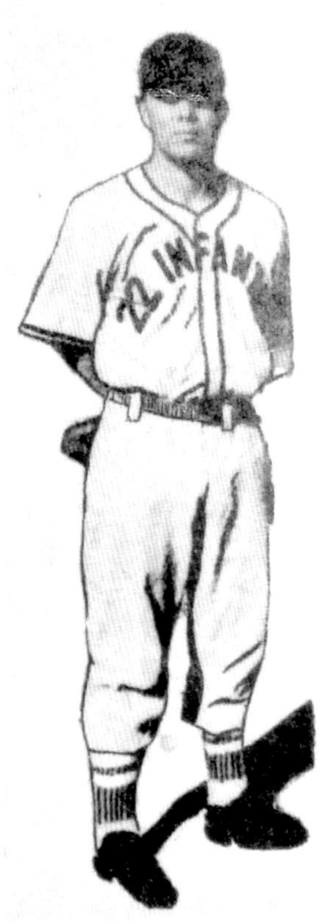

Chano Gaitan played ball with the 22nd Regiment. He grew up in East Los Angeles playing along with his brothers Joe and Tony. After leaving the service, Chano signed a professional contract with the Pittsburgh Pirates organization. He was assigned to the Arizona-Texas League. The following year, he was promoted to the Modesto Reds of the California League. His children are college graduates in the fields of law and business. (Courtesy of Ray Gaitan.)

IN GRATEFUL MEMORY OF

Antonio Corrall Lugo

WHO DIED IN THE SERVICE OF HIS COUNTRY AT

U.S. Naval Hospital, Oceanside, California, 10 March 1945

HE STANDS IN THE UNBROKEN LINE OF PATRIOTS WHO HAVE DARED TO DIE

THAT FREEDOM MIGHT LIVE, AND GROW, AND INCREASE ITS BLESSINGS.

FREEDOM LIVES, AND THROUGH IT, HE LIVES—

IN A WAY THAT HUMBLES THE UNDERTAKINGS OF MOST MEN

Franklin D Roosevelt

PRESIDENT OF THE UNITED STATES OF AMERICA

Antonio Corrall Lugo from East Los Angeles lost his life during World War II. He was badly wounded at the Battle of Saipan and eventually died from his wounds. Lugo was the father of Tony Lugo, an outstanding community and Garfield High School player. Tony took small comfort that the office of Pres. Franklin Delano Roosevelt sent a signed letter to the family. (Courtesy of Richard Lugo.)

Pedro Barrios was born in 1908 and raised on Gallardo Street (known as "G Street"). It bordered Brooklyn Avenue (now Cesar Chávez Avenue) and Mission Road. Pedro, the oldest of five children, married Consuelo Chacon Demson at 19. They had three children. He worked nights so he could play ball during the day. He played for Monterey in the Mexican League and was an outstanding switch-hitter. He umpired for years in East Los Angeles. His brother, Manuel, played ball but gave it up to work as a meat inspector. Manuel married at the age of 50 and had nine children, eight of them boys. (Courtesy of Pete Barrios Jr.)

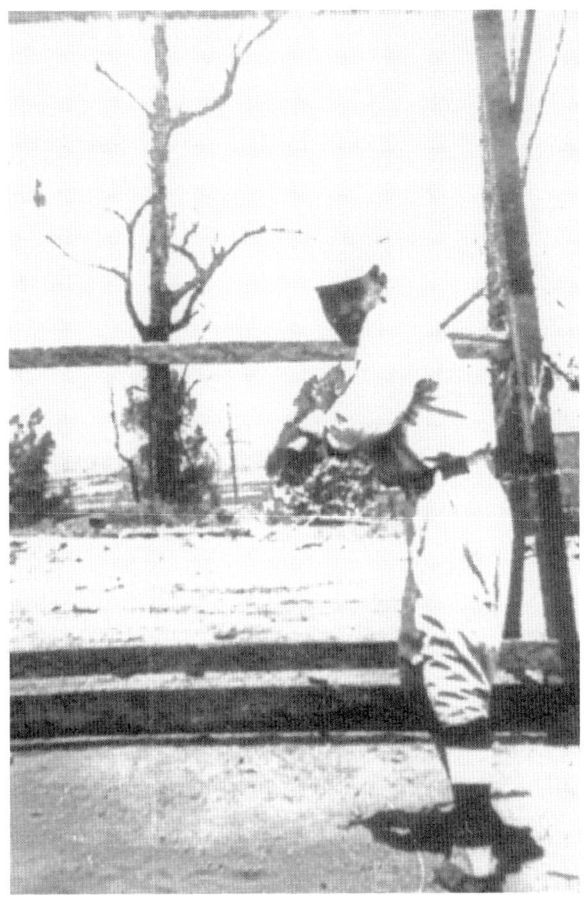

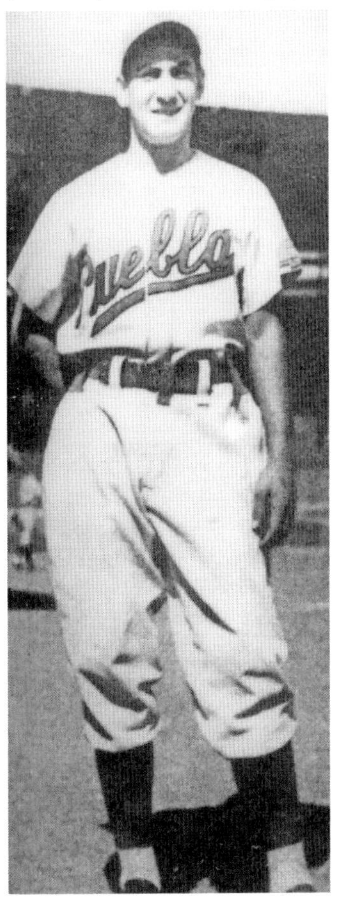


Freddy González was born in 1922 in Yuma, Arizona. The family moved to Boyle Heights shortly after his birth. He played lots of ball in parks and schools and received a scholarship to the University of Santa Clara. He played in Puebla, Mexico, before he went into the service and played ball with the Coast Guard during World War II. His four brothers, Joe, James, Ernest, and John, served as well. Ernest was killed at the Battle of the Bulge, and John was wounded in action. After the war, Freddy played for the Pacific Coast League's Hollywood Stars before leaving for Mexico again. He ran a heating and air-conditioning business in Atascadero and was an avid golfer. As a young man, he won an amateur golf championship. (Courtesy of Jim González.)

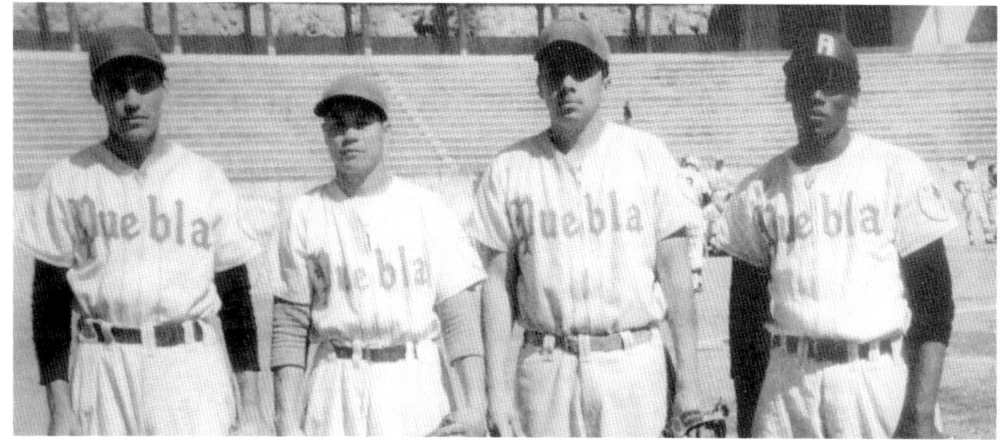

A native of East Los Angeles, Armando Pérez (third from left) played for Puebla in Mexico during the 1950s. He recalled that his Spanish was limited, making it awkward to communicate with other players and fans, but his language skills eventually improved so much that he was able to conduct media interviews in Spanish. Many Mexican Americans who played in Mexico remarked that they learned much about their language, culture, and history, including visiting the hometowns of their parents and grandparents for the first time. (Courtesy of Armando Pérez.)

DE LA REPUBLICA MEXICANA, A. C.

CONTRATO UNIFORME DE DEPORTISTA PROFESIONAL

JUGADOR DE BEISBOL

I. PARTES CONTRATANTES

EMPRESA PROMOCIONES Y ESPECTACULOS DE ENSENADA S. A. DE C. V.

Domicilio Calle 4ta. # 238-5

Representada por Ramón Inzunza Ramos

JUGADOR DE BEISBOL Nicolas Escamilla

Nacionalidad ______ Fecha de nacimiento ______

Estado Civil ______ Domicilio ______ Ciudad ______ Tel. ______

II. DENOMINACIONES

Los partes contratantes aceptan que de aquí en adelante, en el curso de este Contrato, ellas y los organismos del beisbol profesional que en el mismo se mencionan, se denominen:

EMPRESA PROMOCIONES Y ESPECTACULOS DE ENSENADA S. A. DE C. V. será "EL C

JUGADOR DE BEISBOL Nicolas Escamilla, será "EL JUGADOR

ASOCIACION DE LIGAS PROFESIONALES DE BEISBOL DE LA REPUBLICA MEXICANA, A. C., será "LA ASOCIACION".

LA LIGA Norte de Sonora "AA" será "LA LIG

EL COMISIONADO DEL BEISBOL será "EL COMISIONADO".

Nicky Escamilla was an outstanding youth player in El Sereno and at Wilson High School. He was an excellent hitter, often batting in the clean-up spot, and had a rifle of an arm when throwing out runners from the outfield. He also played first base. He was recruited in the 1980s to play in Mexico. This is a copy of his contract when he played in Nogales and Ensenada. Later in his career, he joined a Mike Brito All-Star team and played against Los Potros in Tijuana. He played for semiprofessional teams playing against the Long Beach Rockets, Pasadena Red Birds, and San Bernardino Spirits. (Courtesy of Nicky Escamilla.)

Mark García has played baseball with several teams as a second baseman including in the Development Golden Baseball League, Bishop Amat High School, Pasadena City College, Australian Development Baseball League, El Monte Brocs in the Mike Brito League, and the semi-pro Pasadena Red Birds. After his playing days, Mark became a professional baseball scout with several teams including working as a territorial scout in the Southern California region for the Milwaukee Brewers ball club; an administrative assistant in the International Operations for the California Angels, and an international scout for the Boston Red Sox covering all of the Far East and Latin American markets including Mexico, Venezuela, Puerto Rico, the Dominican Republic, Japan, Korea, Taiwan, Australia, and Russia. Mark's father is Adolfo García, who was an outstanding player and coach in El Sereno for many years. (Courtesy of Mark García.)

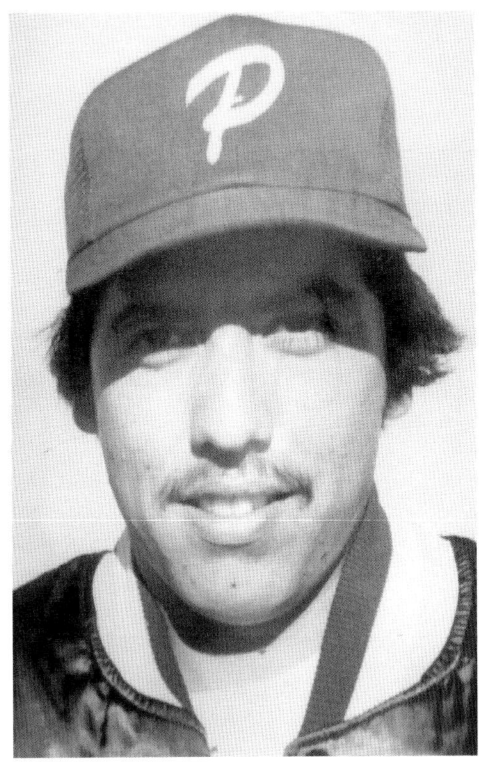

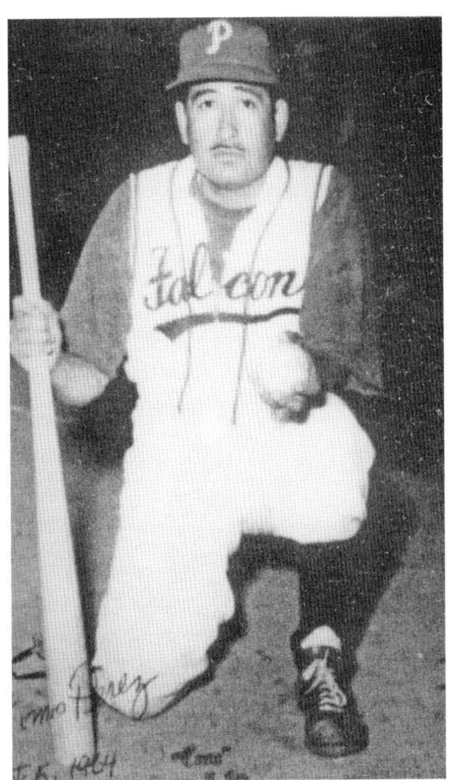


Tom Pérez Jr. was player-manager for Jean's Falcons in the 1960s. The Los Angeles–based team played against teams in Baja California for years. Several Mexican American teams had agreements with teams in Mexico to play home and away games with each other. Some Mexican Americans decided to play their entire careers in Mexico due to high salaries, bigger stadiums, cultural familiarity, extensive press coverage, better competition, and a huge fan base. Tom attended Garfield High School, while most of his teammates were Roosevelt alumni. Tom's father, Tom Sr., was an outstanding East Los Angeles player and manager in the 1930s and 1940s. Tom Jr.'s eight children and 17 grandchildren have continued the rich family baseball history. His wife, Alice, is the foundation of this amazing baseball family. (Courtesy of Tom Pérez Jr.)

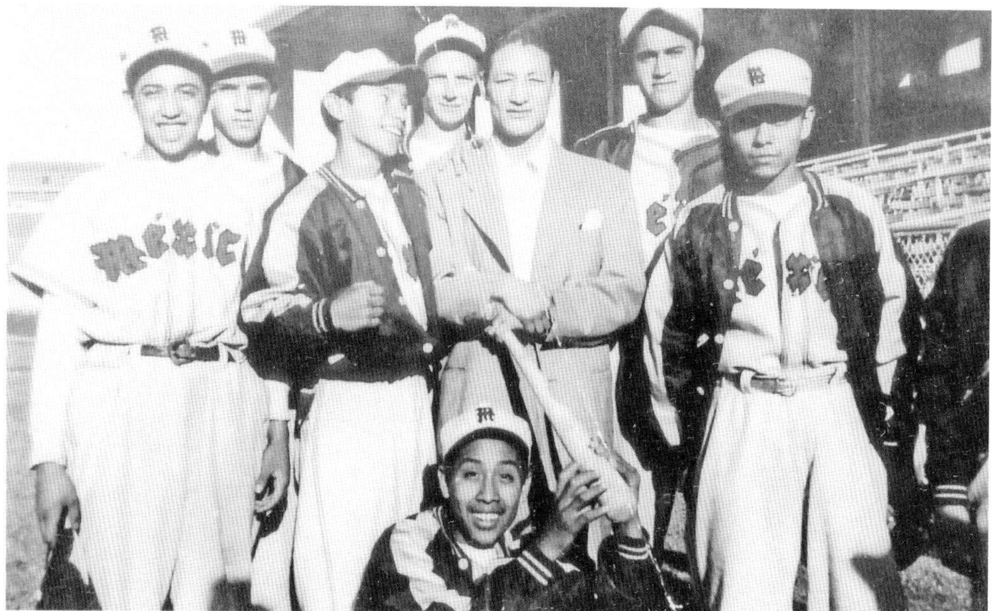

Enrique Bolanos (sports jacket) is surrounded by a team from Mexico at Wrigley Field in Los Angeles, the home of the Pacific Coast League Angels. Bolanos was a huge baseball fan and an outstanding boxer. He fought Ike Williams three times for the lightweight championship at Wrigley Field in 1946, 1947, and 1949. Bobby Recendez (not shown), an outstanding baseball player in East Los Angeles, became Bolanos's biographer. (Courtesy of Bobby Recendez.)

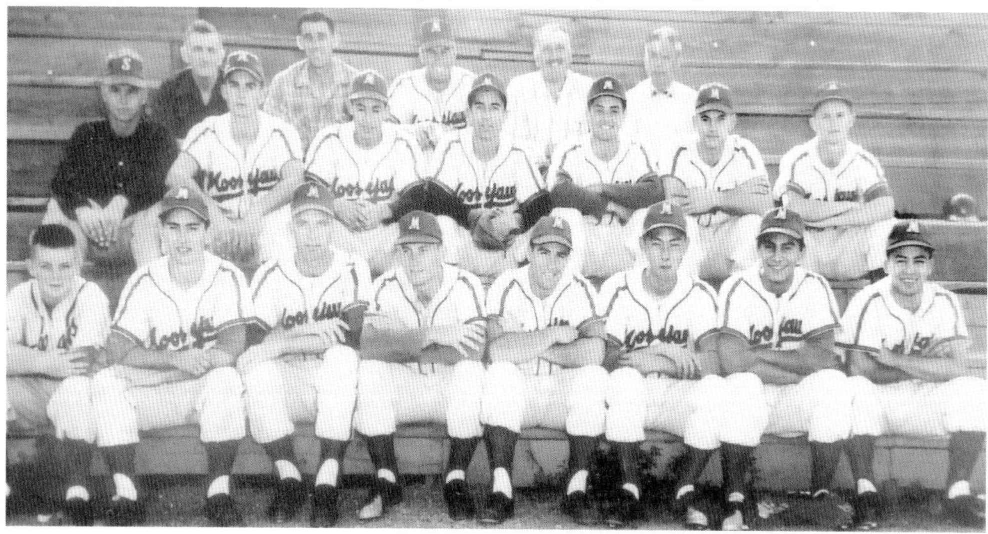

The 1956 Moosejaw, Saskatchewan, team was comprised of college players representing different campuses. There are three East Los Angeles players: Joe Gaitan (first row, far right), Conrad Muñatones (second row, third from right), and Ernie Rodríguez (second row, fourth from right). Gaitan played at Garfield High School and Fresno State, while Muñatones and Rodríguez played at Roosevelt High School and UCLA. Muñatones and Rodríguez went on to sign professional contracts. (Courtesy of Joe Gaitan.)

Tom Robles was an outstanding player from East Los Angeles. After a successful baseball career at Garfield, he was drafted by the US Army in 1958. Robles did his basic training in the Deep South and remembers vividly going into a barbershop for a haircut and being refused and told to go to the "colored" barbers. He played for the divisional artillery team at Fort Lewis in Seattle. Before being drafted, Tom signed with the Pittsburgh Pirates and played on their minor-league team in Merida, Mexico, which was a cultural shock for Tom. (Courtesy of Mary Robles.)

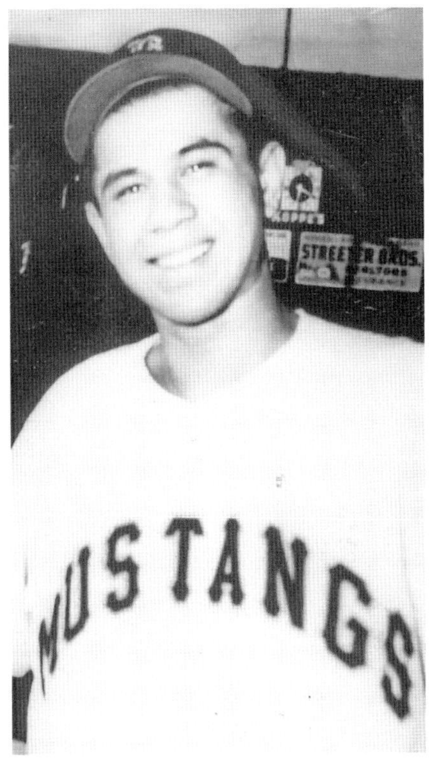


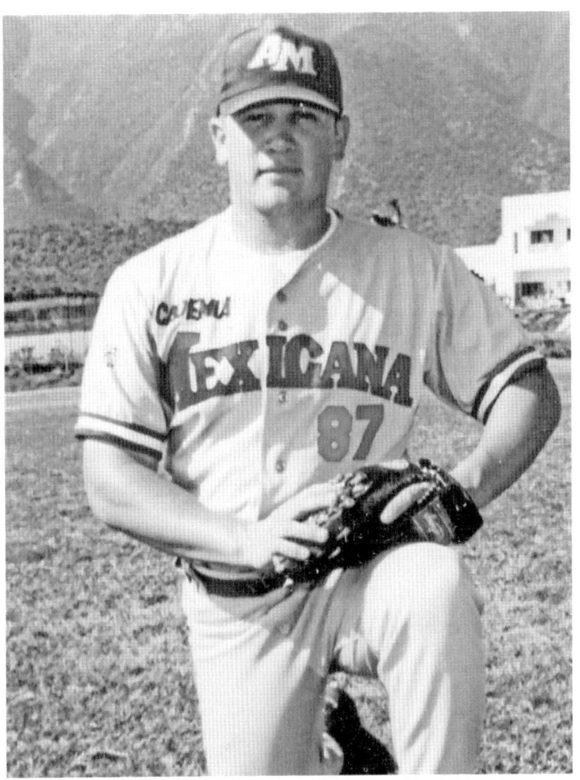


Ray Ruiz was part of a group of talented ballplayers from the Los Angeles area who traveled to play teams in Mexico. He remembers a tournament that took the Los Angeles team to Guaymas, Hermosillo, and Navajoa. Javier Burruel and his family sponsored the trip, and Javier was a major influence in Ray's life. Several players from the Los Angeles area went on to play in major-league organizations, including Peter Cervantes (Dodgers), Cesar Castañeda (Rangers), Steve Toriz (Expos), Andres Torres (Blue Jays), and Alex Chavez in Mexico. One player who did not play professionally but is making a name for himself is coach Mark Viramontes at the University of San Diego. (Courtesy of Ray Ruiz.)

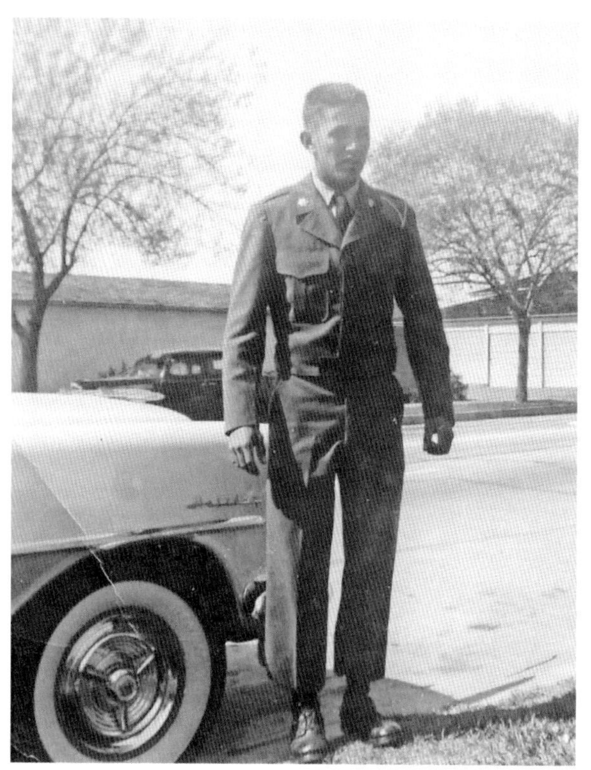

Fernando Farfán joined the US Army and was stationed in Germany after the Korean War. He traveled throughout Europe playing against other military teams. Farfán remembers that there were several professional ballplayers in the service at the time, including a pitcher from the St. Louis Cardinals on his team. He caught for this pitcher, and in one game, an inside pitch broke his wrist, ending Fernando's dreams of playing in the major leagues after the military. He later played at East Los Angeles Junior College and with local semipro teams, including Los Chorizeros. He was one of the youngest players in their lineup and one of the youngest inducted into their hall of fame. (Courtesy of Damon Farfán.)

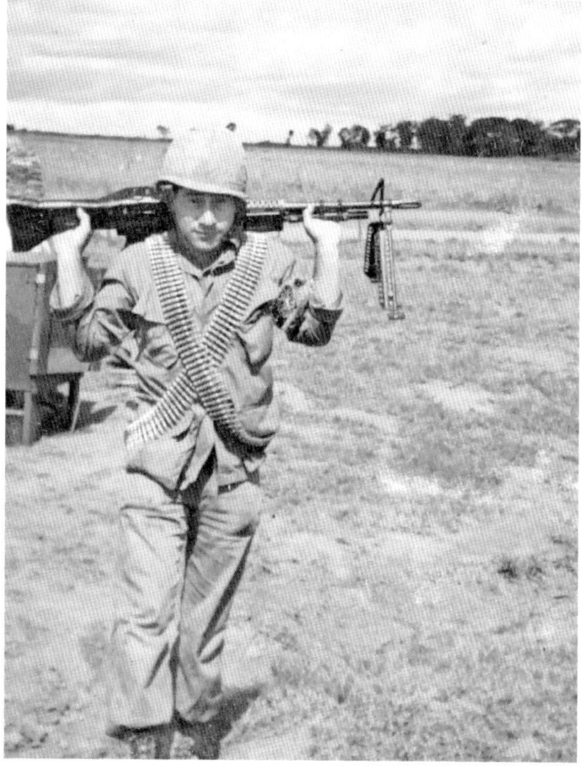

William Pimentel is shown in Vietnam. As a youth, he played baseball on East Los Angeles teams including the Belvedere Pee Wees, the Brooklyn Ford Market, and Ramírez Mortuary. His twin brothers, Joe Luís and Jesús, also played youth ball and later were inducted into the Boxing Hall of Fame. William served in Vietnam in 1966–1967 as crew chief of the 4th Infantry, 42nd Battalion, Battery D. He is now a pastor in East Los Angeles. William received his master's degree in theology at the Fuller Seminary in Pasadena, California. He also earned his PhD in psychology. He married Mary Zambrano and they have three children, Rachel, David, and Steven. (Courtesy of Victor Pimentel.)

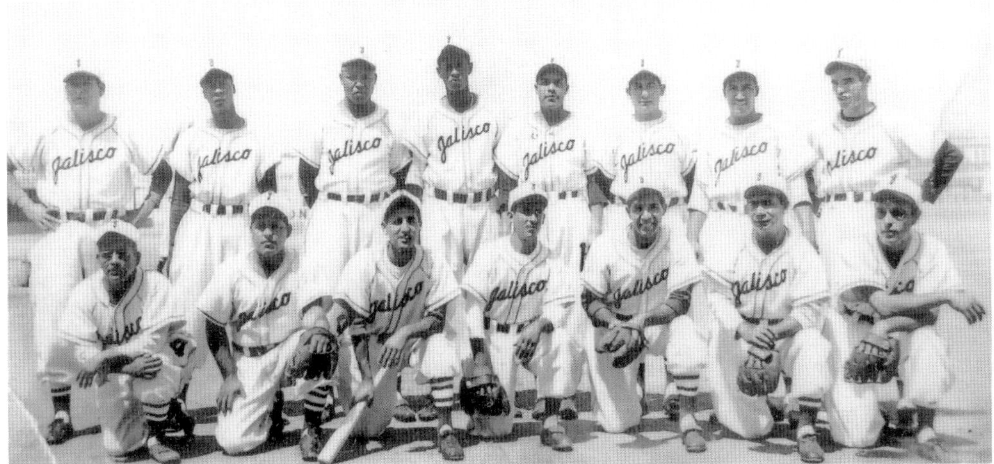

Ray Alderete (first row, third from left) was born in 1921 in Las Cruces, New Mexico, and when he was six months old, his family moved to East Los Angeles. As a youth, he played ball at Evergreen Park, at Stevenson Junior High, and at Roosevelt High School. His father, Antonio, and his brothers had a team, and Ray was the batboy. Ray played ball in Jalisco, Mexico, until 1950. (Courtesy of Ray Alderete.)

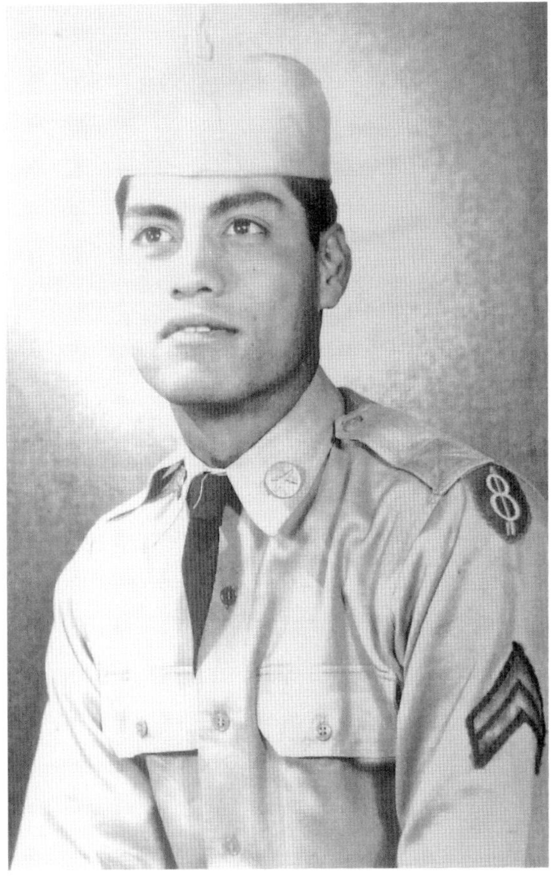

In September 1953, Charlie Mena was drafted into the US Army. Mena was attending USC at the time and pitching for the team. He was stationed for 21 months at Fort Carson, Colorado. He played for two years on the base team. One of his teammates was shortstop Billy Martin, who had just played on the New York Yankees' 1952 championship team. After his enlistment, Charlie returned to USC, where legendary coach Rod Dedeaux had kept his scholarship for him. The Trojans made a goodwill tour throughout Asia, entertaining the troops by playing US military teams and Japanese teams in Hawaii, Korea, and Japan. (Courtesy of Charlie Mena.)

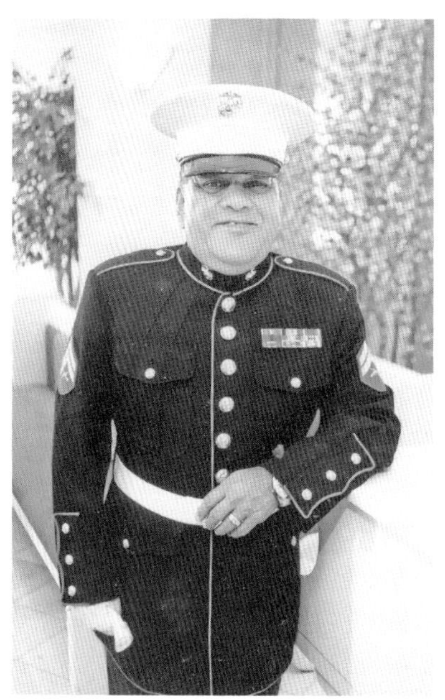

Gil Pérez grew up with baseball. He played Little League in East Los Angeles and at Garfield High School as a catcher in the 1960s before hurting his throwing arm. His father was Manuel "Shorty" Pérez, a revered coach for four decades in East Los Angeles. Gil was drafted by the military and served as a Marine in Vietnam. He was decorated with several medals and ribbons, including the Bronze Star and a medal for valor. He is seen here wearing his uniform for his wedding. He credits his mother, Juanita, and his wife, Lucille, for his wonderful life. Lucille was born in East Los Angeles and attended Stevenson Junior High School and Monte Vista High School. Gil and Lucille raised two boys, Robert and Danny, and have 12 grandchildren and 4 great-grandchildren. (Courtesy of Gil Pérez.)

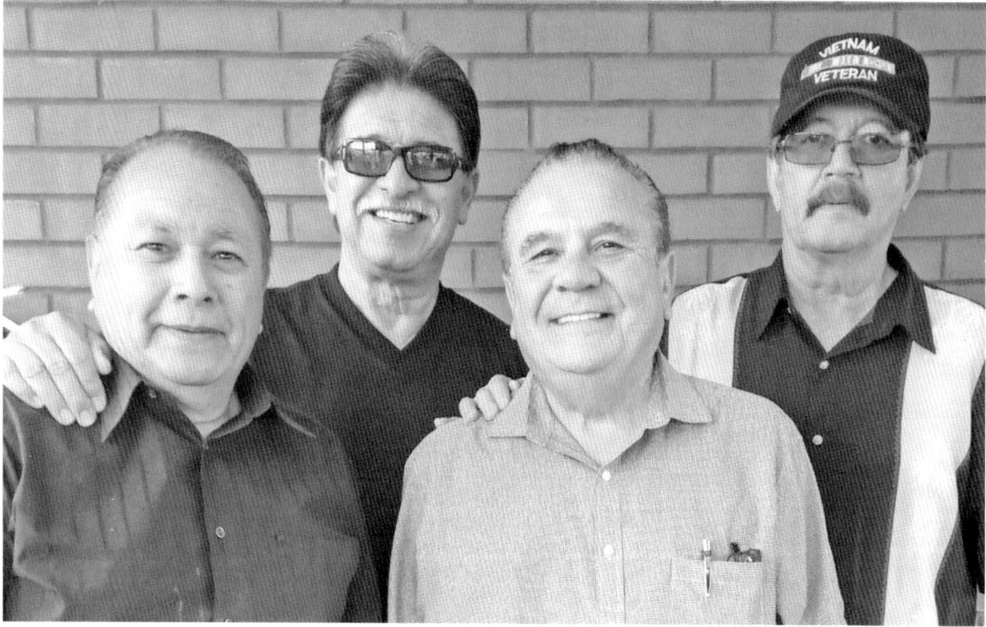


On Saturday, May 21, 2016, Garfield High School unveiled the Memorial Wall, saluting Vietnam-era veterans. The ceremony was glorious. Nearly 600 names grace this shrine to those who served their nation in the 1960s and 1970s. Seventeen of these brave young men were killed in action in Vietnam. Los Angeles County supervisor Hilda Solís and Los Angeles School Board member Mónica García spoke from their hearts. Bishop Jon Bruno, a Bulldog alum, gave the official blessing. From left to right are Joe Valle, Joe Ronquillo, Monte Pérez, and Armando Valdez. A close friend, Richard Télles (not pictured) played ball with the Laguna Park Giants and at Roosevelt. Except for Pérez, they all served in Vietnam. (Courtesy of Ray Ronquillo.)

# Field of Dreams

From its humble beginnings, the Latino Baseball History Project has paid tribute to veteran players and their supportive families and friends. These sentimental activities have included first-pitch ceremonies, oral interviews, library exhibits, luncheons, certificates of recognition, reunions, press conferences, parades, and public symposiums. For the legendary players and their diehard supporters, the Latino Baseball History Project is truly *El Campo de los Sueños* (Field of Dreams).

On August 14, 2014, the Latino Baseball History Project sponsored its fourth annual Baseball Reunion on the campus of California State University at San Bernardino. These reunions bring together players and their loyal followers, shedding light on their extraordinary careers so long ago. There is music, food, speakers, library exhibits, book signings by players, and the additional collection of memorabilia. Families generously donate uniforms, equipment, and other precious items to the project. Moreover, California State University at Pomona sponsors annual luncheons and exhibits that have included showcasing women ballplayers, individuals who played ball in the military, and teams and players from both the Pomona Valley and East Los Angeles. California State University at Channel Islands in 2015 saluted women players from Ventura County. Needless to say, there is not a dry eye at these emotional events.

For surviving ballplayers, especially those now in their 80s and 90s, this overdue acknowledgement, in the ninth inning of their lives, has instilled an awareness in them that their noteworthy contributions to the American pastime are now being publicly acknowledged and chronicled. Family members have observed that this newfound attention has invigorated the physical and cerebral lives of these players, becoming heroes and celebrities again in their families, neighborhoods, and the larger community. More special is that their children, grandchildren, and great-grandchildren are also basking in the glory of their baseball and softball ancestors. Everyone is upbeat, overjoyed, and on cloud nine.

This generational inspiration and appreciation especially rings true with the widespread influence women players have had on their daughters, granddaughters, great-granddaughters, goddaughters, and nieces. Families now have a better understanding and appreciation of how these female trailblazers impacted the game and the groundbreaking roles that baseball and softball players had on the struggle for gender equality in sports.

Sadly, countless players have gone to play in the big ballpark in the sky. Each passing day sees more of the old-timers joining the lineup with the big club in heaven. These once bright lights in Mexican American communities slowly grow dim. They are mourned and eulogized, and they will be greatly missed, but their well-documented legacy will live forever thanks to the Latino Baseball History Project. And wherever people play ball in East Los Angeles, these amazing angels will be on the field with them spiritually.

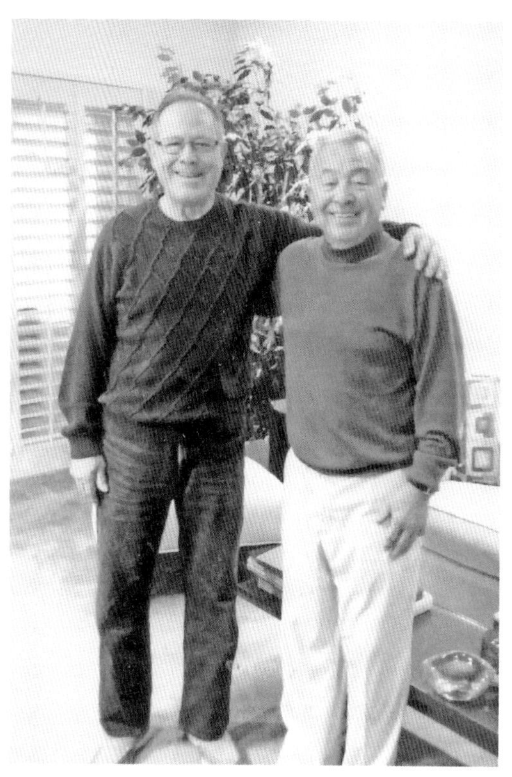

Joe Gaitan (right) and Bobby Recendez (left) have been friends since their playing days in the 1950s. As youngsters, they were archrivals, since Bobby attended Roosevelt High School and Joe attended Garfield. Both were outstanding players at all levels of baseball. These boyhood and girlhood relationships are an important part of the East Los Angeles baseball and softball story. There are countless groups of men and women who still meet on a regular basis for breakfast and lunch around East Los Angeles to keep in touch and remember the honest-to-goodness days of their youth. (Courtesy of Richard A. Santillán.)

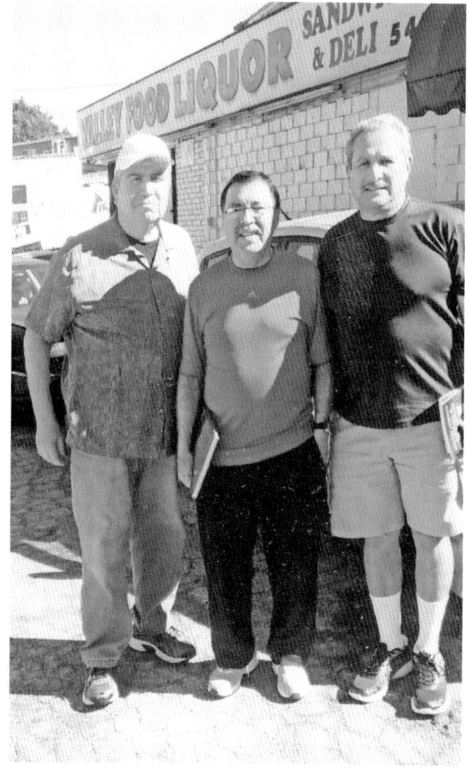


From left to right, George Caro, Raúl Cardoza, and David Escarciga played baseball at Cantwell High School in the 1960s. They still recall their playing days as if they were yesterday. They talk about how sports helped them live clean lives and achieve successful careers. Like many of their peers, they have given a lifetime of support back to their school and community. In every corner of East Los Angeles, former players have far-reaching influence on young people. These generations also helped wear down discrimination through their superhuman efforts. Raúl Cardoza graduated from California State University Los Angeles in mathematics and earned a master's in psychology. He earned his PhD in education from UCLA and was a college administrator for 36 years, including campus president at Chabut College in Hayward, California. (Courtesy of Richard A. Santillán.)

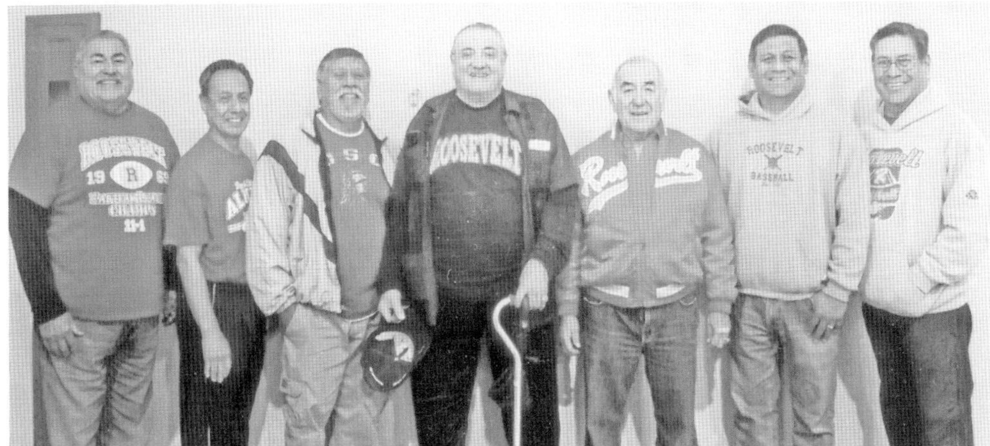

This 2016 photograph shows four De La Rosa brothers with their coaches from Roosevelt High School. From left to right are Mario Esparza, Al and Elías De La Rosa, coaches Conrad Muñatones and Ernie Rodríguez, and Rubén and Frank De La Rosa. Al and Frank also coached at Roosevelt. Elías played ball in the military and earned a Bronze Star in Vietnam. Rubén was a firefighter for over 30 years and played softball on the firefighter team. Mario is an attorney from New Mexico and has raised scholarships for Roosevelt students for over 40 years. (Courtesy of De La Rosa family.)

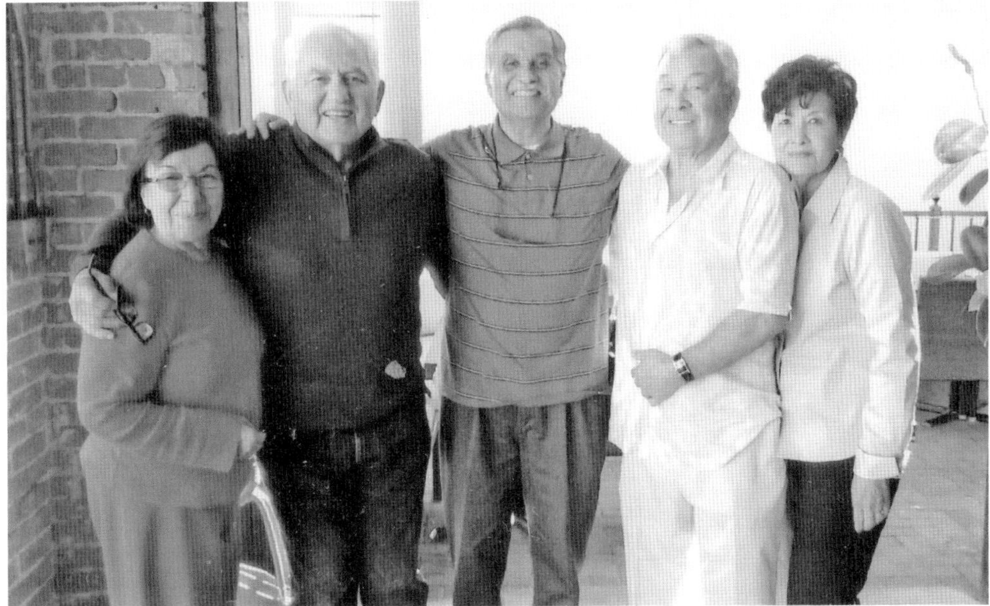

Bill and Mary Ellen Miranda, Joe Gaitan, and Mary Robles represent the importance of wives and baseball. Like many wives, Mary Ellen, Lillian (not pictured), and Mary supported their husbands Bill, Joe, and Tom (not pictured) through thick and thin. Wives rallied the entire family and neighbors by the truckloads in support of their husbands' teams. Over and over again, the majority of ballplayers give credit for their good fortune to their spouses. Ballplayers still recall that their wives were their biggest fans, especially when they were in slumps. Richard A. Santillan is seen here in the middle. (Courtesy of Richard A. Santillán.)

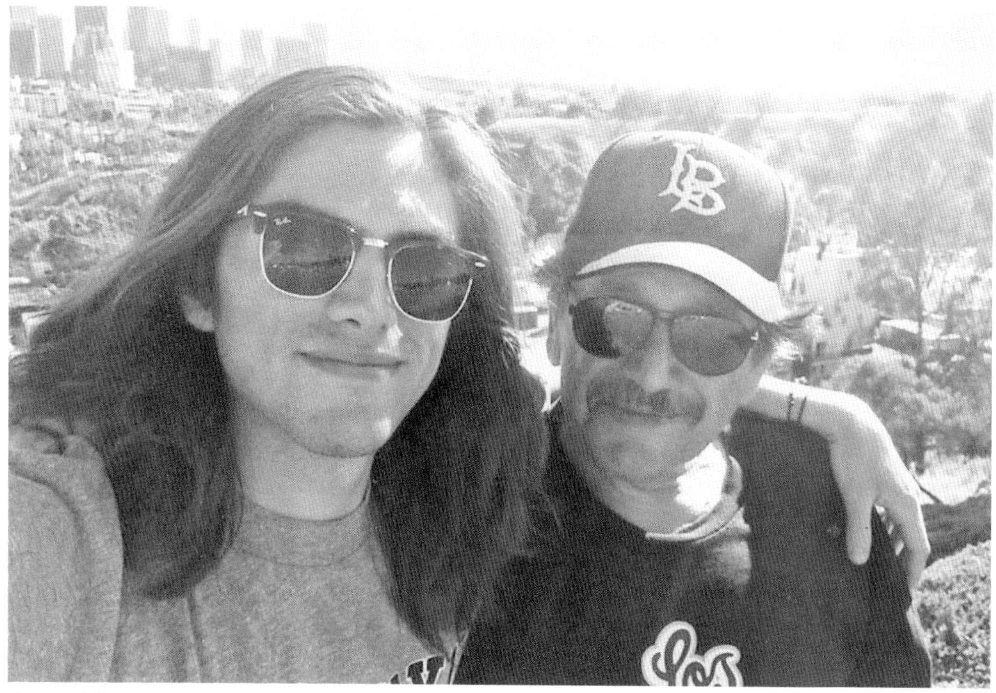

One of the most poignant moments is when a dad takes his sons to their first ballgame. Fathers have taken sons to Gilmore Stadium, Wrigley Field in Los Angeles, the Coliseum, and Dodger and Angel Stadiums for decades. Tomas J. Benítez (right) and his son Lucas are at the opening game at Dodger Stadium in 2015. Lucas was only four months old in 1994 when Tomas took him to his first opening game. Another father-son ritual took place when Tomas and Lucas shared their first beer together at the game when Lucas was 21. Richard A. and Teresa M. Santillán, coauthors of this book, have taken their three grandchildren, Alec, Román, and Rhiannon, to every Dodger opening game since the late 1990s. Richard still remembers his dad Carlos taking him to his first Dodger game at the Coliseum in 1958. (Courtesy of Tomas J. Benítez.)

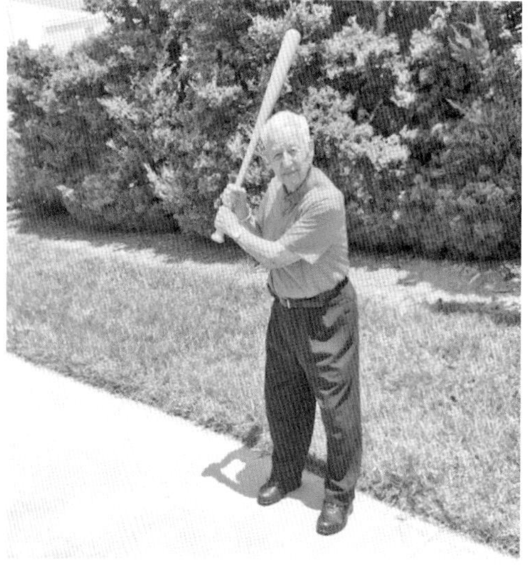

Ray Alderete shows off his famous batting stance at the age of almost 96 in May 2016. Ray is believed to be the oldest East Los Angeles player alive. He played in the 1930s. Eons ago, these players were majestic, gifted, dyed-in-the-wool daredevils with nerves of steel and beauty and poise on the field. They still wear their baseball caps as badges of honor. Their legacies still reverberate throughout the fields of East Los. Father time was the only opponent they could not defeat. (Courtesy of Ray Alderete Jr.)

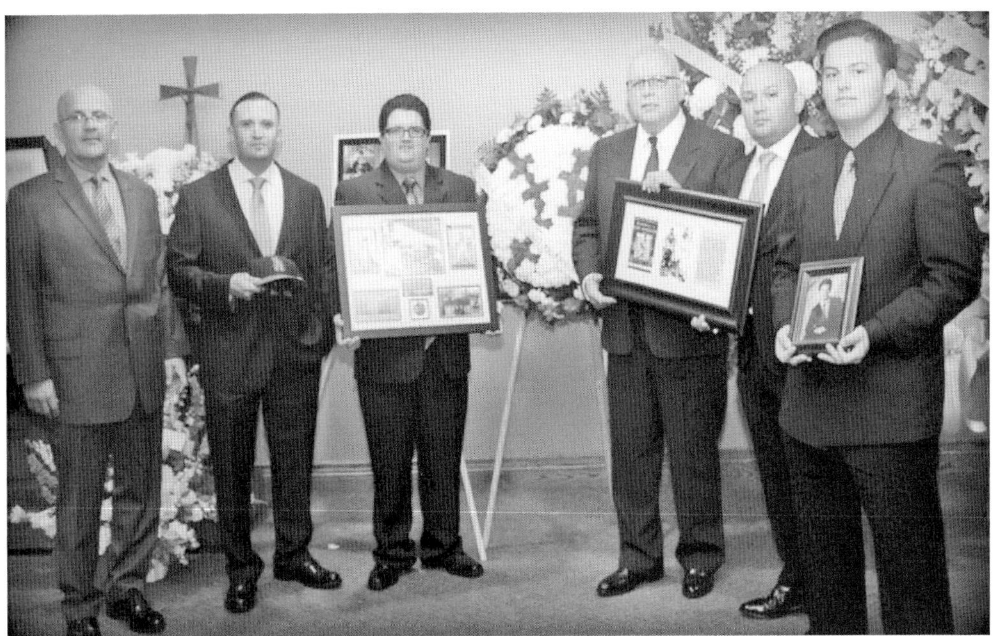

The Latino Baseball History Project has paid tribute to thousands of players over the last 10 years. The saddest part of the project's work is learning that a player has died. Several have passed away in 2016, including Tony Lugo (Garfield High School). The funeral service was baseball-themed, including a ball signed by his boyhood friend Edwin "Duke" Snider in his casket. From left to right are Tony's son Raymond Lugo, grandson Michael Lugo, grandson Andrew Lugo-Rice, son Richard Lugo, grandson Anthony Lugo, and grandson Ryan Lugo-Rice holding a photograph of his late older brother Ricky Lugo-Rice. (Courtesy of Richard Lugo.)

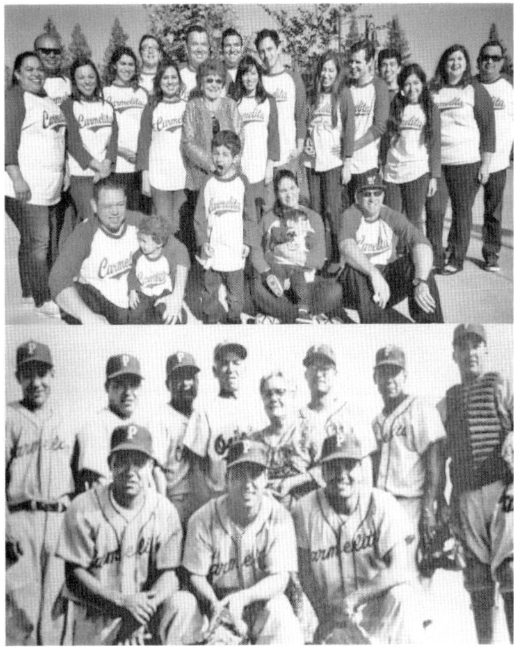

Richard Peña was one of the staunchest supporters of the Latino Baseball History Project since its inception in 2006. Without the extraordinary help of Richard, his brothers, Al Padilla, and Bob Lagunas, the project would have struck out in the first inning. Richard (Roosevelt High School) passed away in 2016. Tony Lugo and Richard Peña were longtime buddies. The Lugo and Peña families are very close, especially their children. Some of the family members (top) are wearing Carmelita Chorizeros t-shirts, honoring the team Richard played for. On the back is the number 30, representing the year he was born, 1930. At bottom, the nine Peña brothers are pictured with their mother Victoria and father William. (Courtesy of the Peña family.)

# LATINO BASEBALL HISTORY PROJECT ADVISORY BOARD

José M. Alamillo
Eduardo B. Almada T.
Richard Arroyo
Gabriel "Tito" Ávila Jr.
Francisco E. Balderrama
Tomas J. Benítez
Anna Bermúdez
Juan J. Canchola-Ventura
Terry A. Cannon
Raúl Cardoza
Gene Chávez
David Contreras Jr.
Juan D. Coronado
Christopher Docter
Peter Drier
Robert Elias
Luís F. Fernández
Maria García
Gregory Garrett
Jorge Iber
Rumado Z. Juárez
Alfonso Ledesma
Enrique M. López
Jody L. and Gabriel A. López
Susan C. Luévano
Amanda Magdalena
Rod Martínez
Douglas Monroy
Carlos Muñoz Jr
Eddie Navarro
Victoria C. Norton
Mark A. Ocegueda
Alan O'Connor
Monica Ortez
Al Padilla
Richard Peña
Al Ramos
Samuel O. Regalado
Vicki L. Ruiz
Anthony Salazar
Richard A. Santillán
Teresa M. Santillán
Marcelino Saucedo
Ray P. Serra
Monserrath Segura
Alicia S. Stevens
Joe Talaugon
Carlos Tortolero
Sandra L. Uribe
Elisa Urmston
David Vargas
Alejo L. Vásquez
Angelina F. Veyna
Alfonso Villanueva Jr.
Robert Zamora

# BIBLIOGRAPHY


Alamillo, José M. *Making Lemonade Out of Lemons: Mexican American Labor and Leisure in a California Town, 1880–1960*. Urbana and Chicago, IL: University of Illinois Press, 2006.

———. "Mexican American Baseball: Masculinity, Racial Struggle and Labor Politics in Southern California, 1930–1960." *Sports Matters: Race, Recreation, and Culture*. New York, NY: New York University Press, 2002.

———."Peloteros in Paradise: Mexican American Baseball and Oppositional Politics in Southern California, 1930–1950." *Western Historical Quarterly* XXXIV: 2, 191–212.

———. "Playing Across Borders: Transnational Sports and Identities in Southern California and Mexico, 1930–1945." *Pacific Historical Review* vol. 79, no. 3 (2010): 360–392.

*Chavez Ravine: A Los Angeles Story*. PBS Independent Lens Film, 2003.

Latino Baseball History Project. Special Collections, John M. Pfau Library, California State University, San Bernardino.

Magdalena, Amanda. "Peloteras de Casa: Baseball's Role in Creating Gender Capital for Mexican American Women." Master's thesis, Tulane University, 2011.

Normark, Don. *Chavez Ravine 1949: A Los Angeles Story*. Vancouver, BC: Raincoast Books, 1999.

*Oral Histories Interviews: Mexican American Baseball in Los Angeles: From the Barrios to the Big Leagues*. Special Collections, John F. Kennedy Library, California State University, Los Angeles.

Regalado, Samuel O. "Baseball in the Barrios: The Scene in East Los Angeles Since World War II." *Baseball History* (Summer 1986): 47–59.

———. "Dodger Béisbol Is on the Air: The Development and Impact of the Dodgers' Spanish Language Broadcasts, 1958–1994." *California History* LXXIV (Fall 1995): 3, 280–289.

———. *Viva Baseball: Latin Major Leaguers and Their Special Hunger*. Urbana and Chicago, IL: University of Illinois Press, 1998.

Santillán, Richard A. *From the Battlefields to the Ballfields: Mexican Americans and Military Ball: World War II, Korea, and Vietnam*. Unpublished manuscript, 2014.

———. "Mexican Americans and Military Baseball during World War II." *Journal of the West: Latinos and Sports in the American West* vol. 54, no. 4 (Fall 2015).

———. "Mexican Baseball Teams in the Midwest, 1916–1965: The Politics of Cultural Survival and Civil Rights." *Perspectives in Mexican American Studies* VII: 132–151. Tucson, AZ: University of Arizona Press, 2000.

Santillán, Richard A. and Francisco E. Balderama. "Los Chorizeros: The New York Yankees of East Los Angeles and the Reclaiming of Mexican American Baseball History." *The National Pastime—The Endless Season: Baseball in Southern California*. Cleveland, OH: Society for American Baseball Research, 2011.

———. *Mexican American Baseball in Los Angeles*. Charleston, SC: Arcadia Publishing, 2011.

Uribe, Sandra. *Una Liga of Their Own: Mexican American Women and the Struggle for Gender Equality on the Diamond, 1930s–1960s*. Unpublished manuscript, 2014.

———. "The Queens of Diamonds: Mexican American Women's Amateur Softball in Southern California, 1930–1950." Unpublished paper, 2005.

Consistent with our mission to preserve history on a local level, this book was printed in South Carolina on American-made paper and manufactured entirely in the United States. Products carrying the accredited Forest Stewardship Council (FSC) label are printed on 100 percent FSC-certified paper.

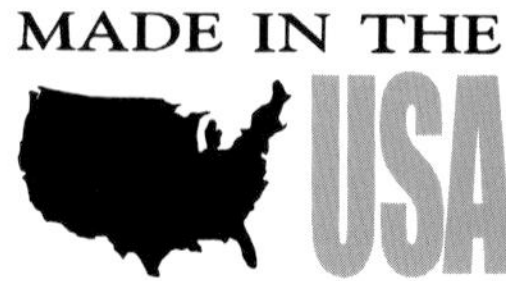